ADOBE® ACROBAT® 9

Covers Standard, Pro, and Pro Extended

CLASSROOM IN A BOOK®

The official training workbook from Adobe Systems

www.adobepress.com

Adobe

WHAT'S ON THE CD

Here is an overview of the contents of the *Classroom in a Book* CD.

Lesson files ... and so much more

The *Adobe Acrobat 9 Classroom in a Book* disc includes the lesson files that you'll need to complete the exercises in this book, as well as other content to help you learn more about Adobe Acrobat and use it with greater efficiency and ease. The diagram below represents the contents of the disc, which should help you locate the files you need.

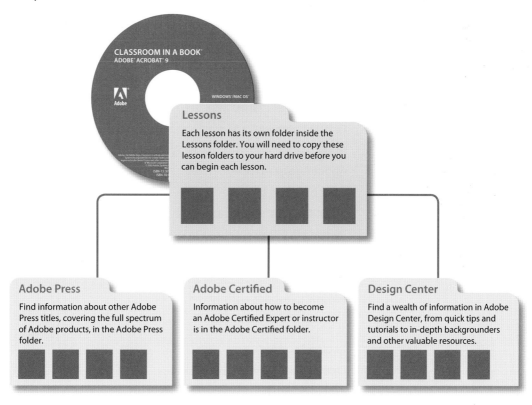

CLASSROOM IN A BOOK
ADOBE ACROBAT 9

WINDOWS/MAC OS

Lessons
Each lesson has its own folder inside the Lessons folder. You will need to copy these lesson folders to your hard drive before you can begin each lesson.

Adobe Press
Find information about other Adobe Press titles, covering the full spectrum of Adobe products, in the Adobe Press folder.

Adobe Certified
Information about how to become an Adobe Certified Expert or instructor is in the Adobe Certified folder.

Design Center
Find a wealth of information in Adobe Design Center, from quick tips and tutorials to in-depth backgrounders and other valuable resources.

CONTENTS

3 CREATING ADOBE PDF FILES

4 CREATING ADOBE PDF FROM MICROSOFT OFFICE FILES (WINDOWS)

8 ADDING SIGNATURES AND SECURITY

9 USING ACROBAT IN A REVIEW CYCLE

10 WORKING WITH FORMS IN ACROBAT

14 USING ACROBAT IN PROFESSIONAL PRINTING

15 WORKING WITH 3D IN PDF FILES

GETTING STARTED

Adobe® Acrobat® 9 is an essential tool in today's electronic workflow. You can use Acrobat Standard, Acrobat Pro, or Acrobat Pro Extended to create virtually any document in Adobe Portable Document Format (PDF), preserving the exact look and content of the original, complete with fonts and graphics. Additionally, Acrobat now provides native support for Adobe Flash technology, so you can be sure that multimedia components in a PDF will play smoothly.

You can unify documents, spreadsheets, presentations, email, rich media, and more into a single, cohesive PDF Portfolio. In fact, you can manipulate the files in a PDF Portfolio without affecting the PDF Portfolio as a whole—or the original file itself.

You can distribute PDF documents reliably and securely by email or store them on the web, an intranet, a file system, a CD, or a web service such as Acrobat.com. With shared reviews, you and your colleagues can collaborate easily as you perfect a document. Reviewers can view and comment on your work, regardless of the platform they work on. Acrobat makes it easy to collect and organize data from reviews or from forms.

Acrobat Pro and Acrobat Pro Extended offer improved print production controls, for a faster, more reliable print workflow. And some features that were previously found only in Acrobat Pro are now available in Acrobat Standard. For example, you can use any version of Acrobat 9 to create interactive forms and enable users of the free downloadable Adobe Reader® 9 software to save the completed form.

About Classroom in a Book

Adobe Acrobat 9 Classroom in a Book® is part of the official training series for Adobe graphics and publishing software. The lessons are designed to let you learn at your own pace. If you're new to Adobe Acrobat, you'll learn the fundamental concepts and features you'll need to master the program. If you've been using Acrobat for a while, you'll find *Classroom in a Book* teaches many advanced features and includes lessons targeted specifically for architects, engineers and construction professionals; legal professionals; and print professionals.

The lessons in this edition include information on a host of Adobe Acrobat features, including:

- Using the Organizer to manage your PDF files.

- Creating PDF Portfolios.

- Creating Adobe PDF files with a single click.

- Saving websites and other clipboard content as PDF files.

- Repurposing the content of Adobe PDF files for use in other applications (if permitted by the author).

- Editing PDF documents.

- Creating multimedia presentations.

- Reviewing and commenting on Adobe PDF documents, using streamlined workflows and tools, including the ability to share a document for live review.

- Creating, distributing, and gathering data from forms.

- Obtaining measurements with tools designed for engineering and technical users.

- Redacting information and using Bates numbering, for legal professionals.

- Securing PDF documents.

- Working with 3D objects in PDFs.

Although each lesson provides step-by-step instructions for specific projects, there's room for exploration and experimentation. You can follow the book from start to finish or do only the lessons that match your interests and needs.

Acrobat Pro, Acrobat Pro Extended, and Acrobat Standard

This book covers features included in Acrobat Pro, Acrobat Pro Extended (available for Windows only), and Acrobat Standard. We've noted where a tool or feature described in this book is not available in Acrobat Standard. The only lesson that requires Acrobat Pro Extended is Lesson 15, "Working with 3D in PDF Files."

Features available only in Acrobat Pro and Pro Extended include:

- Preflighting documents and other print production tasks.

- Adding headers and welcome screens to PDF Portfolios.

- Converting layered and large-format engineering drawings to Adobe PDF.

- Modifying the reflow order of objects on a page to optimize accessibility.
- Adding video and sound files to PDF documents.
- Applying Bates numbering and redaction.

Prerequisites

Before beginning to use *Adobe Acrobat 9 Classroom in a Book*, you should have a working knowledge of your computer and its operating system. Make sure you know how to use the mouse, standard menus, and commands, as well as how to open, save, and close files. If you need to review these techniques, see the printed or online documentation included with your system.

Installing Adobe Acrobat

Before beginning to use *Adobe Acrobat 9 Classroom in a Book*, make sure that your system is set up correctly and that you've installed the required software and hardware. You must purchase Adobe Acrobat 9 software separately. For system requirements, see the Adobe website at www.adobe.com/products/acrobat/main.html.

You must install the application from the Adobe Acrobat 9 CD onto your hard drive; you cannot run Acrobat 9 from the CD. Follow the onscreen installation instructions.

Starting Adobe Acrobat

You start Acrobat just as you would any other software application.

- **On Windows:** choose Start > Programs or All Programs > Adobe Acrobat 9 Standard, Adobe Acrobat 9 Pro, or Adobe Acrobat 9 Pro Extended.
- **On Mac OS:** open the Adobe Acrobat 9 Standard folder or the Adobe Acrobat 9 Pro folder, and double-click the program icon.

Copying the Classroom in a Book files

The *Adobe Acrobat 9 Classroom in a Book* CD includes folders that contain all the electronic files for the lessons. Each lesson has its own folder, and you must copy the folders to your hard drive to work through the lessons. To save room on your drive, you can install only the folder necessary for each lesson as you need it, and remove the folder when you're done.

To copy the Classroom in a Book files:

Note: If you overwrite the lesson files as you work through the lessons, you can restore the original files by recopying the corresponding lesson folder from the Classroom in a Book CD to the *AA9_CIB* folder on your hard drive.

1 Insert the *Adobe Acrobat 9 Classroom in a Book* CD into your CD-ROM drive.

2 Create a folder named **AA9_CIB** on your hard drive.

3 Copy all the lessons, or only those you want to work with now, to the hard drive:

- To copy all of the lessons, drag the Lessons folder from the CD into the AA9_CIB folder.

- To copy a single lesson, drag the individual lesson folder from the CD into the AA9_CIB folder.

Additional resources

Adobe Acrobat 9 Classroom in a Book is not meant to replace documentation provided with the Adobe Acrobat 9 program. Only the commands and options used in the lessons are explained in this book. For comprehensive information about program features, refer to these resources:

- Adobe Acrobat 9 Help, included with the Adobe Acrobat 9 software, which you can view by choosing Help > Adobe Acrobat 9 Help. This help system contains a complete description of all features.

- The Adobe website at www.adobe.com/products/acrobat.

- The Acrobat knowledge base, which you can view by choosing Help > Online Support > Knowledge Base if you have a connection to the World Wide Web.

Adobe certification

The Adobe training and certification programs are designed to help Adobe customers improve and promote their product proficiency skills. The Adobe Certified Expert (ACE) program, which is designed to recognize the high-level skills of expert users, is the best way to master Adobe products. For information on Adobe-certified training programs, visit the Partnering with Adobe website at http://www.adobe.com/support/certification/ace.html.

1 INTRODUCING ADOBE ACROBAT 9

Lesson Overview

In this lesson, you'll do the following:

- Get acquainted with the Adobe PDF document format and Acrobat 9.

- Take a first look at the Acrobat work area.

- View examples of PDF documents designed for printing and for viewing online.

- Examine some formatting and design decisions you need to make when creating an electronic publication.

- View a PDF in Full Screen mode.

- Learn to use Adobe Acrobat 9 Help.

 This lesson will take approximately 45 minutes to complete. Copy the Lesson01 folder onto your hard drive if you haven't already done so.

About Adobe PDF

Adobe Portable Document Format (PDF) is a universal file format that preserves all of the fonts, formatting, colors, and graphics of any source document, regardless of the application and platform used to create the original document. Adobe PDF files are compact and secure. They can be shared, viewed, navigated, and printed by anyone with the free Adobe Reader. You can extend additional rights to Adobe Reader users, allowing them to fill in and save a PDF form, and to digitally sign a PDF. If you're using Acrobat Pro or Pro Extended, you can also enable Reader users to participate in PDF review and commenting processes.

- Adobe PDF preserves the exact layout, fonts, and text formatting of electronic documents, regardless of the computer system or platform used to view these documents.

- PDF documents can contain multiple languages, such as Japanese and English, on the same page.

- PDF documents print predictably with proper margins and page breaks.

- PDF files can be secured to prevent undesired changes or printing, or to limit access to confidential documents.

- You can change the view magnification of a PDF page in Acrobat or Adobe Reader, which is especially useful for zooming in on graphics or diagrams containing intricate details.

About Adobe Acrobat

Acrobat lets you create, work with, read, and print PDF documents.

Creating Adobe PDF files

Almost any document—a text file, a file created in a page-layout application, a scanned document, a web page, or a digital photo—can be converted to Adobe PDF using Acrobat software or third-party authoring applications. Your workflow and document type determine the best way to create a PDF.

- Use the Create PDF commands in the Acrobat File menu to quickly convert a variety of file formats to Adobe PDF and open them in Acrobat. You can also access the Create PDF commands from the Create button in the Tasks toolbar. You can convert files one at a time, or convert multiple files at once. You can combine converted files into a single, compact PDF file, or assemble them in a PDF Portfolio with built-in navigation tools. You can also create a blank PDF page using the PDF Editor.

- Use the Adobe PDF printer to convert almost any file to Adobe PDF from within any application. In most applications, you can adjust settings for the Adobe PDF printer from within the Print dialog box.

- Use Acrobat PDFMaker from Microsoft Office and other popular applications for Windows. When you install Acrobat, Acrobat PDFMaker is added automatically to supported applications that are installed on the computer. Simply click the Create PDF button (🖶) on the Acrobat ribbon (Office 2007) or the Convert to Adobe PDF button (📷) on the authoring application's toolbar. You can change settings to include bookmarks, hyperlinks, and accessibility features.

- Scan paper documents and convert them to Adobe PDF.

- Use the Create PDF From Web Page command to download web pages and convert them to Adobe PDF.

Lesson 3, "Creating Adobe PDF Files," Lesson 4, "Creating Adobe PDF from Microsoft Office Files," and Lesson 14, "Using Acrobat in Professional Printing," give step-by-step instructions for creating Adobe PDF using several of these methods.

Working with PDF files

Working with PDF files has never been easier.

- Use the Organizer feature to manage your PDF files. (Lesson 2, "Looking at the Work Area.")

- Configure the Acrobat work area to suit your needs. The user interface in Acrobat 9 features customizable toolbars and a navigation pane. (Lesson 2, "Looking at the Work Area.")

- Assemble multiple documents into a PDF Portfolio, in which the individual files are maintained as separate documents that can be read, edited, and printed independently. (Lesson 5, "Combining Files in PDF Portfolios.")

- Convert web pages to editable and searchable PDF files, keeping links intact. (Lesson 3, "Creating Adobe PDF Files.")

- Convert email messages to Adobe PDF in Microsoft Outlook and in Lotus Notes on Windows. You can convert an individual email to PDF, or convert an entire folder of messages into a merged PDF or a PDF Portfolio. (Lesson 4, "Creating Adobe PDF from Microsoft Office Files.")

- Run a simple search from the Find toolbar, or run a more complex search from the powerful Search window. (Lesson 6, "Reading and Working with PDF Files.")

- Rotate and crop PDF pages, insert PDF files and pages into a document, customize bookmarks, and renumber pages. (Lesson 7, "Enhancing and Editing PDF Documents.")

- Make minor edits to PDF content using the TouchUp Text tool and, in Acrobat 9 Pro or Pro Extended, the TouchUp Object tool. Re-use the content of a PDF file in other applications (if allowed by the creator of the document) by saving the contents to other file formats, extracting images, and converting PDF pages to image formats. (Lesson 7, "Enhancing and Editing PDF Documents.")

- Approve the contents or certify the validity of a document by adding your digital signature. You can also add sophisticated protection to a confidential PDF file, preventing users from copying text and graphics, printing the document, or even opening the file. (Lesson 8, "Adding Signatures and Security.")

- Add comments and mark-up text in an electronic document review cycle. In Acrobat 9, you can set up email, web, or shared reviews. You can collaborate live using features on the new Acrobat.com service. And if you're using Acrobat 9 Pro or Pro Extended, you can invite Adobe Reader users to participate in reviews. (Lesson 9, "Using Acrobat in a Review Cycle.")

- Create interactive PDF forms from any electronic document or a scanned paper form. You can enable forms so that Adobe Reader users can complete and save them, too. Tools in Acrobat also help you distribute forms, track responses, and analyze form data. (Lesson 10, "Working with Forms in Acrobat.")

- Use Acrobat 9 Pro or Pro Extended to create sophisticated multimedia presentations. Embedded video, animation, or sound files require no additional software for viewing. The PDF file includes everything the recipient needs to view the file in Acrobat 9 or the free, downloadable Adobe Reader 9. (Lesson 11, "Creating Multimedia Presentations.")

- Process and deliver legal documents electronically. To serve the needs of courts and law offices, Acrobat 9 Pro and Pro Extended include a redaction feature for removing privileged content from a PDF document and a Bates numbering feature for labeling documents. (Lesson 12, "Using the Legal Features.")

- Share technical drawings and documents with clients and colleagues, using review and commenting tools designed for the needs of architects, engineers, and construction professionals. (Lesson 13, "Using the Engineering and Technical Features.")

- Generate high-quality PDF files with Acrobat 9. Specialized prepress tools in Acrobat 9 Pro and Pro Extended enable you to preview color separations, adjust how transparent objects are imaged, and print color separations from PDF files. The new Standards pane identifies PDF/X, PDF/A, and PDF/E files, and a redesigned Preflight feature makes it easier to verify that a PDF file meets your criteria before printing. (Lesson 14, "Using Acrobat in Professional Printing.")

- Use Acrobat 9 Pro Extended to convert 3D PDF files directly from supported 3D CAD files, edit 3D content in native file formats, and interact with 3D models, creating camera views, adding comments, and creating content-rich documentation. (Lesson 15, "Working with 3D in PDF Files.")

Reading PDF files

You can read PDF documents using Adobe Reader, Acrobat Standard, Acrobat Pro, or Acrobat Pro Extended. You can share your PDF files using network and web servers, CDs, DVDs, other removable media, and the Acrobat.com web service.

Adobe PDF on the web

The web has greatly expanded the possibilities for delivering electronic documents to a wide and varied audience. Because web browsers can be configured to run other applications inside the browser window, you can post PDF files as part of a website. Your users can download or view these PDF files inside the browser window using Adobe Reader.

When including a PDF file as part of your web page, you should direct users to the Adobe website so that the first time they encounter a PDF, they can download Adobe Reader, free of charge, if necessary.

PDFs can be viewed one page at a time and printed from the web. With page-at-a-time downloading, the web server sends only the requested page to the user, decreasing downloading time. In addition, the user can easily print selected pages or all pages from the document. PDF is a suitable format for publishing long electronic documents on the web. PDF documents print predictably, with proper margins and page breaks.

You can also download and convert web pages to Adobe PDF, making it easy to save, distribute, and print web pages. (For more information, see Lesson 3, "Creating Adobe PDF Files.")

Adding Adobe Reader installers

Adobe Reader is available free of charge for distribution with your documents, making it easier for users to view your PDF documents. It's important either to point users to the Adobe Reader installers on the Adobe website at www.adobe.com, or to include a copy of the Adobe Reader installers on the CD, if that's how you're distributing documents.

If you're including the Adobe Reader installers on a CD-ROM, you should include a ReadMe text file at the top level of the CD that describes how to install Adobe Reader and provides any last-minute information. If you're posting the Adobe Reader installers on a website, include the Adobe Reader installation instructions with the link to the downloadable software.

If you're distributing documents on the web, you'll probably want to point users to the Adobe website for the downloadable Adobe Reader software.

You may make and distribute unlimited copies of Adobe Reader, including copies for commercial distribution. For complete information on distributing and giving your users access to Adobe Reader, visit the Adobe website at http://www.adobe.com/products/acrobat/.

A special logo is available from Adobe for use when distributing Adobe Reader.

A first look at the work area

Publishing a document electronically is a flexible way to distribute information. Electronic PDF documents can be used for printing, for multimedia presentations, or for distribution on a CD or online. First you'll take a look at some PDFs in Acrobat to get acquainted with the Acrobat 9 interface and to get a feel for electronic document design considerations.

1   In Acrobat, choose File > Open. Select the file named Hilaptorex.pdf in the
    Lesson01 folder, and click Open.

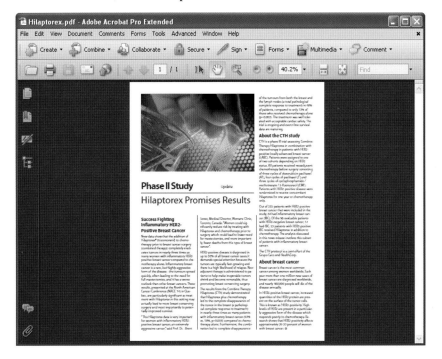

This document is a one-page article that has been converted to Adobe PDF for easy
electronic distribution.

2   Take a look at the work area.
    It includes a menu bar at the
    top of the screen. Click any
    of the menu names to see
    a menu of commands. We
    clicked on Tools.

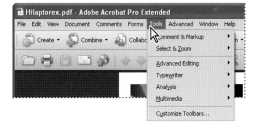

The menu bar is usually open when you're working in Acrobat. If you ever do
close the menu bar by choosing View > Menu Bar, you won't be able to access any
menu commands to reopen it. To reopen the menu bar, press F9 (Windows) or
Shift+Command+M (Mac OS) on your keyboard.

3   Notice the two rows of docked toolbars directly
    under the menu bar. Each toolbar has a grabber bar
    to its left. Move the cursor over one of the grabber
    bars to view a toolbar's name.

The toolbars organize the Acrobat tools into task-related groups. Only selected
toolbars are displayed by default. You'll learn how to show and hide toolbars and
add individual tools in Lesson 2, "Looking at the Work Area."

4   Notice that the upper row consists of a
    single toolbar, the Tasks toolbar. Click the
    arrow to the right of the Create button
    on the Tasks toolbar to see a menu of
    related commands. Choosing one of these
    commands initiates a process for creating a
    PDF file. Click outside the menu to close it
    without selecting a command.

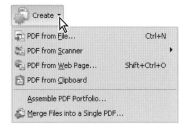

The buttons on the Tasks toolbar differ from the individual tool buttons on other
toolbars because they offer you additional menus.

5   Notice that each toolbar on the lower
    row of toolbars contains buttons,
    representing tools. Move your cursor
    over a button to view its name or
    function.

Only a selection of the Acrobat tools are displayed by default. You'll learn about
displaying additional tools and toolbars in Lesson 2, "Looking at the Work Area."

6   Move your cursor down to the bottom left of the
    document pane to reveal the size of this page.
    (The document pane is the part of the workspace that
    displays an open document.) The page size display
    disappears when you move the cursor away from the
    area.

Notice that the page size is a standard 8.5-by-11 inches. The designer chose this
size so that the page could be printed on a desktop printer in addition to being read
electronically.

7   Choose File > Open, and open the Application.pdf file, located in the
    Lesson01 folder. Notice that the file opens in a separate workspace with its
    own set of toolbars. You can switch between viewing the two open documents,
    Hilaptorex.pdf and Application.pdf, using the Window menu.

8 Choose Window, and select the Application.pdf file from the list of open files at the bottom of the menu. Later you'll learn how to tile windows so that you can view several files at once.

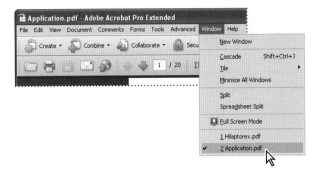

9 Click the Bookmarks button in the navigation pane on the left side of the work area. Click on the Harry Tanaka CV bookmark in the Bookmarks panel to jump directly to that bookmark's destination page in the document.

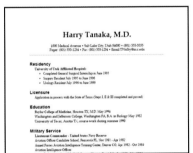

The navigation pane displays the default navigation panels, including the Bookmarks panel. To open additional navigation panels, choose View > Navigation Panels. You'll learn more about the navigation pane and its panels in Lesson 2, "Looking at the Work Area."

10 With the Application.pdf file active, choose File > Close, and close that file without saving any changes. Close the Hilaptorex.pdf file in the same way.

You've had a brief look at the major components of the Acrobat 9 work area—the menu bar, the toolbars, task buttons and tools, the document pane, and the navigation pane. You'll learn more about these elements as you work through this book.

Viewing PDF presentations in Full Screen mode

In Full Screen mode, the menu bar and toolbars are hidden.

1   Choose File > Open, and double-click the Aquo_Financial.pdf file, located in the Lesson01 folder.

2   Click Yes in the Full Screen message box to open this document in Full Screen mode.

Notice that in Full Screen mode the document occupies all available space on the monitor. All the Acrobat toolbars, menus, and panels have disappeared.

This document is an informational presentation, designed to be viewed exclusively onscreen. The graphics, large type size, and horizontal page layout have been designed for optimal display on a monitor.

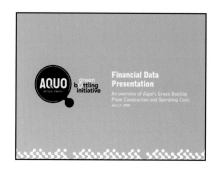

When you create or edit a PDF file, you can set it to appear in Full Screen mode when viewed in Acrobat. To set a file to open in Full Screen mode, choose File > Properties, click the Initial View tab in the Document Properties dialog box, select Open In Full Screen Mode, and click OK. Then save the document.

For more information, see Lesson 11, "Creating Multimedia Presentations."

You can view any PDF file in Full Screen mode by opening the document in Acrobat and choosing View > Full Screen Mode.

3   Press Enter or Return to page through the presentation.

4   Press the Escape key to exit Full Screen mode.

5 To ensure that navigation controls are always accessible to you, even in Full Screen mode, choose Edit > Preferences (Windows) or Acrobat > Preferences (Mac OS) and select Full Screen from the list of categories in the Preferences dialog box. Select the Show Navigation Bar option, and click OK to apply your changes.

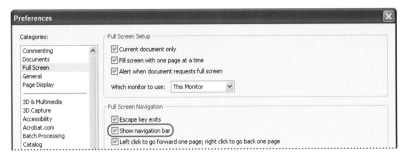

From this point on, whenever you open a document in Acrobat on your computer in Full Screen mode, Acrobat will display Next Page, Previous Page, and Exit Full Screen View buttons at the bottom left of the document pane. The buttons appear when you first view the document in Full Screen mode, and then disappear so that they don't obstruct the presentation. To access the buttons, move the pointer over the bottom-left corner of the screen. Keep in mind that Full Screen viewing preferences are specific to the computer on which you run a PDF presentation, not to the document.

6 Choose File > Close, and close the file without saving any changes.

Designing documents for online viewing

If you've decided to post your documents online, you need to make the design and production decisions that will help make the publication attractive and easy to use. If you're simply converting an existing paper document to electronic format, you'll inevitably weigh the benefits of reworking the design against the time and cost required to do so. If your publication will be viewed both onscreen and on paper, you'll need to be sure that the design accommodates the requirements of both.

First, you'll take a look at a printed document that was converted unchanged to electronic format. Converting a document to Adobe PDF is a good way to distribute the document cheaply and easily. It also enables you to use features such as links and bookmarks to make navigation of a longer document, such as a company FAQ, both easy and intuitive.

▶ **Tip:** Reading mode maximizes the screen space available to a document in Acrobat to give you more space to read. Choose View > Reading Mode to hide all the elements of the work area except the document and the menu bar. When you're done reading, choose View > Reading Mode again to restore the work area.

1 Choose File > Open, and open the Aquo_FAQs_Print.pdf file, located in the Lesson01 folder.

Notice that this long and narrow document is difficult to read onscreen. You must scroll down to read the entire page.

2 To view the entire page in the document pane, choose View > Zoom > Fit Page or click the Single Page button (⊞).

Even though the page fits onscreen, you can see that this document was designed for print. The long and narrow page is inconveniently shaped for the screen, and the small image and type sizes make reading a strain for the user.

Now you'll look at the same document redesigned and optimized for online reading.

3 Choose File > Open, and double-click the Aquo_FAQs_Web.pdf file.

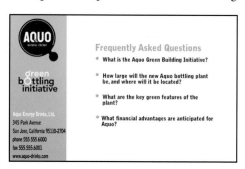

Notice that the horizontal page orientation makes this document better-suited for display on a monitor than the vertical orientation of the previous document.

4 Click the Bookmarks button in the navigation pane to open the Bookmarks panel.

5 Click the bookmark labeled "Size and location of the plant."

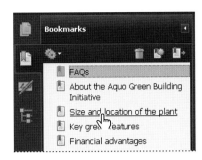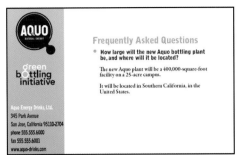

The question and answer about the plant's size and location appear. Notice how the larger type and different page size make this document easier to view than the document designed for print.

6 Click the bookmark labeled "FAQs."

7 Click one of the questions to jump to its page.

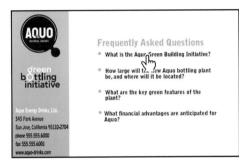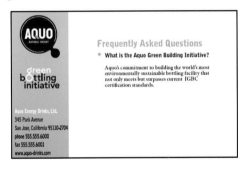

Each question on the first page of the document is a link that takes the viewer to the corresponding question. The original document has been redesigned to accommodate a navigational structure based on self-contained, screen-sized units.

The formatting considerations of onscreen publications—fonts, page size, layout, color, and resolution—are the same as those of other kinds of publications; however, each element must be re-evaluated in the context of onscreen viewing. Decisions about issues such as color and resolution, which in traditional publishing may require a trade-off between quality and cost, may require a parallel trade-off between quality and file size in electronic publishing. Once you have determined the page elements that are important to you, you need to choose the publishing tools and format that will best maintain the desired elements.

8 Choose File > Close to close each open PDF file.

In this part of the lesson, you have examined a variety of electronic documents designed in different file formats for different purposes, while getting acquainted with working in the Acrobat 9 work area. Later in this book, you'll get some hands-on practice in creating and tailoring electronic documents.

Getting help

Acrobat offers complete, accessible resources to help you learn and use the program:

- Adobe Acrobat 9 Help contains in-depth information about all the Acrobat commands and features.

- From Acrobat, you have a direct link to up-to-date support resources online at the Adobe website.

Using Adobe Acrobat 9 Help

The lessons in this book focus on commonly used tools and features of Acrobat 9. You can get complete information on all the Acrobat tools, commands, and features for both Windows and Mac OS systems from Adobe Acrobat 9 Help. Adobe Acrobat 9 Help is easy to use because you can look for topics in several ways:

- Scan the table of contents.

- Search for keywords.

- Jump from topic to topic using related topics links.

You'll use Acrobat 9 Help to find information about the application.

1   Choose Help > Adobe Acrobat 9 Help to open the Adobe Acrobat 9 Help in your
    default browser.

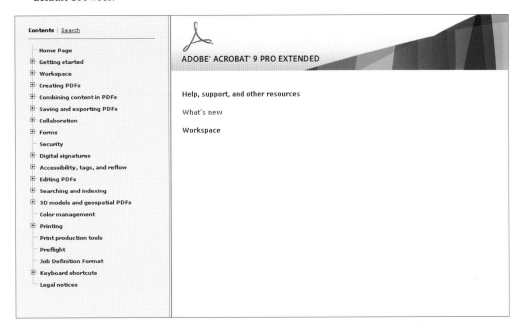

The help content is displayed in the right pane—the topic frame; the navigation
information is displayed in the left pane—the navigation frame.

2   If necessary, click the Contents link at the top of the navigation pane to show
    a table of contents in the navigation pane. Click the icons to the left of the
    headings to expand them.

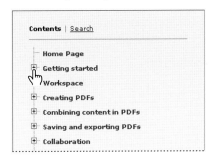 

3 Click on any heading or subheading to view help content in the topic pane on the right.

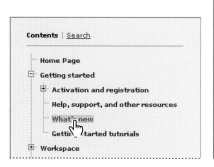

4 Use the headings in the navigation pane, or use the navigational buttons in the topic pane to browse through the content.

5 Click the Search link at the top of the navigation pane to start a search. The Search feature offers another way to find content in Help.

● **Note:** The search is not case-sensitive.

6 Type the word or words you want to search for, such as **PDF Portfolio** and click the Search button.

The search results are listed in the navigation pane.

7 To print a help topic, choose File > Print or click the Print button on the toolbar of your browser application.

You can view the help topics onscreen, or you can print them.

8 Close the browser to close Acrobat 9 Help.

9 Quit Acrobat by choosing File > Exit (Windows) or Acrobat > Quit Acrobat (Mac OS).

Now that you've been introduced to Acrobat, you can move through the lessons in this book and learn how to create and work with Adobe PDF files.

Review questions

1 Name one way you can create a PDF document.

2 Name two advantages of PDF documents.

3 How can you return to your usual work area from Full Screen mode?

Review answers

1 You can use the Create command in Acrobat, use the Adobe PDF printer from any application, use Acrobat PDFMaker from Microsoft Office in Windows or another supported application, scan a document and convert it to PDF, or create a PDF file from a web page using the From Web Page command in Acrobat.

2 Adobe PDF provides several advantages, including the following:

- Adobe PDF preserves the exact layout, fonts, and text formatting of electronic documents, regardless of the computer system or platform used to view these documents.

- PDF documents can contain multiple languages, such as Japanese and English, on the same page.

- PDF documents print predictably with proper margins and page breaks.

- PDF files can be secured to prevent undesired changes or printing, or to limit access to confidential documents.

- You can change the view magnification of a PDF page in Acrobat or Adobe Reader, which is especially useful for zooming in on graphics or diagrams containing intricate details.

3 To exit Full Screen mode and return to your normal work area, press the Esc key on your keyboard.

2 LOOKING AT THE WORK AREA

Lesson Overview

In this lesson, you'll do the following:

- Customize the display and arrangement of the Acrobat toolbars and tools.

- Add hidden tools to toolbars.

- Use the navigation pane to jump directly to specific pages in an open document.

- Change the view of a document in the document pane.

- Explore Organizer, an Acrobat feature designed to help you manage your files.

 This lesson will take approximately 30 minutes to complete. Copy the Lesson02 folder onto your hard drive if you haven't already done so.

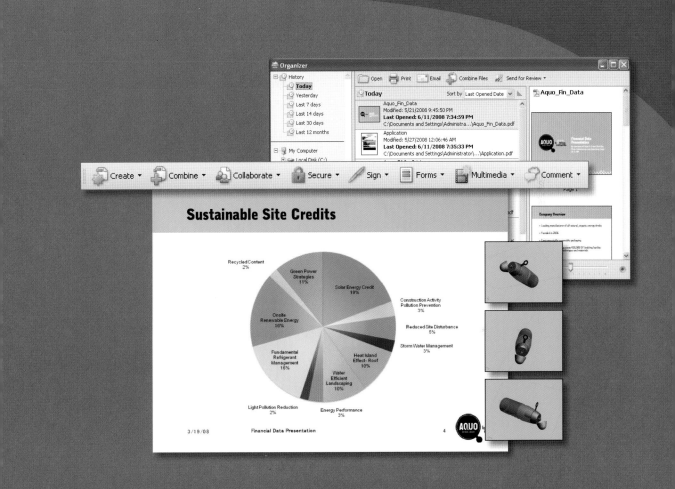

Opening a PDF file in the work area

The default Acrobat 9 work area is streamlined to ensure easy access to the tools you'll use most often as you work with PDF files.

1 Start Acrobat.

2 Choose File > Open. Select the Aquo_Fin_Data.pdf file in the Lesson02 folder, and click Open.

▶ **Tip:** In Windows, you can move between open PDF documents by clicking a file's icon in the Windows Taskbar.

Default toolbars are visible at the top of the work area. In Acrobat 9, each open document has its own work area and toolbars.

Working with Acrobat tools and toolbars

The default Acrobat toolbars contain commonly used tools and commands for working with PDF files. The toolbars are organized by function, with each toolbar displaying tools related to particular tasks, such as file management, page navigation, and page display.

In addition to the default toolbars, other toolbars are available from the Toolbars menu. As you work through the lessons in this book, you will use some of these additional toolbars.

You can customize the toolbars to fit your needs by floating and docking toolbars, rearranging toolbars, opening additional toolbars, and hiding toolbars to maximize your work area. You can also control which tools appear on a toolbar.

The majority of tools and toolbars are available across the Acrobat family—Acrobat Pro Extended, Acrobat Pro, and Acrobat Standard. If a particular tool or toolbar is not available in all three products, we'll note it.

Acrobat can open in two different ways—as a stand-alone application or in a web browser. The associated work areas differ in small but important ways. This book assumes that you are using Acrobat as a stand-alone application.

Reviewing the toolbars

This section introduces the default tools and toolbars. As you work through the lessons in this book, you'll learn more about each tool's function. You can view the name of a toolbar by moving your pointer over the toolbar's grabber bar. To see the name or description of a tool, hover your pointer over any button in a toolbar.

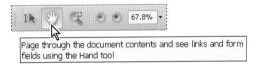

The default toolbars are File, Page Navigation, Select & Zoom, Page Display, Find, and Tasks. Each of these toolbars displays all or a subset of its available tools. The Tasks toolbar displays a series of buttons that give you quick access to commands related to a particular task. For information on the Tasks toolbar, see "Working with Acrobat task buttons" later in this lesson.

The File toolbar displays the Open, Print, Save, Email, and Upload Documents to Acrobat.com buttons.

The Page Navigation toolbar displays the Previous Page button, Next Page button, and Page Number display.

The Select & Zoom toolbar displays the Select, Hand, Marquee Zoom, Zoom Out, and Zoom In tools, and Zoom Value display.

The Page Display toolbar displays the Scrolling Mode and Single Page buttons.

The Find toolbar displays the Find text box.

1 On the Acrobat menu bar, choose View > Go To > Last Page.

2 In the document pane, click on the bottle.

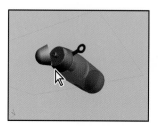

The 3D toolbar opens automatically when you activate 3D content in a PDF document.

3 Drag the bottle up and down and around to experience 3D PDF.

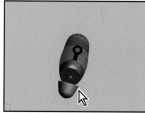

For information on the 3D toolbar and manipulating models, see Lesson 15, "Working with 3D in PDF Files."

4 On the Acrobat menu bar, choose View > Go To > First Page to return to the first page of the document.

Showing and hiding toolbars

The default work area purposely does not display all available toolbars nor does each toolbar display all the tools available. This allows you to work in an uncluttered space with plenty of room for your document and the tools you use most. If you need a tool or toolbar that is not displayed by default, you can quickly add it to your workspace. You also can hide toolbars that you don't use often to give yourself more working space.

1 Choose View > Toolbars to see the available toolbars. Check marks appear next to the toolbars that are currently displayed.

2 Select Edit from the menu to display the Edit toolbar.

The Edit toolbar appears in the work area, floating on top of the open document. Leave it there for now.

The Edit toolbar displays the Spell Check tool (for checking spelling in comments and form fields), and the Undo, Redo, and Copy tools (for editing text in Sticky Notes).

Now you'll hide a toolbar.

3 Choose View > Toolbars. To hide the Find toolbar, which is displayed in the toolbar area by default, select Find.

The Find toolbar disappears from the toolbar area. You can always display it again by choosing View > Toolbars > Find.

Docking, floating, and rearranging toolbars

You can dock and undock toolbars in the toolbar area, and rearrange docked toolbars to suit your needs.

1 To dock the floating Edit toolbar, drag the toolbar by its title bar or grabber bar to the row of docked toolbars at the top of the work area. Move the Edit toolbar into an empty area and release your mouse. Or move it over one of the toolbar grabber bars, and release your mouse when the grabber bar changes color.

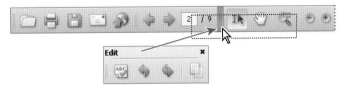

The Edit toolbar is now docked with the other toolbars.

2 To move the Edit toolbar to another place in the toolbar area, drag it by its grabber bar and drop it into an empty space or over one of the grabber bars of a docked toolbar.

You can also convert any docked toolbar to a floating toolbar by dragging it out of the toolbar area by its grabber bar.

3 Drag the Edit toolbar back into the document pane.

> **Tip:** To hide all toolbars in the work area to better view a large document, choose View > Toolbars > Hide Toolbars. To restore the toolbars to the work area in the same configuration, choose View > Toolbars > Show Toolbars. To hide all but the command bar, choose View > Reading Mode. Choose View > Reading Mode to exit the reading mode.

Hiding button labels

If your toolbar area becomes cluttered as you add hidden toolbars, you can create more space by hiding tool button labels.

Choose View > Toolbars > Button Labels. Choose No Labels to hide all labels, choose All Labels to display all labels that fit in the toolbar area, or choose Default Labels to display selected labels. Even if you choose All Labels, Acrobat automatically hides some labels if the toolbar area becomes full.

Locking toolbars

▶ **Tip:** If you have several PDFs open, you can customize the toolbars for each PDF independently. The different customized states persist as you switch between PDFs.

If you customize the arrangement of toolbars in the toolbar area, you can preserve your arrangement by locking the toolbars. Locking the toolbars maintains the configuration of docked toolbars and tools, even after you close and restart Acrobat. (You cannot lock the position of a floating toolbar.)

1 Choose View > Toolbars > Lock Toolbars.

When toolbars are locked, the grabber bars are hidden.

2 Choose View > Toolbars > Lock Toolbars again to unlock the toolbars.

Resetting the toolbars

Don't hesitate to rearrange your toolbars. If you don't like the result, you can revert to the Acrobat default toolbar arrangement at any time, with one simple command.

1 Choose View > Toolbars > Reset Toolbars.

Note that the Reset command does not work if your toolbars are locked. You must unlock your toolbars before you can reset them. The reset command does not restore the default setting for button labels.

2 Choose View > Toolbars > Button Labels > Default Labels to restore the default label configuration.

Selecting tools

The default tool in Acrobat is the Select tool (I▶).

To select a tool from a toolbar, click the tool button on the toolbar. A selected tool usually remains active until you select another tool. You'll try out a few tools in this section.

1 Click the Next Page button (↓) in the Page Navigation toolbar three times to page forward in the document to page 4.

2 Click the Marquee Zoom tool button
(🔍) on the Select & Zoom toolbar to
select that tool. Drag diagonally across
a portion of the page to zoom in on that
area.

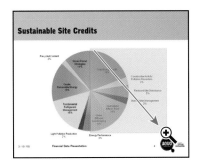

The Zoom tools do not change the actual size of a document. They change only its
magnification on your screen.

3 Hold down the spacebar on your keyboard and drag in the document pane. This
moves the magnified document around in the document pane so you can see
other parts of the document. Release the spacebar, reactivating the Marquee
Zoom tool.

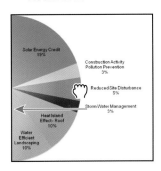 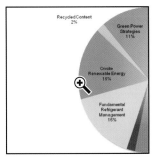

Holding down the spacebar when you have a tool selected temporarily switches the
focus to the Hand tool.

4 Click the arrow to the right of the
Zoom Value text box, and choose
100% from the menu to see the
document at 100%.

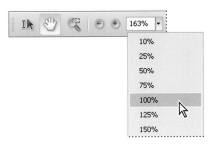

A black arrow to the right of a tool
indicates that there is a menu associated
with that tool. Click on the arrow to
reveal that menu.

Accessing hidden tools and toolbars from the Tools menu

The Tools menu offers another way to access hidden tools and toolbars. The Tools menu lists several commonly used toolbars and the full range of tools for those toolbars. Not all the tools listed in the menu are displayed when you show the toolbar.

The Tools menu is a convenient way to access hidden tools without cluttering the toolbar area with toolbars.

1   Drag the Select & Zoom toolbar out of the toolbar area and down towards the bottom of the document pane. The toolbar contains several tools and a text box.

2   Now choose Tools > Select & Zoom. Notice that this menu gives you access to additional tools.

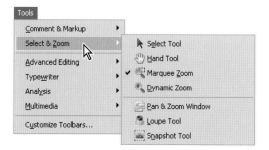

3   Select the Dynamic Zoom tool () from the Select & Zoom menu. Drag downwards in the document pane to reduce the view of the document; drag upwards to enlarge the view.

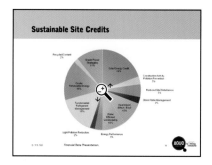
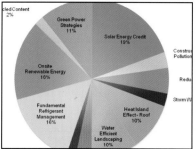

Tools can be selected from either the toolbar or the Tools menu.

4   Select the Hand tool on the toolbar.

Adding tools to a toolbar

As you just saw, some of the default toolbars have hidden tools associated with them. You can customize any of your toolbars by adding one or more hidden tools to them, or by removing some of the tools that you don't use.

1   Right-click (Windows) or Control-click (Mac OS) on the grabber bar of the Page Navigation toolbar.

The context menu lists all of the tools that you can display in the Page Navigation toolbar. Items with check marks are currently shown on the toolbar. Items without check marks are not shown on the toolbar.

2   Select First Page to add the First Page button to the Page Navigation toolbar.

3   Click the First Page button (⊼) to go to the cover page of the document.

4   To remove a tool from a toolbar, right-click (Windows) or Control-click (Mac OS) the tool, and in the menu, select the tool to be removed. We removed the First Page button.

The preceding method is an efficient way to add a hidden tool to a toolbar if you know which tool you want to add and which toolbar it is on. If that's not the case, try the following method of adding a hidden tool to a toolbar.

5   Choose Tools > Customize Toolbars.

The More Tools dialog box lists all of the Acrobat toolbars and the tools. Tools with check marks are shown; tools without check marks are hidden.

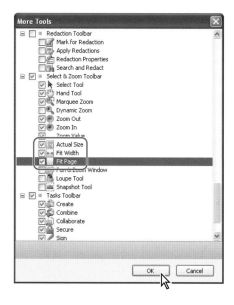

6 Scroll down through the More Tools dialog box until you see Select & Zoom Toolbar.

7 Click the boxes next to the Actual Size (![actual size icon]), Fit Width (![fit width icon]), and Fit Page (![fit page icon]) icons. Click OK.

These three tools are added to the Select & Zoom toolbar in your work area. Click each to explore how they affect the display of the document in the work area.

8 To reconfigure the toolbars to display only their default tools, choose View > Toolbars > Reset Toolbars.

Using keyboard shortcuts to select tools

You can set your Acrobat preferences so that you can use a keyboard shortcut to select a tool.

1 Choose Edit > Preferences (Windows) or Acrobat > Preferences (Mac OS), and select General in the left pane.

2 Select the Use Single-Key Accelerators To Access Tools option. A check mark appears in the box when this option is selected.

3 Click OK to apply the change.

Now when you position the pointer over some of the tools, you'll see a letter or Shift+[letter] in parentheses following the tool name. This is the keyboard shortcut for that tool.

4 Move your pointer over the Marquee Zoom tool in the Select & Zoom toolbar, and notice that the tool tip now contains the letter "Z." This is the keyboard shortcut.

5 Move the pointer into the document pane, and press "Z" on the keyboard. The pointer changes from a hand to a zoom tool.

6 Click the Hand tool or press "H" on the keyboard to return to the Hand tool.

Working with Acrobat task buttons

The Tasks toolbar is slightly different from the other toolbars. Each button on this toolbar relates to a particular task and has a menu of task-related commands.

You can show, hide, float, and dock the Tasks toolbar just like any other toolbar. Note, however, that the Tasks toolbar has no hidden tools or commands associated with it.

1 Click the Comment button ( ) on the Tasks toolbar.

The Comment button menu lists items related to the task of reviewing a document. All of the buttons on the Tasks toolbar have a similar task-oriented menu, making it easy to initiate tasks in Acrobat.

2 From the Comment button menu, choose Add Sticky Note ( ). A note is added automatically in the document pane. If necessary, click inside the note to create an insertion point, and type a short comment about the document. We typed "I'm testing the sticky note tool."

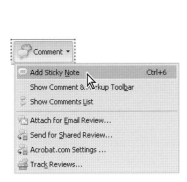

3 Click outside the note to deselect it. Click the close button to close the note window. You can drag the sticky note and the note icon anywhere on the document page. You'll learn more about commenting on documents in Lesson 9, "Using Acrobat in a Review Cycle."

Working with the navigation pane

Another major component in the Acrobat 9 work area is the navigation pane.

Reviewing the navigation pane buttons

The buttons along the left side of the document pane are the default navigation pane buttons. Each of the buttons opens a different panel in the navigation pane.

1 Move your pointer over each of the default buttons to display its name and description.

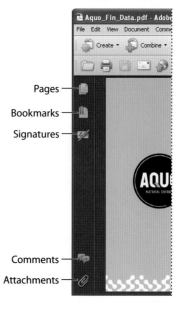

2 To view additional navigation panels, choose View > Navigation Panels. Click outside the menu to close it without making a selection.

Using the navigation pane

1 Click the Pages button (▤) in the navigation pane.

The Pages panel opens, showing a thumbnail image of each of the pages in the open document.

You click on a page thumbnail in the Pages panel to jump to that page in the PDF file.

2   Click the arrow next to the magnification box on the Select & Zoom toolbar, and select 150%. Then click the page thumbnail for page 5 to display that page in the document pane. (You may have to scroll down in the Pages panel to see the page 5 thumbnail.)

 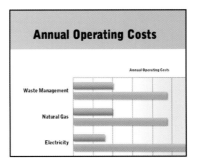

3   Drag the top border of the red bounding box on the page thumbnail up and down or right and left to move the corresponding page the same direction in the document pane.

 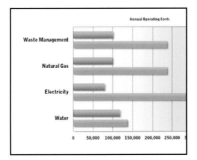

The red bounding box indicates the area displayed in the document window.

Page thumbnails not only let you navigate through your document, but they also let you change the view of the page in your document pane. You'll learn more about using page thumbnails in Lesson 7, "Enhancing and Editing PDF Documents."

4   Click the Bookmarks button ( ) in the navigation pane.

5 Click the Construction Costs & Sustainable Site Credits bookmark icon in the Bookmarks panel to jump to that page in the open document.

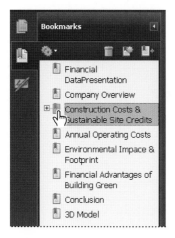

Nested bookmarks have a plus sign or triangle next to them. You expand or collapse a nested bookmark by clicking the icon to the left of the bookmark.

Notice that the buttons for the Attachments and Comments panels are located near the bottom of the navigation pane. Both of these panels open horizontally across the bottom of the work area.

You can change the orientation of any panel to either vertical or horizontal. To orient a panel vertically, drag its button to the upper part of the navigation pane, near the buttons of other vertically oriented panels. To orient a panel horizontally, drag its button to the lower part of the navigation pane, near the buttons of other horizontally oriented panels.

6 Click the Comments button.

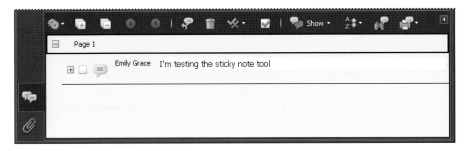

The Comments List in the Comments panel has a unique set of buttons and commands that help you manage comments in a PDF document. See Lesson 9, "Using Acrobat in a Review Cycle."

7 Choose View > Navigation Panels > Reset Panels to reset the navigation pane buttons to their default configuration.

As you work through later lessons in this book, you'll learn more about the functions of each of the panels in the navigation pane.

8 Choose File > Close and close the file without saving your work.

▶ **Tip:** You can change the width of an open navigation panel by dragging its right border.

Using Organizer

Organizer is a powerful feature for locating and managing your PDF files in Acrobat. Organizer displays the history of PDF files you have accessed by date; it lets you group your PDF files into collections and favorites; and it allows you to browse through documents page-by-page, without having to open them to find exactly what you're looking for.

In addition you can use the buttons on the Organizer toolbar to open a PDF file, print it, email it, or send it for review. You can even combine PDF files from within Organizer. In this lesson, you'll review the basics of the Organizer feature.

If you did not work through Lesson 1 today, please navigate to the Lesson01 folder and open and close each file in that folder at least once.

First you'll look at how you can use Organizer to get fast and easy access to all of your PDF documents.

1 Choose File > Organizer > Open Organizer to open the Organizer window.

2 Select Today under History in the left pane. Notice that the Organizer window has three panes: the Categories pane, the Files pane, and the Pages pane.

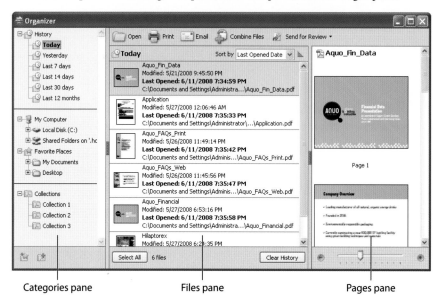

Categories pane   Files pane   Pages pane

The Categories pane (on the left) is divided into three areas.

- The History area limits the display of files to files opened today, yesterday, or within the last week, two weeks, month or year.

- The My Computer area displays the hierarchy of folders and drives on your computer system, including locations you've marked as Favorite Places for quick access.

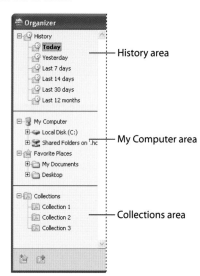

- The Collections area lists PDF files that you've associated with one another for a particular task or by subject matter. Collections can include files located in different places on your computer system, so you can quickly access related files without having to move them into the same folder.

The Files pane (in the center) lists all the PDF files included in any selection that you make in the Categories pane.

The Pages pane (on the right) displays thumbnails of the pages in the PDF files selected in the Files pane.

Locating and sorting PDFs in Organizer

First you'll look at the History component of the Categories pane.

1   Make sure that Today is still selected in the History area and that Last Opened Date is selected in the Sort By menu in the Files pane.

2   Notice that all the files you used today—the files you used earlier in this lesson and in Lesson 1—are now listed in the Files pane in the center of the Organizer work area. Select the last file you opened, Aquo_Fin_Data.pdf.

Look at the Pages pane on the right. All the pages in Aquo_Fin_Data.pdf are displayed there as thumbnail images.

3   Drag the slider at the bottom of the Pages pane to reduce the view so you can see all of the Aquo_Fin_Data.pdf page thumbnails without having to scroll down.

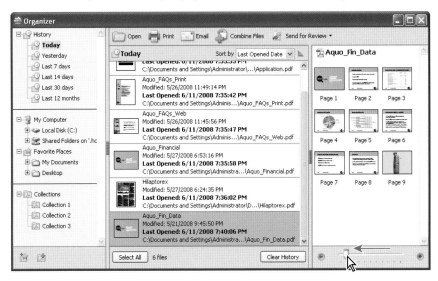

4   Double-click any page in the Pages pane to open the Aquo_Fin_Data.pdf file to that page in Acrobat.

You just opened a PDF file in Acrobat directly from the Pages pane of the Organizer. You can also open PDF files by double-clicking any file in the Files pane of the Organizer.

5   In the Organizer, click the arrow next to the Sort By menu at the top of the Files pane, and select Filename from the sort criteria. The files you selected using the History category are now sorted alphabetically in the Files pane.

Now you'll see how you can use the Organizer to quickly scan for a particular page in a file.

6   To display all the pages of all the files that you used today in the Pages pane, click the Select All button at the bottom of the Files panel.

7   Use the scroll bar on the right of the Panes panel to scroll through all the pages in all the selected files. It may take a few moments for the display to catch up with the scroll bar.

This is a quick way to scan multiple PDF files to find a particular page.

8   Drag the pointer on the Zoom bar at the bottom of the Pages pane to reduce or magnify the view of the pages in the Pages pane.

9   In Acrobat, close any open files. Leave the Organizer open.

▶ **Tip:** The Clear History button clears the Files pane. This operation cannot be undone.

Creating a collection

Now you'll create a collection of PDF files. A collection can include any number of PDF files. The files do not have to be in the same folder or even on the same system. For the purpose of this lesson, you'll create a collection that contains all the files in the Lesson01 folder.

1   Go to the Collections area at the bottom of the Categories pane in the Organizer. Right-click (Windows) or Control-click (Mac OS) on the Collection 1 icon. From the context menu, choose Rename Collection and type **My_Lesson_1** as the name for your new collection. Then click outside the label.

Organizer gives you several empty Collections icons to get you started. You can rename these collections or you can create new collections using the New Collection button (▣) at the bottom of the Categories pane.

Now you'll add the files from the Lesson01 folder to the collection.

2   Right-click (Windows) or Control-click (Mac OS) again on the My_Lesson_1 collection icon, and choose Add Files from the context menu.

3   In the Select Files To Add To Your Collection dialog box, navigate to the Lesson01 folder. Shift-click on the top and bottom files in the list to select all the files in the Lesson01 folder. Click Add.

You can add more files to the collection from another location on your system the same way.

You can delete a file from a collection by selecting the file in the Files pane, right-clicking (Windows) or Control-clicking (Mac OS), and choosing Remove From 'collection name' from the context menu.

4 When you're finished, click the close button in the Organizer window. Then exit Acrobat.

The lesson files used in this book are organized in folders, so you don't really need the capabilities of Organizer to keep track of your PDF lesson files. When you start creating your own PDF files and receiving files from other people, you'll find that Organizer is a powerful management tool.

▶ **Tip:** You can determine the actual physical location of a file in Windows Explorer or in the Mac OS Finder by right-clicking (Windows) or Control-clicking (Mac OS) on the file icon or on a file name in the Files pane, and choosing Show in Windows Explorer (Windows) or Show in Finder (Mac OS).

Review questions

1 How do you display a hidden toolbar in the work area?

2 How do you dock a floating toolbar?

3 Describe two ways to add a hidden tool to a toolbar.

4 How do you reset all toolbars and tools to their default configuration?

Review answers

1 To display a hidden toolbar, choose View > Toolbars, and select the hidden toolbar's name from the Toolbars menu.

2 To dock a floating toolbar, drag the floating toolbar by its title bar or grabber bar to the row of docked toolbars in your work area. Move it over one of the toolbar grabber bars, and release your mouse when the grabber bar changes color.

3 To add a hidden tool to a toolbar, right-click (Windows) or Control-click (Mac OS) on a toolbar in your work area, and select the desired tool from the context menu. Alternatively, choose Tools > Customize Toolbars. In the More Tools dialog box, select the tool name and click OK.

4 To reset all toolbars and tools to their default configuration, choose View > Toolbars > Reset Toolbars.

3 CREATING ADOBE PDF FILES

Lesson Overview

In this lesson, you'll do the following:

- Convert a TIFF file to Adobe PDF using the Create PDF command.

- Convert a file to Adobe PDF using the authoring application's Print command.

- Convert email messages to Adobe PDF.

- Convert web pages to Adobe PDF from Acrobat and directly from Internet Explorer (Windows).

- Convert multimedia files to Adobe PDF files.

- Explore the Adobe PDF settings used to convert files to Adobe PDF.

- Reduce the size of a PDF file.

 This lesson will take approximately 60 minutes to complete. Copy the Lesson03 folder onto your hard drive if you haven't already done so.

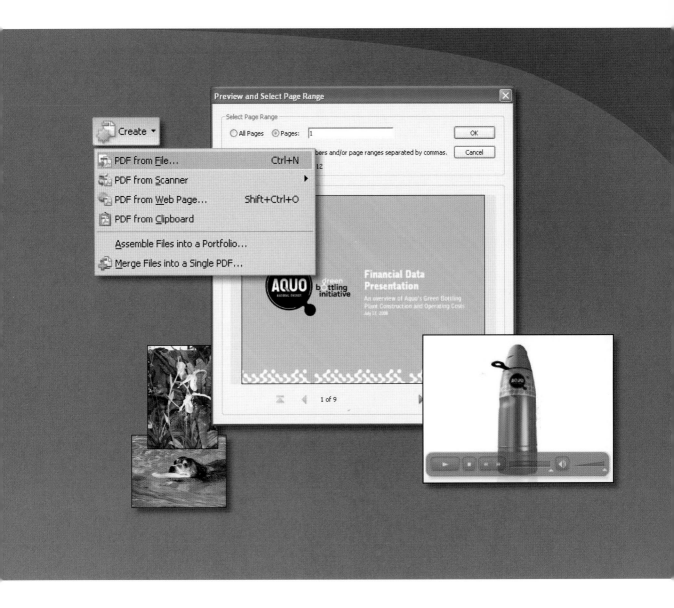

About creating Adobe PDF files

You can convert a variety of file formats to Adobe PDF, preserving all the fonts, formatting, graphics, and color of the source file, regardless of the application and platform used to create it. You can create PDFs from blank pages, document files, websites, scanned paper documents, and clipboard content.

If the document you want to convert to PDF is open in its authoring application (for example, a spreadsheet is open in Excel), you can usually convert the file to PDF without opening Acrobat. But if Acrobat is already open, you don't have to open the authoring application to convert a file to PDF.

You also need to consider PDF file size and quality (image resolution, for example). When such factors are critical, you'll want to use a method that allows you to control conversion options. Dragging and dropping files on the Acrobat icon to create PDF files is fast and easy, but if you want more control over the process, you'll want to use another method, such as using the Create PDF menu in Acrobat or printing to the Adobe PDF Printer in the authoring application. After you set conversion settings, the settings apply across PDFMaker, Acrobat, and Acrobat Distiller until you change them.

● **Note:** When you're creating a PDF from within Acrobat, you must have the application that created the original file installed on your system.

Lesson 4, "Creating Adobe PDF from Microsoft Office Files (Windows)," describes how to create Adobe PDF files directly from a variety of Microsoft Office files using PDFMaker in Windows. Lesson 14, "Using Acrobat in Professional Printing," covers the creation of press-quality PDF files.

Increasingly the content of Adobe PDF files is being reused when the security settings applied by the creator of the document allow for such reuse. Content can be extracted for use in another authoring application or the content can be reflowed for use with handheld devices or screen readers. The success with which content can be repurposed or reused depends very much on the structural information contained in the PDF file. The more structural information a PDF document contains, the more opportunities you have for successfully reusing the content and the more reliably a document can be used with screen readers. (For more information, see Lesson 6, "Reading and Working with PDF Files.")

Using the Create PDF command

You can convert a variety of different file formats to Adobe PDF using the Create PDF command in Acrobat.

In this section of the lesson, you'll convert a single TIFF file to an Adobe PDF file. You can use this same method to convert a variety of both image and non-image file types to Adobe PDF.

1 Open Acrobat.

2 Do one of the following:

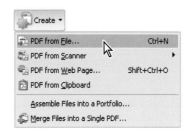

- On Windows, click the Create button on the Tasks toolbar, and choose PDF From File.

- On Mac OS, choose File > Create PDF > From File. (On Mac OS, the Tasks toolbar is not available until you have a PDF document open.)

3 In the Open dialog box, click the arrow to display the Files Of Type (Windows) or Show (Mac OS) menu, and choose TIFF for the file type. (The menu lists all the file types that can be converted using this method.)

4 Click Settings to open the Adobe PDF Settings dialog box.

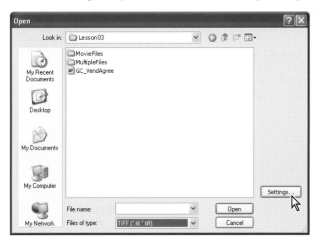
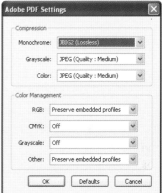

This is where you set the compression that will be applied to color, grayscale, and monochrome images, and where you select the color management options used when the file is converted to Adobe PDF. Resolution is determined automatically.

5 Click Cancel to leave the options unchanged for now.

You can also review and edit the conversions settings used to convert your files to PDF in the Convert To PDF panel of the Preferences dialog box.

6   In the Open dialog box, navigate to the Lesson03 folder, select the GC_VendAgree.tif file, and click Open.

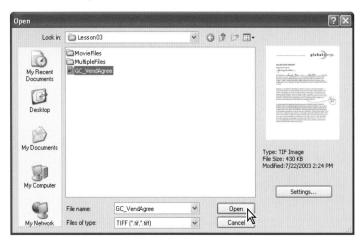

Acrobat converts the TIFF file to Adobe PDF and opens the PDF file automatically.

7   Select View > Zoom > Fit Page or click the Single Page button (⊞) on the toolbar so that you can see the entire agreement.

Notice the handwritten note that the signer of the agreement has added is preserved in the Adobe PDF file.

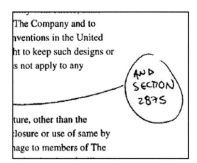

8   Choose File > Save As, name the file **GCVend_Agree1.pdf**, and save it in the Lesson03 folder. Choose File > Close to close the PDF file when you are finished.

On Windows, you can create and consolidate Adobe PDF files using the Convert To Adobe PDF command or the Combine Supported Files In Acrobat command. See "Exploring on your own: Creating Adobe PDF from the context menu" later in this lesson.

Dragging and dropping files

You can create Adobe PDF files from a variety of files by simply dragging the file onto the Acrobat icon or by dragging the file into the document pane in Acrobat (Windows). Note that the conversion settings used are the last ones you defined.

Experiment with dragging the Orchids.jpg file and the H2O_Dog.jpg files into the Acrobat document pane (Windows), onto the Acrobat icon on your desktop, or onto the Acrobat icon in the Dock (Mac OS). Close any open PDF files when you are finished.

Creating Adobe PDF from Microsoft Office files (Mac OS)

In Acrobat 9, you convert Microsoft Office files to Adobe PDF just as you would convert any other file. You can use the Print command in Microsoft Office combined with the Adobe PDF printer. You can use the Create PDF menu in Acrobat. Or you can drag the file onto the Acrobat icon on your desktop. Acrobat 9 does not offer PDFMaker for Mac OS. For more information, see the relevant topics in this lesson and "Creating PDFs" in the Adobe Acrobat 9 Help.

Converting and combining different types of files

You can use the Assemble Files Into A Portfolio command or the Merge Files Into A Single PDF command on the Create button menu to easily convert different types of files to Adobe PDF and assemble them into a PDF Portfolio or combine them into one PDF file. For information on assembling files into a PDF Portfolio, see Lesson 5, "Combining Files in PDF Portfolios."

In this part of the lesson, you'll convert a file to Adobe PDF and combine it with several other PDF files.

Assembling the files

1   In Acrobat, click the Create button or the Combine button on the Tasks toolbar, and choose Merge Files Into A Single PDF. (On Mac OS, choose File > Create PDF > Merge Files Into A Single PDF.)

The Combine Files dialog box is where you assemble your documents.

2   Click the Add Files button in the Combine Files dialog box.

The Add Files menu lets you add files, all files in a folder, files that you have combined into PDF files in other sessions, and any open files.

Now you'll select the files that you want to convert and combine. The types of files that you can convert varies depending on whether you are working on Windows or Mac OS.

3   Choose Add Files, and in the Add Files dialog box navigate to the MultipleFiles folder in the Lesson03 folder. Make sure that All Files is selected in the Files of Type menu (Windows) or All Supported Formats is selected in the Show menu (Mac OS). Select the bottle.jpg file. Ctrl-click (Windows) or Command-click (Mac OS) to add the following files to your selection:

*   Analysis.xls.pdf

*   Ad.pdf

*   Data.ppt.pdf

*   Install.pdf

*   Application.pdf

4   Click Add Files.

It doesn't matter in what order you add these files, because you can rearrange them in this window. You can also use the Remove button to remove any unwanted files.

5 Select each file in turn, and use the Move Up and Move Down buttons to arrange the files in the following order:

- Ad.pdf

- Data.ppt.pdf

- Analysis.xls.pdf

- Application.pdf

- Install.pdf

- bottle.jpg

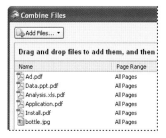

You can convert all pages in a file, or you can select a specific page or range of pages to convert.

6 Select the Data.ppt.pdf file in the Combine Files dialog box, and click the Choose Pages button. Use the page controls in the Preview And Select Page Range dialog box to review the pages in this document.

7 Select the Pages option, and enter **1** in the text box to convert only the first page of the presentation. Click OK. Notice that the entry in the Page Range column has changed.

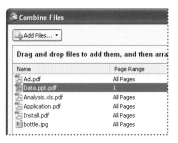

Converting and consolidating the files

For this lesson, you'll use the Default File Size conversion setting to convert the assembled files into one PDF file.

Use the File Size option to specify the size of your PDF file—small, medium, or large.

1   Click Combine Files.

You'll see the progression of the conversion and consolidation process.

2   In the Save As dialog box, rename the file **Aquo.pdf**. Click Save, and save your work in the Lesson03 folder.

The consolidated Adobe PDF file, named Binder1.pdf by default and renamed Aquo.pdf, opens automatically.

3   Use the Next Page ( ) and Previous Page ( ) buttons to page through your consolidated documents.

Without leaving Acrobat, you have converted a JPEG file to Adobe PDF and combined it with several other PDF files.

4   Choose File > Close to close the file.

Creating a PDF document from a blank page

In Acrobat, you can create PDF files from blank pages, which makes it easy to create a cover page for a project, for example.

1   In Acrobat, choose File > Create PDF > From Blank Page.

2   Begin typing. Use options on the New Document toolbar to change text attributes.

3   Choose File > Save As to save the document.

4   To continue editing, choose Document > Resume Editing.

5   To prevent anyone from editing the PDF, choose Document > Prevent Further Edits. (This action cannot be undone.)

Text is converted to tagged PDF.

You set the default font, margins, and page size for blank pages in the New Document preferences.

Using the Print command to create Adobe PDF files

As you saw earlier in this lesson, you can easily create Adobe PDF files using the Acrobat Create PDF command or the Create button on the Tasks toolbar. Additionally, authoring applications, such as Adobe InDesign, Adobe Photoshop, and Adobe PageMaker, have special commands such as the Export command and the Save As command that also allow you to convert a file to Adobe PDF. To make full use of these latter commands, consult the documentation that came with your authoring application.

While not all file types are supported by the Create PDF command and the Create button in the Tasks toolbar, and while not all authoring applications have special buttons or commands for converting files to Adobe PDF, you can still create an Adobe PDF file from almost any application file by using the application's Print command in conjunction with the Adobe PDF printer. The Adobe PDF printer uses the same conversion options as Distiller.

The Adobe PDF printer isn't a physical printer like the one sitting in your office or on your desk. Rather, it is a simulated printer that converts your file to Adobe PDF instead of printing it to paper. The printer name is Adobe PDF.

Printing to the Adobe PDF printer

In this part of the lesson, you'll convert a text file to Adobe PDF using the File > Print command in conjunction with your Adobe PDF printer. You can use this technique from almost any application, including the Microsoft and Adobe applications that have built-in Convert To Adobe PDF buttons and Export or Save As Adobe PDF commands. You should be aware, however, that the Adobe PDF printer creates untagged PDF files. (A tagged structure is required for reflowing content to a handheld device and is preferable for producing reliable results with a screen reader.)

From your desktop, navigate to the Lesson03 folder, and double-click the Memo.txt file.

The text file should open in a text editor such as NotePad on Windows or TextEdit on Mac OS.

Follow the steps for your platform, Windows or Mac OS, to convert the file to Adobe PDF.

On Windows:

Steps may vary depending on whether you are using Windows XP or Vista. These steps assume that you are using Windows XP Professional.

1   In a text-editing program, such as NotePad, choose File > Page Setup.

2   In the Page Setup dialog box, click the Printer button.

3   Click the arrow next to the Name text box to display the list of available printers. Select Adobe PDF. If you want to change the settings used in the conversion of the text file to Adobe PDF, you would do so by clicking the Properties button in this Page Setup dialog box. For more information, see "About the Adobe PDF Settings (presets)," later in this lesson.

4   Click OK, and click OK again to return to the memo.

5   Choose File > Print, make sure that the Adobe PDF printer is selected, and click Print.

6   Save the file using the default name (Memo.pdf) in the Lesson03 folder, and click Save in the Save PDF File As dialog box.

7   If the PDF file doesn't open automatically, navigate to the Lesson03 folder, and double-click the Memo.pdf file to open it in Acrobat. When you have reviewed the file, close it and exit NotePad (or the application you were using).

The Adobe PDF printer is an easy and convenient way to create a PDF file from almost any document. However, if you're working with Microsoft Office files, you should use the Create Adobe PDF buttons or the Acrobat ribbon (which use PDFMaker) for best results. If you use the Adobe PDF printer, your PDF files will be untagged and won't include bookmarks and hypertext links.

8   Close any open files.

On Mac OS:

1   Choose File > Print, and make sure that the Adobe PDF printer (Adobe PDF 9.0) is selected from the Printer menu.

If you want to change the settings used in the conversion of the text file to Adobe PDF, you would do so by choosing PDF Options from the pop-up menu below Presets.

2   Click the PDF button at the bottom of the dialog box, and choose Save As PDF.

3 In the Save dialog box, you can rename the PDF file and choose where to save it. For this lesson, save the file as **Memo.pdf** in the Lesson03 folder.

4 Click Save.

5 If the PDF file doesn't open automatically, navigate to the Lesson03 folder, and double-click the Memo.pdf file to open it in Acrobat. When you have reviewed the file, close it and quit the TextEdit (or equivalent) application.

You have just converted a simple text document to an Adobe PDF document using the authoring application's Print command.

6 Close any open files.

About the Adobe PDF Settings (presets)

In this portion of the lesson, you'll look at the Adobe PDF conversion settings (or presets) that allow you to create an Adobe PDF file that best balances quality and size for your needs. For example, a PDF file created for high-quality commercial printing requires different conversion settings than a PDF file intended only for onscreen viewing and quick downloading over the Internet.

The Adobe PDF settings or presets—the settings that control the conversion of files to Adobe PDF—can be accessed and set from a number of different places. You can access the Adobe PDF settings from Distiller, from the Adobe PDF printer, from the Adobe PDF menu in Microsoft Office applications (Windows), and from the Print dialog box in many authoring applications. Regardless of where you access the settings from, the Adobe PDF Settings dialog box and the options it contains are the same. To access the Adobe PDF Settings dialog box, do one of the following:

• In Acrobat, choose Advanced > Print Production > Acrobat Distiller to open Distiller. The predefined presets are available in the Default Settings menu, and you can customize settings by choosing Settings > Edit Adobe PDF Settings.

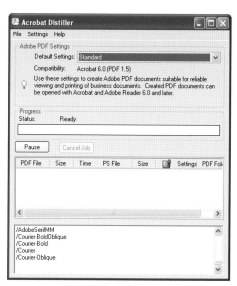

- On Windows, open a file in an authoring application such as Adobe FrameMaker or Microsoft Word, choose File > Print, and choose Adobe PDF from the printer menu. Depending on your application, click the Properties or Preferences button. (In some applications, you may need to click Setup in the Print dialog box to access the list of printers and the Properties or Preferences button.) The predefined presets are available in the Default Settings menu, along with any customized settings that you have defined using Distiller. You can also customize settings by clicking the Edit button.

- In Office 2007, choose Acrobat > Preferences.

▶ **Tip:** Regardless of how you access the Adobe PDF Settings dialog box, you should check your settings periodically.

- On Mac OS, open a file in an authoring application such as Microsoft Word or TextEdit, choose File > Print, and choose Adobe PDF 9.0 from the Printer menu. Select PDF Options from the pop-up menu (Copies & Pages) below the Presets menu to access the Adobe PDF Settings. The predefined presets are available in the Adobe PDF Settings menu, along with any customized settings that you have defined using Distiller.

For information on changing the Adobe PDF Settings in PDFMaker on Windows, see Lesson 4, "Creating Adobe PDF from Microsoft Office Files (Windows)."

Reducing file size

The size of a PDF file can vary tremendously depending on the Adobe PDF settings used to create the file. For example, files created using the High Quality Print preset will be larger than files created using the Standard or Smallest File Size presets. Regardless of the preset used to create a file, you can often reduce the file size without having to regenerate the PDF file.

In this section, you'll use the Reduce File Size command to dramatically reduce the size of the Ad.pdf file.

1 In Acrobat, open the Ad.pdf file in the Lesson03/MultipleFiles folder.

2 Choose Document > Reduce File Size.

3 Select Acrobat 8.0 And Later for file compatibility, and click OK.

When you choose the compatibility level, be aware that the newer the version of Acrobat that you choose, the smaller the file. If you choose compatibility with Acrobat 9, however, you should be sure that your intended audience does indeed have version 9 installed.

4 Name the modified file **Ad_Reduce.pdf**. Click Save to complete the process.

It is always a good idea to save a file using a different name so that you don't over-write an unmodified file.

Acrobat automatically optimizes your PDF file, a process that may take a minute or two. Any anomalies are displayed in the Conversion Warnings window. If necessary, click OK to close the window.

5 Minimize the Acrobat window. Use Windows Explorer (Windows) or the Finder (Mac OS) to open the MultipleFiles folder in the Lesson03 folder and view the size of the Ad_Reduce.pdf file. The file size is smaller.

You can repeat steps 1-5 using different compatibility settings to see how they affect file size. Note that some settings might actually increase the file size.

PDF Optimizer offers more opportunities to control quality trade-offs.

6 Choose File > Close to close your file.

About compression and resampling

Many factors affect file size and file quality, but when you're working with image-intensive files, compression and resampling are important.

You can choose from a variety of file compression methods designed to reduce the file space used by color, grayscale, and monochrome images in your document. Which method you choose depends on the kind of images you are compressing. The default Adobe PDF presets use automatic (JPEG) compression for color and gray-scale images and CCITT Group 4 compression for monochrome images.

In addition to choosing a compression method, you can resample bitmap images in your file to reduce the file size. A bitmap image consists of digital units called pixels, whose total number determines the file size. When you resample a bitmap image, the information represented by several pixels in the image is combined to make a single larger pixel. This process is also called downsampling because it reduces the number of pixels in the image. (When you downsample or decrease the number of pixels, information is deleted from the image.)

Neither compression nor resampling affects the quality of text or line art.

Creating files from the clipboard

In Windows, you can copy content from any type of file and then choose File > Create PDF > From Clipboard in Acrobat to create a new PDF file. The Create PDF From Clipboard command uses Distiller to convert content to PDF, and PDF content created in this way is fully searchable; it is not an image. (On Mac OS, use the From Clipboard Image command to convert screen shots.)

In Windows, you can also easily add text and graphics that you have copied to the clipboard to an existing PDF. Open the PDF file, and choose Document > Insert Pages > From Clipboard.

Inserting multimedia files

If you are using Acrobat Pro or Pro Extended, you can use the 3D tool, the Flash tool, the Sound tool, or the Video tool to add content to an existing PDF file.

1   In Acrobat Pro or Pro Extended, navigate to the MovieFiles folder in the Lesson03 folder and open the file Aquo_Blank.pdf.

This is the file into which you'll insert a video clip. (If you're using Pro Extended, the file will be converted to Flash format.)

2   Click the Multimedia button on the Tasks toolbar, and select the Video tool.

3   Drag a box to the right of the text. Size and location of the box are not critical. You can resize and reposition the box later. When you release the mouse, the Insert Video dialog box opens.

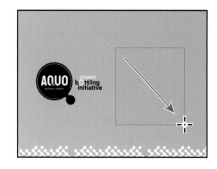

4 In the Insert Video dialog box, click Browse or Choose, navigate to the Lesson03/ MovieFiles folder, and select the Bottle.mov file. Click Open.

5 Do one of the following, depending on the version of Acrobat you have:

- **In Acrobat Pro Extended:** Click OK in the Insert Video dialog box. Acrobat transcodes the file, converting it from a QuickTime movie to an FLV file that will be fully embedded within the PDF file. Acrobat displays a progress box, and then inserts a poster image in the box you drew.

If you select Show Advanced Options in the Insert Video dialog box, you can specify whether the movie plays automatically or only when a user clicks it, whether it plays in the preview window or in a floating window, and more. You'll learn more in Lesson 11, "Creating Multimedia Presentations." For this lesson, you'll use the default settings.

- **In Acrobat Pro:** Click Continue to clear the message box that warns you that viewers will need an external player, such as QuickTime, to view the movie. In the Add Movie dialog box, click OK.

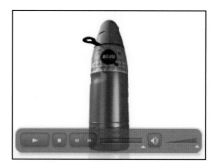

6 Select the Hand tool, and then click on the poster image to start the video clip. If you are using Acrobat Pro, Acrobat asks whether you trust the content before it accesses an external player; select an option and click Play.

7 When you have finished watching the clip, choose File > Close to close the file without saving any changes.

Adding 3D content, Flash content, and sound is equally easy with Acrobat 9 Pro or Pro Extended.

3D Reviewer (Pro Extended only)

You can use Adobe 3D Reviewer to edit most 3D models in native file formats and in PDF, which is useful if you want to change or remove entities from a 3D model and you don't have the source application installed.

Scanning a paper document

Scanning paper documents to PDF is much improved in Acrobat 9. You can scan to PDF or PDF/A from a broad range of scanners, add metadata while scanning, and optimize your scanned PDF. On Windows, you have presets for black and white, grayscale, color documents, and color images. These presets optimize the quality of your scanned document. You can also define your own conversion settings.

If you do not have a scanner connected to your system, skip this section of the lesson.

1 Insert any one-page document into your scanner, and push the Scan button on the scanner. This automatically opens a dialog box on your system asking which program to launch to execute the scan. Choose Acrobat. Alternatively, do one of the following:

   • **On Windows:** In Acrobat, choose File > Create PDF > From Scanner and select a preset for your document.

   • **On Mac OS:** Choose File > Create PDF > From Scanner, select options in the Acrobat Scan dialog box, and click Scan.

The scan occurs automatically.

2 When prompted, click OK to confirm that the scan is complete.

The PDF of the scan is displayed in Acrobat.

3 Choose File > Save, and save the scan in the Lesson03 folder as Scan.pdf.

4 On Windows, to see the settings that were used for the conversion, choose File > Create PDF > From Scanner > Configure Presets. In this dialog box, you can specify a number of options including single- or double-sided scanning, paper size, prompt for more pages, file size, application of optical character recognition, and addition of metadata in the Document Properties dialog box. Click Cancel to exit the dialog box without making any changes.

5 Choose File > Close and close your document.

Converting emails to PDF (Windows)

To complete this section of the lesson, you need to be using the commonly used Microsoft Outlook or Lotus Notes as your email program and to be working on the Windows platform. You will use your own email files as you work through the lesson.

It can be useful to have emails in a form that is independent of your email application, either for archival purposes or just for the convenience of having a more portable and a more easily searchable file. Acrobat adds buttons and commands to the Outlook and Lotus menus and toolbars that allow you to convert individual emails or email folders to Adobe PDF. PDFMaker is used for the conversion.

If you don't see the Acrobat button or commands in Outlook or Lotus Notes, consult the online Adobe Acrobat 9 Help, " Show or activate PDFMaker in Microsoft Office and LotusNotes."

You can convert one message, several messages, or even a folder of messages to Adobe PDF.

Converting email folders

At the completion of any personal or business project, you'll often have a folder or several folders full of project-related email messages. With Acrobat 9 you can easily convert these folders to a fully searchable Adobe PDF file that is completely independent of your email application.

Each email message in the folder is converted as a separate file and saved by default in a PDF Portfolio.

1   In Microsoft Outlook or Lotus Notes, select any folder (we selected the Inbox folder), and click the Create Adobe PDF From Folders button (Outlook) or Convert Selected Folder(s) To Adobe PDF (Lotus Notes) on the email application toolbar.

It can take some time to convert very large email folders, so for this lesson you might want to select folders that don't contain many messages.

2   In Outlook, in the Convert Folder(s) To PDF dialog box, you can select additional folders that you want to convert. Use the Convert This Folder And All Sub Folders option to automatically include all subfolders. Alternatively, expand the folder and manually select the required subfolders. We selected the Inbox folder and left the Convert This Folder And All Sub Folders option unselected. Click OK.

3   In the Save Adobe PDF File As dialog box, click Save to save the PDF file in the Lesson03 folder under the email folder name (Inbox.pdf). You may need to allow access to the email application program.

Your converted emails open automatically in a PDF Portfolio in Acrobat.

Setting up automatic archiving

Automatically backing up your email messages is easy with Acrobat 9.

1   In Outlook, choose Adobe PDF > Setup Automatic Archival. In Lotus Notes, choose Actions > Setup Automatic Archival.

2   In the Acrobat PDFMaker dialog box, click the Automatic Archival tab and select Enable Automatic Archival.

Now you'll specify how often the backup operation will run. You'll set the options to back up your email weekly on Saturday at 12:00 PM.

3   For Frequency, select Weekly and choose Saturday from the adjacent menu.

4   For Run At, choose 12:00 PM. You can use the arrow keys to increment or decrement the time, or you can select the hours, minutes and AM/PM entry and type in new values.

You'll leave the other options at their default values.

5   To select the folders to archive, click Add.

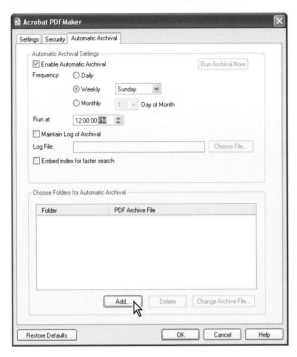

▶ **Tip:** The Embed Index For Faster Search option is useful when you archive folders containing many emails. This option creates an index for the entire email collection. Searching this index is faster than searching the PDF files one by one.

6   In the Convert Folder(s) To PDF dialog box select the folders to be archived. We selected the Inbox folder, the Outbox folder, and the Sent Items folder. Expand any folders that have subfolders (indicated by a plus sign next to the folder name) to verify that you want to convert all the subfolders.

If you select the Convert This Folder And All Sub Folders option, then you will automatically archive any and all folders in the Inbox. We selected the option. If you don't want to convert all subfolders, you must deselect this option and then manually deselect subfolders that you don't want to convert.

7   When you have finalized your selection, click OK, and enter a name for the archive file in the Save PDF Archive File As dialog box. We saved the archive file in the Lesson03 folder using the name EmailArc. Then click Open.

8   Click OK to finish. Your email files in the specified folders will be automatically
    archived every Saturday at 12:00 PM.

Be aware that this archiving process will overwrite the archive file from the previous
week.

In order to see what the archive file looks like, you can run an archive operation
now.

9   Choose Adobe PDF > Setup Automatic Archival. In the Acrobat PDFMaker
    dialog box, click the Automatic Archival tab and click Run Archival Now. Your
    PDF files are automatically created and stored in the named file.

At any time, you can add or remove folders from the automatic archival process
using the Add and Delete button in the Automatic Archival tab of the Acrobat
PDFMaker dialog box. You can change the name and/or location of the archive file
using the Change Archival File button in this same dialog box.

10 When you are finished, close any open PDF files and close Outlook or Lotus
    Notes.

Converting web pages to Adobe PDF

You can convert or "capture" selected content on a web page, an entire web page,
or several levels of a multipage website. You can define a page layout, set display
options for fonts and other visual elements, and create bookmarks for web pages
that you convert to Adobe PDF. The HTML file and all associated files—such as
JPEG images, cascading style sheets, text files, image maps, and forms—are included
in the conversion process so the resulting PDF behaves much like the original web
page.

Because converted web pages are in Adobe PDF, you can easily save them, print
them, email them to others, or archive them for your own future use and review.

There are no lesson files for this section of the lesson.

Connecting to the web

Before you can download and convert web pages to Adobe PDF, you must be able to
access the web. If you need help with setting up an Internet connection, talk to your
Internet Service Provider (ISP).

When you have a connection to the Internet, you can set your Acrobat Internet preferences for handling web page conversion.

1   To access your Internet Preferences, in Acrobat choose Edit > Preferences (Windows) or Acrobat > Preferences (Mac OS), and select Internet in the left pane of the Preferences dialog box. Click the Internet Settings button (Windows) or Network Settings button (Mac OS) to check your network settings. On Windows, your settings are on the Connections tab. Exit this dialog box without making any changes.

By default, several Internet preference options that control how Acrobat interacts with your web browser are automatically set to be on.

- Display PDF In Browser displays any PDF document opened from the web inside the browser window. If this option is not selected, PDF documents open in a separate Acrobat window.

- Allow Fast Web View downloads PDF documents for viewing on the web one page at a time. If this option is not selected, the entire PDF file downloads before it is displayed. If you want the entire PDF document to continue downloading in the background while you view the first page of requested information, also select Allow Speculative Downloading In The Background.

- Allow Speculative Downloading In The Background allows a PDF document to continue downloading from the web, even after the first requested page displays. Downloading in the background stops when any other task, such as paging through the document, is initiated in Acrobat.

2   When you have finished reviewing your Internet Settings, click OK in the Preferences dialog box to apply any changes you have made, or click Cancel to exit the dialog box without making any changes.

Setting options for converting web pages

You may want to check the options that control the structure and appearance of your converted web pages before you download and convert the pages. You set these options in the Web Page Conversion Settings dialog box. To access this dialog box, in Acrobat, choose File > Create PDF > From Web Page, and click Settings in the Create PDF From Web Page dialog box.

To convert Chinese, Japanese, and Korean (CJK) language web pages to PDF on a Roman (Western) system in Windows, you must have installed the CJK language support files while installing Acrobat. Also, it is preferable to select an appropriate encoding from the HTML conversion settings.

Converting web pages from within Acrobat

Because web pages are updated on a regular basis, when you visit the web pages described in this lesson, the content of the pages may have changed. Even though we have tried to use links that we think will be relatively stable, you may have to use links other than those described in this section. However, you should be able to apply the steps in this lesson to virtually any links on any website. If you are working inside a corporate firewall, for example, you might find it easier to do this lesson substituting an internal site for the Adobe Press site or the Peachpit site.

Now you'll enter a URL in the Create PDF From Web Page dialog box and convert some web pages.

1 If the Create PDF From Web Page dialog box is not open, choose File > Create PDF > From Web Page.

2 For URL, enter the address of the website you'd like to convert. (We used the Adobe Press website at http://www.adobepress.com.)

3 Click the Capture Multiple Levels button.

You control the number of converted pages by specifying the levels of site hierarchy you wish to convert, starting from your entered URL. For example, the top level consists of the page corresponding to the specified URL; the second level consists of pages linked from the top-level page, and so on. You need to be aware of the number and complexity of pages you may encounter when downloading more than one level of a website at a time. It is possible to select a complex site that will take a very long time to download. Use the Get Entire Site option with great caution. In addition, downloading pages over a dial-up modem connection will usually take much longer than downloading them over a high-speed connection.

4 Make sure that the Get Only option is selected, and that 1 is selected for the number of levels.

5 Select Stay On Same Path to convert only pages that are subordinate to the URL you entered.

6 Select Stay On Same Server to download only pages on the same server as the URL you entered.

7   Click Create. The Download Status dialog box displays the status of the download in progress. When downloading and conversion are complete, the converted website appears in the Acrobat document window, with tagged bookmarks in the Bookmarks panel.

If any linked material is not downloadable you will get an error message. Click OK to clear any error message.

8   Click the Single Page button (⊞) on the Acrobat toolbar to fit the view of the converted web page to your screen.

9   Use the Next Page (⬇) and Previous Page (⬆) buttons to move through the pages.

10 Choose File > Save As, name the file **Web.pdf** and save it in the Lesson03 folder.

On Windows, if you're downloading more than one level of pages, the Download Status dialog box moves to the background after the first level is downloaded. The globe in the Create PDF From Web Page button in the toolbar continues spinning to show that pages are being downloaded. Choose Advanced > Web Capture > Bring Status Dialogs To Foreground to see the dialog box again.

The converted website is navigable and editable just like any other PDF document. Acrobat formats the pages to reflect your page-layout conversion settings, as well as the look of the original website.

Downloading and converting linked pages

When you click a web link in the Adobe PDF version of the web page and when the web link links to an unconverted page, Acrobat downloads and converts that page to Adobe PDF.

1   Navigate through the converted website until you find a web link to an unconverted page. We used the "Events & Promotions" link below the AdobePress title bar. (The pointer changes to a pointing finger when positioned over a web link, and the URL of the link is displayed.)

2 Right-click (Windows) or Control-click (Mac OS) on the web link, and choose Append To Document from the context menu.

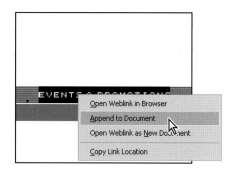

The Download Status dialog box again displays the status of the download. When the download and conversion are complete, the linked page appears in the Acrobat window. A bookmark for the page is added to the Bookmarks list.

3 Choose File > Save As, rename the file **Web1.pdf**, and save it in the Lesson03 folder.

4 When you're finished looking at your converted web pages, exit Acrobat.

Now you'll convert web pages directly from Internet Explorer.

Converting web pages in Internet Explorer (Windows)

If you've ever had the frustrating experience of printing a web page from your browser only to discover portions of the page missing, you'll love the Acrobat feature that allows you to create and print an Adobe PDF version of the web page without ever leaving your browser.

On Windows, Acrobat adds a button with a menu to the toolbar of Internet Explorer (version 6 and later), which allows you to convert the currently displayed web page (or a selected portion of the page) to an Adobe PDF file or convert and print it, email it, or send it for review in one easy operation. When you print a web page that you have converted to an Adobe PDF file, the page is reformatted to a standard page size and logical page breaks are added.

First you'll set the preferences used to create Adobe PDF pages from your web pages.

Looking at the conversion preferences

You set conversion preferences from the menu on the Convert button that Acrobat adds to the Internet Explorer toolbar.

1 Open Internet Explorer, and navigate to a favorite web page. We opened the Peachpit Press home page at http://www.peachpit.com.

2   In Internet Explorer, click the arrow next to the Convert button (), and choose Preferences from the menu.These preferences are the same as described in "Setting options for converting web pages" earlier in this lesson.

If you don't see the Convert button in Internet Explorer, choose View > Toolbars > Adobe PDF.

3   Click Cancel to exit the dialog box without making any changes.

Now you'll convert the Peachpit Press home page to Adobe PDF.

Converting selected portions of web pages to Adobe PDF

1   In Internet Explorer, navigate to the web page that you want to convert. We navigated to the Peachpit Press homepage (www.peachpit.com).

2   Click the Select button () on the toolbar to activate the advanced selection tool.

Notice that as you drag your pointer over the page, content is highlighted with a red box.

You'll select the New Title and Articles content.

3   Move your pointer in the area of the New Titles heading and note that the text block that contains the three book covers is enclosed in a red box. Click in the box to confirm the selection. Then move your pointer in the area of the Articles heading. Again you'll notice that the block of text is enclosed in a red box. Ctrl-click to add this to the selection.

4   Click the arrow next to the Convert button on the Internet Explorer toolbar to expand the drop-down menu, and choose Convert Web Page To PDF.

5   In the Convert Web Page To Adobe PDF dialog box, Navigate to the Lesson03 folder. For the file name, we typed in **PeachpitHome.pdf**. Then click Save.

The default file name used by Acrobat is the text used in the HTML tag <TITLE>. Any invalid characters in the web page filename are converted to an underscore when the file is downloaded and saved.

Your selected text is converted to PDF and the file automatically opens in Acrobat.

6 When you are finished, close Internet Explorer, Acrobat, and any open PDF files.

You can convert a web page to Adobe PDF and email it using the Convert Web Page And Email command in the Convert button menu. (For more information, see the Adobe Acrobat 9 Help.)

Exploring on your own: Creating Adobe PDF from the context menu (Windows)

You can create and consolidate Adobe PDF files using the context menu.

Using the Convert To Adobe PDF command

1 In Windows Explorer, navigate to the Lesson03 folder, and right-click on the Memo.txt file.

2 From the context menu, choose Convert To Adobe PDF.

Text files are converted to Adobe PDF using Web Capture and opened in Acrobat. Different conversion methods are used for other file types, but the conversion method is always determined automatically by Acrobat.

3 Choose File > Save. Name the file and choose where to save it in the Save As dialog box.

When you are finished, close any open Adobe PDF files and exit Acrobat.

Using the Combine Supported Files In Acrobat command

1 In Windows Explorer, navigate to the Lesson03/MultipleFiles folder, and select the bottle.jpg file.

2 Ctrl-click to add one or more files to the selection. We added Application.pdf.

3 Right-click, and from the context menu, choose Combine Supported Files In Acrobat.

Acrobat opens and displays the Combine Files dialog box, with the target files listed. You can add to the list of files, rearrange files, delete files, and convert and consolidate files as described earlier in this lesson.

When you are finished, close any open PDF files and exit Acrobat.

Review questions

1 How can you find out which file types can be converted to Adobe PDF using the Create PDF From File or Create PDF From Multiple Files commands?

2 If you're working with a file type that isn't supported by the Create PDF From File or From Multiple Files command, how can you create a PDF file?

3 Can you use Acrobat to archive your emails?

Review answers

1 Do one of the following:

   • Choose File > Create PDF > From File. Open the Files Of Type (Windows) or Show (Mac OS) menu in the Open dialog box to view the supported file types.

   • Choose File > Create PDF > From Multiple Files. Click the Add Files button, and open the Files Of Type (Windows) or Show (Mac OS) menu in the Open dialog box to view the supported file types.

2 Simply "print" your file using the Adobe PDF printer. In your authoring application, choose File > Print, and choose the Adobe PDF printer in the Print or Page Setup dialog box. When you click the Print button, Acrobat creates an Adobe PDF file rather than sending your file to a desktop printer.

3 Yes. In Windcows, both Microsoft Outlook and Lotus Notes allow you to use Acrobat to archive emails. In Outlook, choose Adobe PDF > Setup Automatic Archival. In Lotus Notes, choose Actions > Setup Automatic Archival.

4 CREATING ADOBE PDF FROM MICROSOFT OFFICE FILES (WINDOWS)

Lesson Overview

In this lesson, you'll do the following:

- Convert a Microsoft Word file to Adobe PDF.
- Convert Word headings and styles to PDF bookmarks and Word comments to PDF notes.
- Change the Adobe PDF conversion settings.
- Insert a 3D model into a PowerPoint file.
- Convert a Microsoft Excel file and send it for review.

 This lesson will take approximately 60 minutes to complete. Copy the Lesson04 folder onto your hard drive if you haven't already done so.

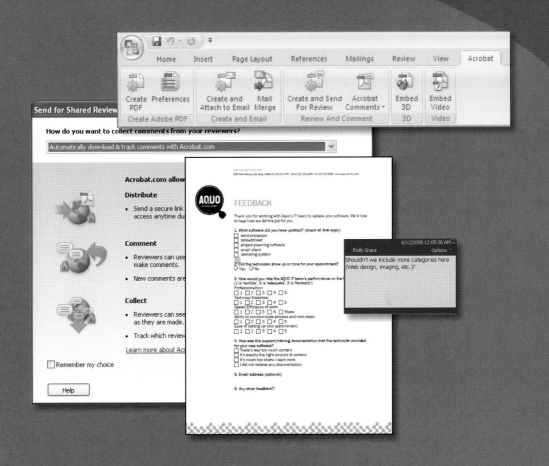

This lesson is designed for Windows users who have Microsoft Office applications such as Microsoft Word, Microsoft PowerPoint, and Microsoft Excel installed on their computers. You need to have one or more of these applications installed on your system to use this lesson. If you do not use these Microsoft Office applications, you should skip this lesson. Visit the Adobe website (www.adobe.com) to see which versions of Microsoft Office are supported.

This lesson assumes you are using Microsoft Office 2007.

For information on converting Outlook files to PDF, see Lesson 3.

About PDFMaker

PDFMaker, which is installed automatically when you install Acrobat, is used to create Adobe PDF files from within Microsoft applications. For Microsoft Office 2007 applications such as Word, Excel, PowerPoint, and Access, the options for creating PDFs are available from the Acrobat ribbon. For earlier versions of Office, Convert To Adobe PDF buttons and an Adobe PDF menu are added automatically to the Microsoft toolbars and menu bars. You use these Adobe PDF menus and buttons to control the settings used in the conversion to Adobe PDF, to email your PDF file, and to set up an email review process without ever leaving your Microsoft application. Acrobat 9 can also attach your Office source file to the PDF file.

PDF files created from Microsoft Office applications using Acrobat 9 have greater fidelity than before, and the conversion is much faster. PDF files are often substantially smaller than the source file. (Complex Excel files may be an exception.) You can also create PDF/A-compliant files from any Office files. (Note, however, that PDFMaker does not support the PDF/A standard for Microsoft Publisher.)

For Office 2007 applications, if you don't see the Acrobat ribbon, choose Add-Ins from the Options dialog box and select Acrobat PDFMaker Office COM Addin. For Office 2003 and earlier, choose Help > About Microsoft "application name." In the dialog box, click Disabled Items. Select Adobe PDF from the list and click Enable. Then close and restart your Microsoft application.

Acrobat installs essentially the same buttons and commands in Word, PowerPoint, and Excel. There are, however, some application-specific differences in the Acrobat/Microsoft Office interface. Despite these application-specific differences, you should be able to complete all sections in this lesson even if you have only one Microsoft Office application, such as Word, installed on your system.

Just follow the steps in each section, avoiding the application-specific steps, and use the lesson file for the Microsoft Office application that you have.

Converting Microsoft Word files to Adobe PDF

Word is a popular authoring program that makes it easy to create a variety of types of documents. Very often, users of Word apply styles to create headings and create hyperlinks to make their documents more usable. In a review process, users may also add Word comments. When you create an Adobe PDF document from your Word document, you can convert Word styles and headings to Acrobat bookmarks and you can convert comments to Acrobat notes. Hyperlinks in your Word document are preserved. Your Adobe PDF file will look just like your Word file and retain the same functionality, but it will be equally accessible to readers on all platforms, regardless of whether or not they have the Word application. (PDF files created from Word files are tagged PDF, making the content easy to repurpose and improving accessibility.)

● **Note:** In Acrobat Pro Extended, PDFMaker includes an option to embed many types of multimedia files in Microsoft Word files. The files are converted to FLV format files. When you convert the document to PDF, the PDF includes a playable FLV file.

About the Microsoft Word file

First you'll look at the Word file that you'll convert to Adobe PDF.

1 Start Microsoft Word.

2 From the Office button menu, choose Open. Select the Feedback.doc file, located in the Lesson04 folder, and click Open. From the Office button menu, choose Save As, rename the file **Feedback1.doc**, and save it in the Lesson04 folder.

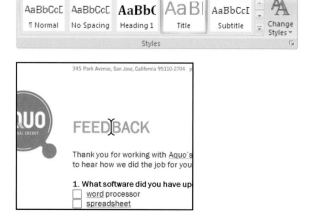

3 Place your pointer on the heading "Feedback" in the open document and click to create an insertion point. Notice that the Word style is "Title." (Styles are located on the Home tab.)

You'll use this information to convert your Word style to a bookmark in Adobe PDF.

Notice also that a Word comment has been added to the document. In the next section you'll verify that this comment converts to an Acrobat comment in the PDF document.

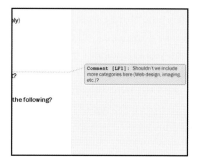

Converting Word headings and styles to PDF bookmarks

If your Word document contains headings and styles that you want to convert to linked bookmarks in Adobe PDF, you must identify these headings and styles in the Acrobat PDFMaker dialog box. (Word Heading 1 through Heading 9 styles are converted automatically.) Because this document isn't formatted using Headings 1 through 9, you'll need to make sure that the style used is converted to a linked bookmark when you create the Adobe PDF file.

1 In Word 2007, click Preferences (🖺) in the Acrobat ribbon.
In earlier versions of Word, on the Word menu bar, choose Adobe PDF > Change Conversion Settings to open the Acrobat PDFMaker dialog box.

The Acrobat PDFMaker dialog box is where you define the settings that control the conversion of your Microsoft application files to Adobe PDF. The tabs available in this dialog box vary with the Microsoft Office application that you are using. Because you are using Microsoft Word in this section of the lesson, the Word tab and the Bookmarks tab are available in the Acrobat PDFMaker dialog box. Later in this lesson, you'll open the Acrobat PDFMaker dialog box from within PowerPoint and Excel. With these applications, you'll see different tabs in this dialog box.

If you are using Acrobat Pro Extended, the PDFMaker dialog box has a new tab, the Video tab, where you set options or multimedia files that are converted to FLV format and inserted into Word or PowerPoint files.

2   Click the Bookmarks tab.

This tab is where you determine which Word headings and styles are converted to Adobe PDF bookmarks.

3   Scroll down the list of bookmarks and styles, until you see the style Title.

4   Move your pointer over the empty square in the Bookmarks column opposite Title, and click in the empty box.

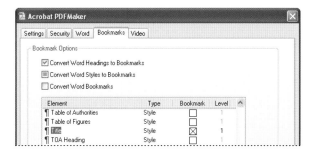

An X appears, indicating that a bookmark will be created for this style. Notice that the level is automatically set to 1. This is the hierarchical level of the PDF bookmark. (If you had a second level of headings, you would set the level to 2.)

5   Scroll through the list again and deselect any other styles that are selected.

Any settings that you make in the Bookmarks tab apply only to the conversion of Word documents.

Converting Word comments to PDF notes

You needn't lose any comments that have been added to your Word document when you convert the document to Adobe PDF. Comments in your Word document are converted to notes in the Adobe PDF document.

1   Click the Word tab in the Acrobat PDFMaker dialog box, and check the Convert Displayed Comments To Notes In Adobe PDF option.

In the Comments window, you'll now see the one comment to be included. Make sure that the box in the Include column is selected.

2 To change the color of the note in the Adobe PDF document, click repeatedly on the icon in the Color column to cycle through the available color choices. We chose blue.

3 To have the note automatically open in the PDF document, click in the box in the Notes Open column. You can always close the note in the PDF document later if you wish.

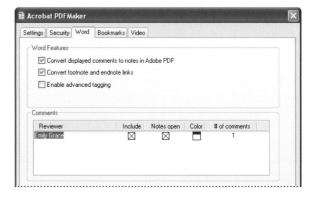

Any settings that you make in the Word tab apply only to the conversion of Word documents.

4 Click the Settings tab.

Looking at the conversion settings

1 In the Acrobat PDFMaker dialog box, click the arrow next to the Conversion Settings menu.

This menu lists the predefined conversion settings used for creating Adobe PDF files. For most users of Acrobat, these predefined settings (or presets) are generally sufficient. If you need to customize the conversion settings you can use the Advanced Settings button to access the Adobe PDF Settings dialog box. Any customized settings that you may have created are also listed in this Default Settings menu.

To see an explanation of the default conversion settings, choose the name of a conversion set in the Default Settings menu. A description is displayed next to the information icon. Use the up and down scroll arrows to move through the text if the description exceeds two lines.

2 After you have finished reviewing the available settings, choose Standard from the Conversion Settings pop-up menu.

3 Verify that the View Adobe PDF Result option is selected. When this option is selected, Acrobat launches automatically and the Adobe PDF file that you create is displayed as soon as the conversion is complete.

4 Make sure that the Enable Accessibility And Reflow With Tagged Adobe PDF option is on (selected). Creating tagged PDF makes your files more accessible.

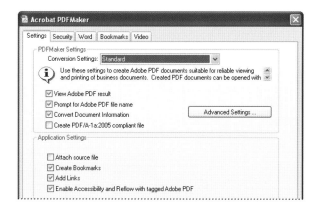

For more information on making your PDF files accessible, see Lesson 6, "Reading and Working with PDF Files."

If you want to attach the source file to the PDF file, check the Attach Source File option in this dialog box.

5 Click OK to apply your settings.

Now that you've defined the settings to be used for the conversion, you're ready to convert your Word file to Adobe PDF, but first you'll save your file.

6 Choose Save As > Word Document from the Office button menu to save your work in the Lesson04 folder.

> **Note:** Adobe PDFMaker will use these conversion settings for converting Word documents until you change them.

Converting your Word file

1 For Microsoft Office 2007 Word, click the Create PDF button (🖼️) on the Acrobat ribbon. For earlier versions of Word, click the Convert To Adobe PDF button (📄) on the Word toolbar.

2 In the Save Adobe PDF As dialog box, name and save your file. We named the file **Feedback1.pdf** and clicked Save to save it in the Lesson04 folder.

Your file is converted to Adobe PDF. The status of the conversion is shown in the Acrobat PDFMaker message box.

3 Acrobat automatically displays your converted file. Notice that the Word comment has been converted to an open Adobe PDF note. You may need to scroll down to see the note.

▶ **Tip:** Acrobat 9 allows you to edit headers and footers in PDF files created from Office 2007 files.

4 After you have read the sticky note, click the close box on the sticky note.

5 Click the Bookmarks button (📖) in the navigation pane, and notice that the bookmark has been created automatically.

▶ **Tip:** If you simply want to convert your Microsoft Office file to Adobe PDF using the current Adobe PDFMaker conversion settings, drag the Office file onto the Acrobat 9 icon on your desktop or into an empty document pane in the Acrobat work area.

In Acrobat 9, when you click on a bookmark in the navigation pane of your PDF file, the link will take you directly to the heading, not the top of the page that contains the heading.

6 If you attached your Word file, click the Attachments button at the bottom of the navigation pane to verify that your original Word file is attached.

7 When you have finished reviewing the file, close it.

8 Choose File > Exit to close Acrobat.

9 Exit Microsoft Word.

Inserting 3D content into PowerPoint presentations (Acrobat Pro Extended)

With Acrobat Pro Extended, you can insert most types of 3D models into Microsoft
Word, Excel, and PowerPoint files. In this part of the lesson, you'll insert a 3D model
into a PowerPoint file, manipulate the model, and then convert the file to PDF.

These steps are similar for inserting a 3D model into an Excel file or a Word file.

1   Open Microsoft PowerPoint and create a new blank slide. In the Click to Add Title box, enter the text **Aquo Water Bottle**.

2   From the Office button menu, choose Save As > PowerPoint Presentation. Save
    your document as **3D_Insert** in the Lesson04 folder. (In PowerPoint 2003 or
    earlier, choose File > Save As.)

3   In your PowerPoint slide, create an insertion point where you want the 3D
    model to appear. We clicked to create an insertion point in the subtitle box.
    Then click the Embed 3D button (⬛) on the Acrobat ribbon. (In PowerPoint
    2003 or earlier, click the insert Acrobat 3D Model button (⬛) on the Acrobat
    PDFMaker 9.0 toolbar.)

The 3D model that you insert into the Office file is represented by a poster image or preview. Clicking on this poster image or preview in the Office application activates the model and gives the user limited ability to manipulate the 3D model. After you convert the Office file to Adobe PDF, clicking on this poster image (or preview) in Acrobat or Adobe Reader gives the user full access to the 3D toolbar for manipulating the model.

4   In the Add 3D Data dialog box, click Browse For Model.

5   In the Open dialog box, navigate to the Lesson04 folder, select the Aquo_Bottle.u3d file, and click Open.

6   Expand the Import Settings Profile menu and choose Visualization/Small File to generate a small PDF file that you can easily exchange with colleagues.

If you wanted to include a JavaScript with the 3D file, you would add it from this dialog box. For this lesson, you'll simply add a 3D model.

7   Click OK to add the 3D model.

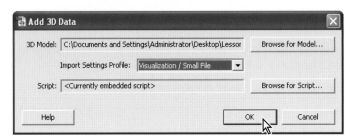

Changing the preview size

Now you'll adjust the size of the preview.

1   Click in the 3D model to select it. Hover the pointer over a corner of the 3D model placeholder until the pointer changes to a double-headed arrow, and Shift-drag the corner of the box to resize the model to fit in the subtitle box. (Shift-dragging resizes the place holder proportionally.) If necessary drag the placeholder to center it under your title text.

 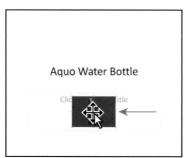

2   From the Office button menu, choose Save to save your PowerPoint slide in the Lesson04 folder. Use the same file name.

Now you'll convert your PowerPoint slide to Adobe PDF to see how the 3D model is handled.

Changing the default view

Before you convert your slide to PDF, you'll change the default view of your 3D model.

1   In PowerPoint 2007, click the View tab and choose Slide Show. The slide opens in Full Screen mode.

2   Move your pointer into the preview window to activate the 3D model and open the Acrobat 3D Control toolbar. You use the tools on this toolbar to manipulate your model. (See Lesson 2, "Looking at the Work Area," for help with these tools.)

3 Select the Rotate tool (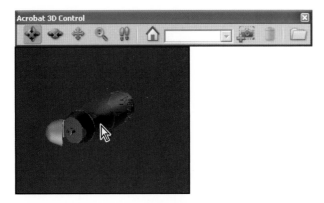) on the far left and drag over the model to change the view.

Now you'll change the background color and the rendering mode.

4 Right-click on the model, and choose Viewing Options > Model Render Mode > Shaded Illustration for the rendering mode.

5 Right-click on the model, and choose Viewing Options > Select A Background Color. Choose a color from the color palette. We chose yellow. Click OK.

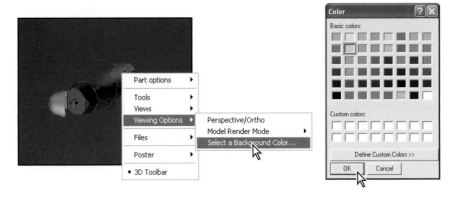

Now you'll make your new view the default view.

6 Right-click on the model, and choose Views > Set As Default View.

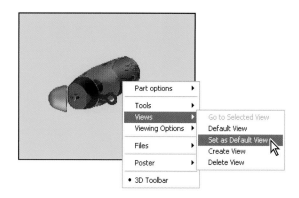

7 Press Esc to exit the Full Screen mode.

8 From the Office button menu, choose Save to save your PowerPoint slide in the Lesson04 folder. Use the same file name.

Converting to Adobe PDF

1 With the 3D_Insert.ppt file open, click Create PDF (🔲) on the Acrobat ribbon. (In Word 2003 or earlier, click the Convert to Adobe PDF button (🔲) on the Acrobat PDFMaker 9.0 toolbar.) Click Save to save the file in the same folder and using the same name but with the PDF extension. The conversion of the PowerPoint file to Adobe PDF is shown in the message box.

2 Your PDF file opens automatically in Acrobat.

Notice that the preview of the 3D model is the new default view that you created.

3 In the Acrobat document pane, click in the model to open the 3D toolbar. Anyone using Acrobat can use the tools on this toolbar to experience the 3D effects.

4 When you are finished, close the PDF file and the PowerPoint file and exit PowerPoint.

In Office 2007 applications, you change the PDF conversion settings by selecting the Preferences button on the Acrobat ribbon. You do this before converting the file to PDF.

About Adobe Presenter
(Acrobat Pro Extended)

Adobe Presenter is an addition to PowerPoint that produces rich media files for use in presentations, training, and education. Presenter slide shows can include video, voice-over narration, interactive quizzes, and other dynamic content to enhance their appeal. Publishing your Presenter slide show to PDF preserves all of the slide show content. It also reduces the file size and allows users to view it offline. Users need Adobe Reader 9 or Acrobat 9 to open Presenter PDFs.

Adding video clips to
Microsoft Office files

With Acrobat 9 Pro or Pro Extended, you can easily add rich media content to your Microsoft Office files.

With Acrobat Pro Extended, you can add video content in a Word or PowerPoint file using the Adobe PDF > Embed Video And Convert To Flash Format command for Office 2003 files. For Office 2007 files, use the Embed Video button on the Acrobat ribbon.

Converting Excel documents and starting a review

In this section, you'll create a PDF file from an Excel document and start a formal review process in which the PDF file is emailed to selected reviewers. In addition to managing the email process, Acrobat also offers powerful file management and comment management tools to facilitate the review.

Acrobat 9 allows you to easily select and order worksheets for conversion, as well as convert all links and bookmarks.

About the Excel file

1   Start Microsoft Excel.

2   Choose Open from the Office button menu, select the Financial2008.xls file, located in the Lesson04 folder, and click Open. Then choose Save As > Excel Workbook from the Office button menu, rename the file **Financial2008_1.xls**, and save it in the Lesson04 folder.

Now you'll review the Excel file. Notice that the first sheet has construction costs.

3   Click the Annual Operating Costs button at the bottom of the Excel spreadsheet. The second sheet has annual operating costs.

 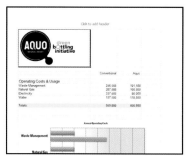

When you create your PDF file, you'll need to convert both these sheets.

Converting the entire workbook

With Office 2007, you can choose to convert an entire workbook, a selection, or selected sheets to PDF. In earlier versions of Office, you must either select the Convert Entire Workbook option in the Adobe PDF pop-up menu (Adobe PDF > Change Conversion Setting) or set the page range in the Adobe PDF Settings dialog box.

1   In Excel 2007, click Preferences in the Acrobat ribbon.

2   In the Settings tab of the Acrobat PDFMaker dialog box, choose Smallest File Size from the Conversion Settings menu because you're going to be emailing the PDF file.

3   Select the Fit Worksheet To A Single Page option.

4   Make sure that the Enable Accessibility And Reflow With Tagged Adobe PDF option is selected. When you create tagged PDF, you can more easily copy tabular data from PDF files back into spreadsheet applications. For more information, see "Exploring on your own" in this lesson. Creating tagged PDF also makes your files more accessible.

5 Select the Prompt For Selecting Excel Sheets option to open a dialog box at the beginning of the file conversion process that allows you to specify which sheets and in what order the sheets will be included.

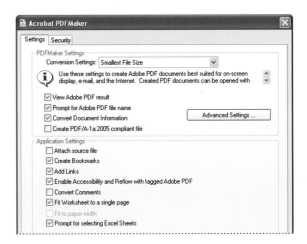

These conversion settings will be used for converting Excel documents until you change them.

6 Click OK to apply your settings.

In Acrobat 9, you can convert an oversized worksheet to a PDF that is one sheet wide and several sheets long. In the Settings tab of the Acrobat PDFMaker dialog box, the Fit Worksheet To A Single Page option adjusts the size of each worksheet so that all the entries on that worksheet appear on the same page of the PDF. The Fit To Paper Width option adjusts the width of each worksheet so that all the columns on that worksheet appear on one page in the PDF.

Starting an email-based review

You can email a file for review using the Create And Send For Review button on the Acrobat ribbon (Excel 2007) or the Convert To Adobe PDF And Send For Review button for earlier versions. The recipient will receive an email with instructions for how to participate in the review and return comments using the Acrobat.com service.

You can also use the Tracker feature in Acrobat to invite additional reviewers to join the process or to send reminders to reviewers. You can invite users of Adobe Reader to participate in the review. For more information on using Acrobat in the reviewing and commenting process, see Lesson 9, "Using Acrobat in a Review Cycle."

1 In Office 2007, from the Acrobat ribbon, select the Create And Send For Review (🖳) button. (For Office 2003 or earlier, choose Adobe PDF > Convert To Adobe PDF And Send For Review.)

2 In the Acrobat PDFMaker dialog box, select whether to convert the entire workbook, selected material, or a sheet. We chose to convert the entire workbook.

3 Click Convert To PDF.

4 In the Save Adobe PDF File As dialog box, click Save to save the file as **Financial2008_1.pdf** in the Lesson04 folder.

The Send For Shared Review dialog box opens to guide you through the process.

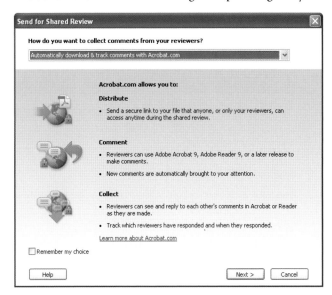

5 From the pop-up menu, choose whether to use Acrobat.com or your own internal server for the review process. Click Next.

The steps vary depending on how you choose to collect data from your reviewers.

6 When you have completed the steps in the wizard and emailed your file, close the PDF file and exit Microsoft Excel.

You cannot experience the email review feature without the help of at least one other participant. We encourage you to experiment with this feature when you have a document to review with colleagues.

Using the spreadsheet split view

When you work with spreadsheets, it is often useful to be able to keep the column or row names in view while scrolling up and down columns or across rows. The Split and Spreadsheet Split commands in Acrobat let you do this.

1   Navigate to the Lesson04 folder and open the GE_Schedule.pdf file.

This schedule is difficult to read onscreen because the type size is small if you have the view set to Fit Page. You'll use the Spreadsheet Split command to look more closely at some of the data. First you'll change the view of the page.

2   Choose Window > Spreadsheet Split to divide the document pane into four quadrants.

You can drag the splitter bars up, down, left, or right to resize the panes.

In Spreadsheet Split view, changing the zoom level changes the zoom level in each quadrant. (In Split Window view, you can have a different zoom level in each of the two windows.)

3   Drag the vertical splitter bar to the left so that the categories fill the left pane.

4   Drag the horizontal splitter bar up so that it is directly below the column headings.

 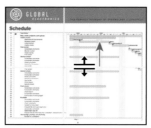 

5   Drag the splitter bars to align with column headers and row labels.

6   Use the vertical scroll bar to scroll down through the categories. Because the column headers remain visible, it is easy to evaluate the schedule for each task.

7   When you are finished exploring the Spreadsheet Split view, choose File > Close and close the GE_Schedule.pdf file without saving your work.

Converting web pages from Internet Explorer

Acrobat 9 adds a button and a menu to the toolbar of Internet Explorer 6 or later that allow you to convert the currently displayed web page or portion of a web page to an Adobe PDF file, convert and print it, or convert and email it in one easy operation. When you print a web page that you have converted to an Adobe PDF file, the page is reformatted to a standard printer page size and logical page breaks are added. You can be sure that your print copy will have all the information on the web page that you see onscreen.

For more information on converting web pages from within Internet Explorer, see Lesson 3, "Creating Adobe PDF Files."

Exploring on your own: Exporting tables from PDF files

You can easily copy and paste tables from a tagged PDF file into spreadsheet applications such as Excel. Earlier in this lesson, you converted an Excel workbook into a PDF file. You'll use that file again to see how easy it is to copy and paste tables from PDF files back into spreadsheet applications.

1 Navigate to the Lesson04 folder, and double-click the Financial2008_1.pdf file to open it in Acrobat.

2 On the Acrobat toolbar, click the Select tool (I).

3 Drag from the top left of the table to the bottom right, selecting all the text in the table, or click in the table. Notice that the pointer changes to indicate a table selection.

4 Right-click in the selected table, and choose the Open Table In Spreadsheet command from the context menu.

Acrobat automatically launches Excel and copies and pastes the table into a new spreadsheet.

5 When you are finished, close the new Excel spreadsheet and exit Excel. Then close Financial2008_1.pdf.

Exploring on your own: Converting and combining multiple Office files

As you saw in this lesson, you can convert Office files to Adobe PDF from within the Office application that you used to author the files. However, if you have several Office files—for example, a Word file, a PowerPoint file, and an Excel file—you can also convert and consolidate the files in one easy step from within Acrobat.

1 In Acrobat, click the Combine button on the Tasks toolbar to open the menu.

2 Choose Merge Files Into A Single PDF. Click Add Files in the dialog box and choose Add Files.

● **Note:** For information on assembling Office files into a PDF Portfolio, see Lesson 5, "Combining Files in PDF Portfolios."

3 In the Add Files dialog box, navigate to the Lesson04 folder.

4 Make sure that All Files is selected for Files Of Type, and then Ctrl-click to select the files, Feedback.doc and Financial2008.xls. Click Add Files.

You can rearrange the files. For this exercise though, you'll simply convert the files.

5 Click Combine Files.

Acrobat converts the files to Adobe PDF and consolidates them into one file. You have more control over the conversion process if you create individual PDF files and consolidate them separately, but if you have a number of similar and simple files, creating a PDF file from multiple source files in this one easy step is convenient.

6 Click Save to save the consolidated and converted file.

Acrobat then opens the consolidated PDF file.

7 When you have reviewed the file, close it without saving your work, and then quit Acrobat.

Review questions

1 How can you be sure that Word styles and headings are converted to Acrobat bookmarks when you convert Word documents to Adobe PDF using PDFMaker?

2 Can you convert an entire Excel workbook to Adobe PDF?

3 How do you change the poster image that represents 3D content in a PDF file?

Review answers

1 If you want Word headings and styles to be converted to bookmarks in Acrobat, you must be sure that the headings and styles are identified for conversion in the Acrobat PDFMaker dialog box. In Microsoft Word, choose Adobe PDF > Change Conversion Settings (in Office 2007 applications, click Preferences in the Acrobat ribbon), and click the Bookmarks tab. Make sure that the required headings and styles are selected.

2 Yes. In Excel 2007, click the Preferences button on the Acrobat ribbon and select the Prompt For Selecting Excel Sheets option in the Acrobat PDFMaker dialog box. In earlier versions of Excel, choose Adobe PDF > Convert Entire Workbook on the Excel toolbar. The option is selected when it has a check mark next to it.

3 In the slide show mode in PowerPoint, click to activate the 3D content. Right-click and change the view using the Viewing Options menu. Then set the new view as the default view using the Views menu.

5 COMBINING FILES IN PDF PORTFOLIOS

Lesson Overview

In this lesson, you'll do the following:

- Quickly and easily combine files of different types into one PDF Portfolio.

- Customize the look and feel of a PDF Portfolio.

- Add a header to a PDF Portfolio (Acrobat 9 Pro and Pro Extended only).

- Add a welcome screen to a PDF Portfolio (Acrobat 9 Pro and Pro Extended only).

- Share a PDF Portfolio.

- Search a PDF Portfolio.

- Modify an existing PDF Portfolio.

- Secure a PDF Portfolio.

- Combine files into a single PDF file without creating a PDF Portfolio.

 This lesson will take approximately 45 minutes to complete. Copy the Lesson05 folder onto your hard drive if you haven't already done so.

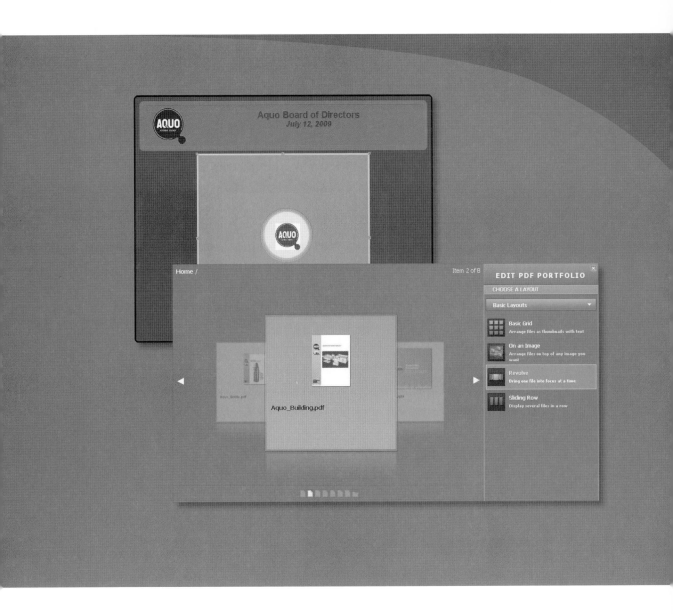

About PDF Portfolios

In Acrobat 9, you can assemble multiple files into an integrated PDF Portfolio. You can combine files of different formats, created in different applications, without converting them to PDF. For example, you could assemble all the documents for a specific project, including text documents, email messages, spreadsheets, CAD drawings, and PowerPoint presentations. The original files retain their individual identities, but are still part of the PDF Portfolio file. Each component file can be opened, read, edited, and formatted without affecting the other files in the PDF Portfolio.

PDF Portfolios offer several advantages over merging multiple files into an ordinary PDF file:

- You can add and remove component documents easily.

- You can quickly preview component files without having to pause for Open or Save dialog boxes.

- You can edit individual files within the PDF Portfolio without affecting the other files. You can also edit non-PDF files in their native applications from within a PDF Portfolio; any changes you make are saved to the file within the PDF Portfolio.

- You can share the PDF Portfolio with others and be sure they receive all the component parts.

- You can sort component files by categories that you can customize.

- You can print one, all, or any combination of components in the PDF Portfolio.

- You can search individual component documents or the entire PDF Portfolio, including non-PDF component files.

- You can add non-PDF files to an existing PDF Portfolio without converting them to PDF.

- The source files of a PDF Portfolio are not changed when you create the PDF, and changes you make to component files do not change the original files.

Getting started

In this lesson, you'll create a PDF Portfolio of documents for the board meeting of a fictitious beverage company. The PDF Portfolio will include a Microsoft Excel spreadsheet, a Microsoft Word document, a Microsoft PowerPoint presentation, and several PDF files. If you're using Acrobat Pro or Acrobat Pro Extended, you'll customize the PDF Portfolio with a header and an animated company logo.

Creating a PDF Portfolio

You'll create a PDF Portfolio, and then add the files you want to include in it.

1 Start Acrobat 9.

2 Choose File > Create PDF Portfolio.

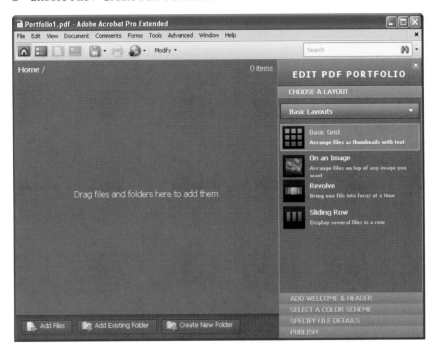

The Edit PDF Portfolio pane appears on the right side of the window. Additionally, the PDF Portfolio toolbar appears below the menu bar. This toolbar appears whenever you open a PDF Portfolio.

3 Click Add Files at the bottom of the window.

4 Navigate to the Lesson05 folder.

The folder contains an Excel spreadsheet, a PowerPoint presentation, a Word document, and several PDF files.

5 Select the Aquo_Bottle.pdf file, and click Open.

Acrobat adds the file you selected to the PDF Portfolio.

6 Click Add Files again.

7 Ctrl-click (Windows) or Command-click (Mac OS) to select the following files in the Lesson05 folder:

- Aquo_Building.pdf

- Aquo_Costs.pdf

- Aquo_Fin_Ana.xls

- Aquo_Fin_Data.pptx

- Aquo_Mkt_Summ.doc

- Aquo_Overview.pdf

8 Click Open to add them to the PDF Portfolio.

When you add a file to a PDF Portfolio, a copy of the original document is included in the PDF file. Some file formats, such as TIFF, are natively supported by Acrobat and Reader. However, to see files in some formats, viewers need to have an application installed that supports the format. Which formats require supporting applications depends on the operating system the viewer is using. For example, if you include a PowerPoint presentation in your portfolio, a viewer using Windows XP must have PowerPoint installed to see it, but one using Windows Vista can view the presentation without having PowerPoint installed.

Organizing files in folders

You can add an entire folder to a PDF Portfolio, or you can combine existing files in a new folder. You'll create a folder for the financial data.

1 Click the Create New Folder button.

2 Name the new folder **Financial data**, and click OK.

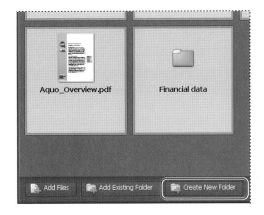

3 Drag the Aquo_Fin_Ana.xls and Aquo_Fin_Data.pptx files into the new folder.

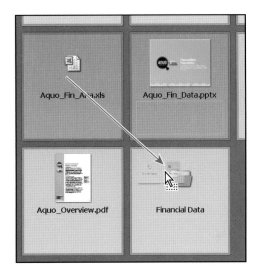

4 Choose File > Save Portfolio. Name the PDF Portfolio **Aquo Board Meeting,** and click Save.

Adding descriptions to component files

You can add descriptions to files and folders in the PDF Portfolio to help viewers find the files they want.

1 Click below the words "Financial data" on the Financial data card. The words "Add Description" appear. Click again to create an insertion point.

2 Type **Financial analysis spreadsheet and financial presentation** in the description box.

Customizing your PDF Portfolio

▶ **Tip:** To edit an existing PDF Portfolio, open it, and then choose Modify > Edit Portfolio from the PDF Portfolio toolbar.

The Edit PDF Portfolio pane includes several options for customizing the look and feel of your PDF Portfolio. You'll choose a layout and select a color scheme to create a more professional-looking document. If you're using Acrobat 9 Pro or Pro Extended, you'll also add a header with the company's logo and include a welcome page with a SWF (Flash animation) file to finish the look.

Selecting a layout

Acrobat 9 includes several layout options for PDF Portfolios. The layouts determine how component documents are displayed on the home page of the PDF Portfolio, and how the viewer navigates through the content. By default, the Basic Grid layout is applied. You'll preview the other layouts and choose one for this PDF Portfolio.

1 Click Choose A Layout in the Edit PDF Portfolio pane.

2 Click Sliding Row.

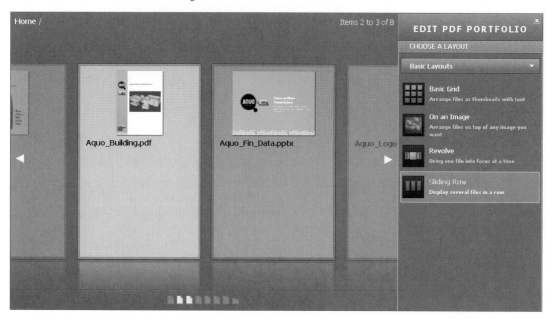

The documents are displayed in a row, with page icons below them to assist in navigation. You can also use the triangles on either side of the window to shift documents to the right or left.

3 Click Revolve.

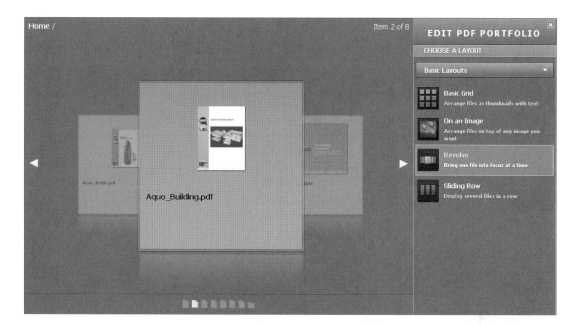

One document is in focus at a time, with two other documents visible behind it. You can navigate through the documents using the page icons or the triangles on either side of the window.

4   Select each of the other layouts to see how they display the documents in the PDF Portfolio.

5   Select Sliding Row for this PDF Portfolio.

Selecting a color scheme

You can further customize a PDF Portfolio by selecting which colors to use for text, backgrounds, and the cards that display component data. You'll select a custom color scheme to match the Aquo logo.

1   Click Select A Color Scheme in the Edit PDF Portfolio pane.

2   Click a Color Scheme swatch to see how it affects the colors.

3   Click Customize Color Scheme.

4   Click Primary Text Color. Then, select a color in the color picker, or type a color number in the box. We used 060606 for black text.

5 Customize the other colors in the scheme. We used 666666 (gray) for secondary text, 617E59 (green) for the background color, 480000 (burgundy) for the card color, and BDC089 (light gray) for the secondary card color.

6 Choose File > Save Portfolio.

Adding a header

If you're using Acrobat 9 Pro or Pro Extended, you can add a header to your PDF Portfolio. The header appears at the top of the layout. You can include text and a graphic in the header, including important information such as a logo, company name, and contact information. You'll add the company logo and the type and date of the meeting to the header.

1 Click Add Welcome & Header in the Edit PDF Portfolio pane.

2 Click Header

There are several header templates, including different text and graphic configurations.

3 Click Logo & Text.

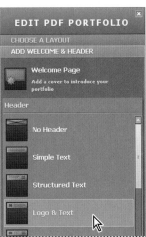

4 Click the Add An Image placeholder on the left side of the header.

5 Navigate to the Lesson05 folder, and double-click the Logo.gif file.

6 Click in the Add a Title panel of the header, and type **Aquo Board of Directors**.

7 Press Enter or Return and type **July 12, 2009**.

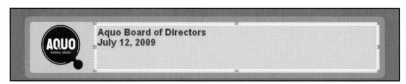

8 Select "Aquo Board of Directors," and then, in the Title Text toolbar, change the font size to 22. Select center orientation.

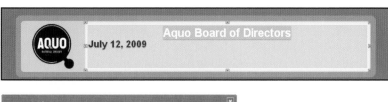

9 Select "July 12, 2009," click the Italic button, and then select center orientation.

10 Click the Background Color swatch on the right side of the toolbar.

11 Select a green that matches or complements the green in the Aquo logo, and click OK. (We chose color 617E59.)

● **Note:** You can also change the scale and opacity of the logo. To do so, click the logo, and then adjust the Scale and Opacity sliders.

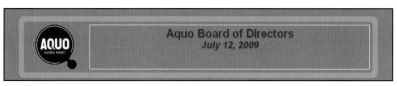

12 Close the Title Text toolbar.

Adding a welcome page

● **Note:** Acrobat welcome pages support SWF files that were created using ActionScript 3. For information about using ActionScript 3 in Adobe Flash files, see Flash Help.

In Acrobat 9 Pro or Pro Extended, you can also include a welcome page to provide information or instructions to PDF Portfolio recipients, or to set a tone. The welcome page appears when the viewer opens the PDF Portfolio. The welcome page can include text, images, or both. It can even include a Flash animation. You'll add an animated logo to the welcome page for this PDF Portfolio.

1　Click Welcome Page in the Edit PDF Portfolio pane.

2　Select Flash Movie.

3　Click the Add A Flash File placeholder.

4　Navigate to the Lesson05 folder, select the Aquo_logo_ani.swf file, and click Open.

5　Move the Scale slider to the right to increase the size of the logo.

6 When you've positioned the movie where you want it, click Done.

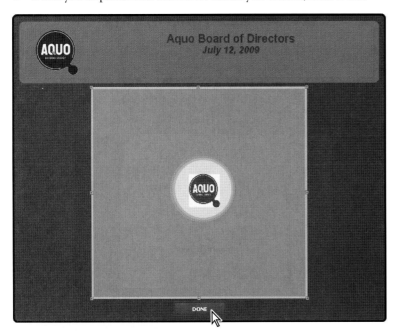

7 Choose File > Save Portfolio to save the PDF Portfolio.

Viewing file details

The File Details view lists PDF Portfolio component files in table format, with columns such as file descriptions, size, and modification dates. To customize the columns that appear in the File Details view, click Specify File Details in the Edit PDF Portfolio pane. Select which columns to display and how to sort them.

Sharing your PDF Portfolio

Note: To download a file from Acrobat.com, recipients must have an Adobe ID, available free. For details about uploading a PDF Portfolio file to Acrobat.com, see the Adobe Acrobat 9 Help.

A PDF Portfolio is a PDF file, so you can share it any way you'd share any other PDF. You can simply save the file and transfer it to a recipient by email, on removable media such as a CD or DVD, or by uploading it to a server or website. However, Acrobat makes it even easier to share PDF Portfolios by email or by posting them to Acrobat.com, a secure web-based service. In this lesson, you'll email the PDF Portfolio to yourself.

1 Click Publish in the Edit PDF Portfolio pane.

2 Click Email.

Your default email application opens, with a new message open. The PDF Portfolio file is included as an attachment.

3 Type your email address in the To line, and add a brief message and subject line.

4 Send the message.

Securing a PDF Portfolio

You can control who opens, prints, or modifies your PDF Portfolio using the same security features you can use with other PDF files. You'll password-protect your PDF Portfolio to restrict how it may be used.

1 Choose Modify > Secure Portfolio from the PDF Portfolio toolbar.

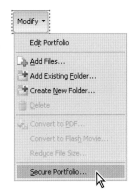

The Security panel of the Document Properties dialog box opens.

2 Choose Password Security from the Security Method menu. The Password Security - Settings dialog box opens.

3 In the Permissions area of the dialog box, select Restrict Editing And Printing.

4 Type a password in the Change Permissions Password box. Make sure it's a password you'll remember.

5 Choose High Resolution from the Printing Allowed menu, and choose None from the Changes Allowed menu. Viewers will be able to print components or the entire PDF Portfolio, but they won't be able to make changes to it unless they have the password.

6   Click OK.

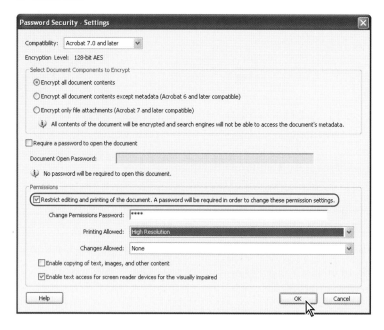

7   Click OK again to close the warning message.

8   Type the password again when prompted to confirm it.

9   Click OK if you see a message informing you that security settings will not be applied until you save the document.

10 If you want to apply the security settings to the PDF Portfolio, choose File > Save Portfolio. If you want to be able to edit the PDF Portfolio without using a password, close the PDF Portfolio without saving it, and then reopen it.

Searching a PDF Portfolio

● **Note:** Acrobat can search any document in a PDF Portfolio as long as it can access the document on that computer. If you cannot preview a PDF Portfolio component because there is no supporting application installed, you also cannot search the component.

You can search for specific words in all the components of a PDF Portfolio, even those that aren't PDF files. You'll search for a quote by a particular person.

1   Click in the Search box on the right side of the PDF Portfolio toolbar.

2   Type **Schneider** to find a quote by the vice president of the company.

3   Click the binoculars icon ().

The search results appear below the search box.

4   Close the PDF Portfolio and any other open files.

Merge to PDF

Sometimes you may want to combine files into a single PDF file without creating a PDF Portfolio. In a merged PDF file, all documents are converted into PDF files and then merged into a single PDF file as sequential pages.

To create a merged PDF file:

1   Choose File > Combine > Merge Files Into A Single PDF.

2   In the upper-right corner of the Combine Files dialog box, make sure that Single PDF is selected.

3   Click Add Files, and then select Add Files or Add Folders.

4   Select the files or folders you want to include, and click Add Files or Add Folders.

5   Arrange the files in the order you want them to appear in the merged PDF file. To reposition a file, select it and click Move Up or Move Down, or drag it into position.

6   If you want to include only some of the pages of a document, select it and click Choose Pages. Then select the pages you want to include.

7   Click Options to specify conversion settings, including whether to add bookmarks or enable accessibility features.

8   Specify a file size by clicking the small, default, or larger page icon.

The small file size uses compression and resolution settings that are appropriate for onscreen display. The default file size creates PDF files for business printing and viewing onscreen. The larger file size uses High Quality Print conversion settings.

9   Click Combine Files.

A status dialog box shows the progress of the file conversions. Some source applications may start and close automatically during the process.

Review questions

1   Name three advantages to creating a PDF Portfolio.

2   Do you need to convert documents to PDF to include them in a PDF Portfolio?

3   What is a welcome page?

4   How can you edit an existing PDF Portfolio?

5   True or False: You can search all documents in a PDF Portfolio, even non-PDF components.

Review answers

1   PDF Portfolios provide several advantages:

   • You can add and remove component documents easily, including non-PDF files.

   • You can preview component files quickly.

   • You can edit individual files within the PDF Portfolio independently.

   • PDF Portfolios contain all the components, so you can share them easily.

   • You can sort component files by categories and arrange them in the order you want.

   • You can print one, all, or any combination of components in the PDF Portfolio.

   • You can search the entire PDF Portfolio, including non-PDF component files.

   • The source files of a PDF Portfolio are not changed when you create the PDF, and changes you make to component files do not change the original files.

2   No. You can combine any documents in a PDF Portfolio, and they remain in their original format.

3   If you are using Acrobat 9 Pro or Pro Extended, you can add a welcome page to a PDF Portfolio. A welcome page appears when a recipient opens a PDF Portfolio. The welcome page may include instructions, information about the PDF Portfolio, or an introductory animation.

4   To edit a PDF Portfolio, choose Modify > Edit Portfolio in the PDF Portfolio toolbar.

5   True. Acrobat can search any document in a PDF Portfolio, as long as an application that can open the file is present on the computer.

6 READING AND WORKING WITH PDF FILES

Lesson Overview

In this lesson, you'll do the following:

- Navigate through an Adobe PDF document using Acrobat's built-in navigational controls.

- Change how an Adobe PDF document scrolls and displays in the document window.

- Search a PDF document for a word or phrase.

- Fill out a PDF form.

- Print all or a portion of a PDF document.

- Examine the accessibility features that make it easier for users with vision and motor impairments to use Acrobat.

 This lesson will take approximately 60 minutes to complete. Copy the Lesson06 folder onto your hard drive if you haven't already done so.

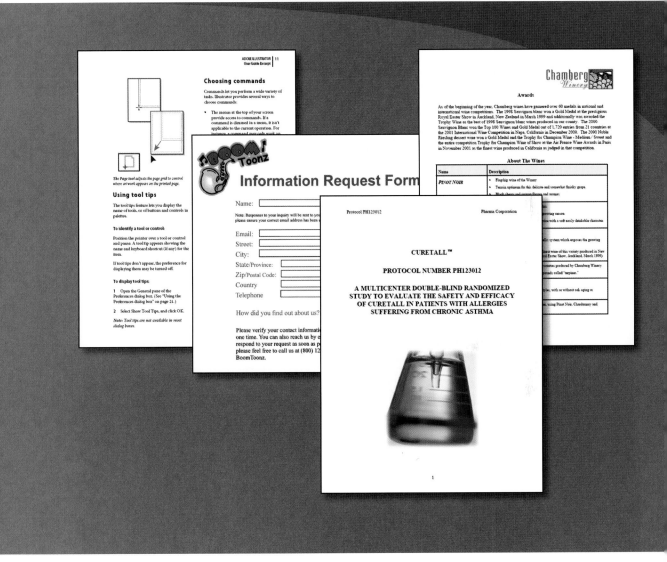

Changing the opening view

You'll open a PDF file and look at the initial view settings and then you'll change those settings to reflect your personal preferences.

1   In Acrobat, choose File > Open, navigate to the Lesson06 folder, and select the Protocol.pdf file. Click Open.

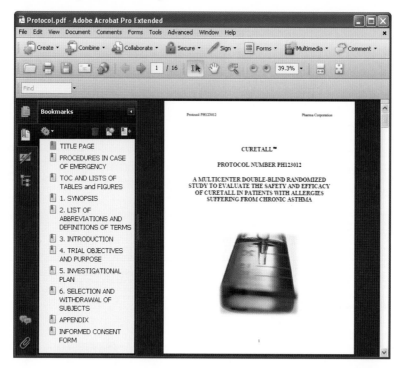

The file opens at the cover page with the navigation pane open and the Bookmarks panel displayed.

2   To see how this initial view is set, choose File > Properties, and in the Document Properties dialog box, click the Initial View tab.

In the Layout And Magnification section, you see that the creator of this document wanted the file to open at page 1, with one page filling the document pane, and with the Bookmarks panel open.

Now you'll experiment with some different opening views.

3   Click the arrow next to the Navigation tab label in this dialog box to open
    the pop-up menu. Choose Page Only to hide the Bookmarks panel when the
    document opens. Change the Page Layout to Two-Up (Facing), and change the
    Magnification to Fit Visible. Click OK to exit the dialog box.

You need to save, close, and then reopen the file for these settings to take effect.

4   Choose File > Save As, and save the file as **Protocol1.pdf** in the Lesson06 folder.
    Then choose File > Close to close the document.

5   Choose File > Open, and select the Protocol1.pdf file. Notice that the navigation
    pane is now hidden and that the document opens with facing pages displayed.

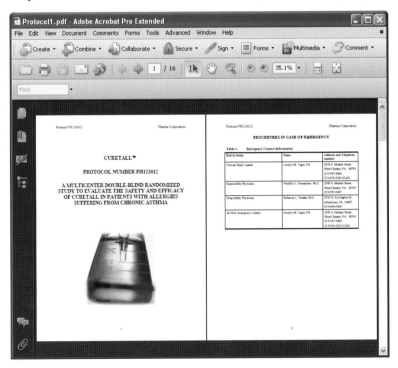

You can use the initial view settings to display documents as you prefer or to set the
initial view of documents that you create and distribute.

6 For the purposes of this lesson, restore the original initial view settings (Bookmarks Panel And Page, Single Page, Fit Page), and then save, close, and reopen your file; or simply close your file and reopen the original work file, Protocol.pdf.

About the onscreen display

Take a look at the Select & Zoom toolbar located at the top of the document window.

▶ **Tip:** To see the printed size of your page, move your pointer into the bottom left of the document pane.

The magnification shown in the Select & Zoom toolbar does not refer to the printed size of the page, but rather to how the page is displayed onscreen. Acrobat determines the onscreen display of a page by treating the page as a 72 ppi (pixels-per-inch) image. For example, if your page has a print size of 2-by-2 inches, Acrobat treats the page as if it were 144 pixels wide and 144 pixels high (72 x 2 = 144). At 100% view, each pixel in the page is represented by 1 screen pixel on your monitor.

How big the page appears onscreen depends on your monitor size and your monitor resolution setting. For example, when you increase the resolution of your monitor, you increase the number of screen pixels within the same monitor area. This results in smaller screen pixels and a smaller displayed page, since the number of pixels in the page itself stays constant.

Reading PDF documents

Acrobat provides a variety of ways for you to move through and adjust the onscreen magnification of a PDF document. For example, you can scroll through the document using the scroll bar at the right side of the window, or you can turn pages as in a traditional book using the Next Page and Previous Page buttons in the Page Navigation toolbar. You can also jump to a specific page.

Using the Reading Mode

The Reading Mode maximizes the screen space available to a document in Acrobat to give you more space to read through the document.

1 Choose View > Reading Mode. This hides all of the elements of the work area except for the document pane and the menu bar.

2 Use the Page Up, Page Down, or arrow keys on your keyboard or use the scrollbar to move through the document.

3 When you're done reading, choose View > Reading Mode again to restore the work area.

Now you'll try some other methods of moving through the document.

Browsing the document

1   If you're not on the first page of the document, enter **1** in the page number box on the Page Navigation toolbar and press Enter or Return.

2   Choose View > Zoom > Fit Width or click the Scrolling Mode button () on the Page Display toolbar to resize your page to fit the width of your screen.

3   With the Hand tool () selected, position your pointer over the document. Hold down the mouse button. Notice that the pointer changes to a closed hand when you hold down the mouse button.

4   Drag the closed hand down and up in the window to move the page on the screen. This is similar to moving a piece of paper around on a desktop.

5   Press Enter or Return to display the next part of the page. You can press Enter or Return repeatedly to view the document from start to finish in screen-sized sections.

6   Choose View > Zoom > Fit Page or click the Single Page button (▦). Click the Previous Page button (⬆) as many times as necessary to return to page 1.

7   Position the pointer over the down arrow in the scroll bar or click in any empty portion of the scroll bar, and click once.

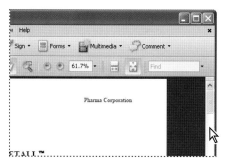
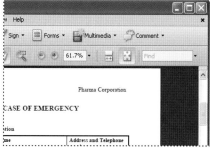

The document scrolls automatically to display all of page 2. In the next few steps, you'll control how PDF pages scroll and display.

You can also access the Actual Size, Fit Page, Fit Width, and Fit Visible commands by clicking the arrow to the right of the magnification pop-up menu in the Select & Zoom toolbar.

8   Click the Scrolling Mode button (🔳) in the Page Display toolbar, and then use the scroll bar to scroll to page 3 of 16.

The Scrolling Mode option displays pages end-to-end like frames in a filmstrip.

9   Choose View > Go To > First Page to go back to the beginning of the document.

10 Click the Single-Page button (🔳) to return to the original page layout.

You can use the page box in the Page Navigation toolbar to move directly to a specific page.

11 Click in the page box until the pointer changes to an I-beam. The current page number is highlighted.

12 Type **15** to replace the current page number, and press Enter or Return.

You should now be viewing page 15.

The scrollbar also lets you navigate to a specific page.

13 Begin dragging the scroll box upward in the scroll bar. As you drag, a page preview box appears. When page 3 of 16 appears in the preview box, release the mouse.

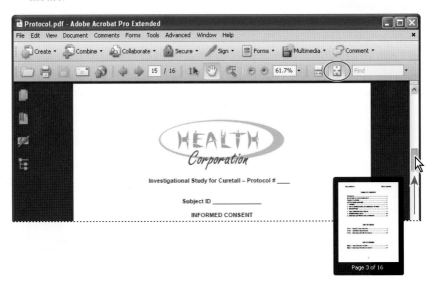

You should now be back at the table of contents in the document.

Browsing with page thumbnails

Page thumbnails are miniature previews of your document pages that are displayed in the Pages panel of the navigation pane.

In this part of the lesson, you'll use page thumbnails to navigate and change the view of pages. In Lesson 7, "Enhancing and Editing PDF Documents," you'll learn how to use page thumbnails to reorder pages in a document.

1   Choose View > Zoom > Fit Width or click the Scrolling Mode button to view the full width of the page. You should still be looking at page 3.

2   Click the Pages button (▤) in the navigation pane to open the Pages panel in the navigation pane.

Page thumbnails for every page in the document are displayed automatically in the navigation pane. The page thumbnails represent both the content and page orientation of the pages in the document. Page-number boxes appear beneath each page thumbnail.

3   Click the page 7 thumbnail to go to page 7. You may need to use the scroll bar to scroll down through the page thumbnails.

The page number for the page thumbnail is highlighted, and a full-width view of page 7 appears in the document window, centered on the point that you clicked.

Take a look at the page 7 thumbnail. The rectangle inside the page thumbnail, called the page-view box, represents the area displayed in the current page view. You can use the page-view box to adjust the area and magnification of the page being viewed.

4   Position the pointer over the lower right-hand corner of the page-view box. Notice that the pointer turns into a double-headed arrow.

5 Drag to shrink the page-view box, and release the mouse button. Take a look at the Select & Zoom toolbar and notice that the magnification level has changed to accommodate the smaller area being viewed.

 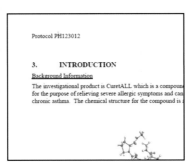

6 Now position the pointer over the bottom border of the page-view box. Notice that the pointer changes to a hand.

7 Drag the page-view box within the page thumbnail, and watch the view change in the document window.

8 Drag the page-view box down to focus your view on the graphic in the middle of the page.

 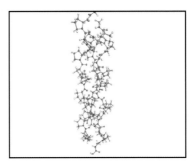

Page thumbnails provide a convenient way to monitor and adjust your page view in a document.

9 Click the Pages button to hide the Pages panel.

Changing the page view magnification

You can change the magnification of the page view using controls in the Select & Zoom toolbar.

1   Choose View > Zoom > Fit Width or click the Scrolling Mode button. A new magnification appears in the Zoom toolbar.

2   Click the Previous Page button (⬆) as many times as necessary to move to page 3. Notice that the magnification remains the same.

3   Choose View > Zoom > Actual Size to return the page to a 100% view.

4   Click the arrow to the right of the magnification pop-up menu in the Select & Zoom toolbar to display the preset magnification options. Choose 200% for the magnification.

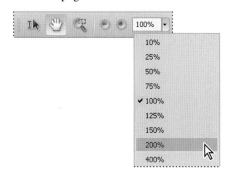

You can also type in a specific value for the magnification.

5   Click the arrow to the right of the magnification pop-up menu in the Select & Zoom toolbar, and choose Actual Size to display the page at 100% again.

Next you'll use the Zoom In button to magnify the view.

6   Select the page number in the Page Navigation toolbar, type **7**, and press Enter or Return to go to page 7.

7   Click the Zoom In (⊕) button once.

8   Click the Zoom In button again to increase the magnification further.

Each click on a Zoom button increases or decreases the magnification by a set amount.

9   Click the Zoom Out button (⊖) twice to return the view to 100%.

Now you'll use the Marquee Zoom tool to magnify the image.

10 Select the Marquee Zoom tool () in the Select & Zoom toolbar. Position the pointer near the top left of the image, and drag over the page as shown in the following illustration.

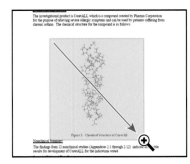
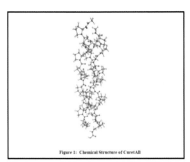

Tip: You can add the Fit Page and the Fit Width buttons to your Select & Zoom toolbar. Right-click or Control-click on the grabber bar of the Select & Zoom toolbar and select the tools you want to add.

The view zooms in on the area you enclosed. This is called marquee-zooming.

11 Choose View > Zoom > Fit Page.

Using the Dynamic Zoom tool

The Dynamic Zoom tool lets you zoom in or out by dragging the mouse up or down.

1 Choose Tools > Select & Zoom > Dynamic Zoom.

2 Click in the document pane, and drag upward to magnify the view, and drag down to reduce the view.

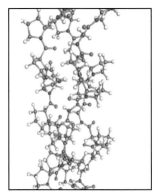

3 When you're finished, select the Hand tool, and then click the Single Page button (⊞).

For information on using the Loupe tool and the Pan & Zoom window, see Lesson 13, "Using the Engineering and Technical Features."

Following links

In a PDF document, you don't have to view pages in sequence. You can jump immediately from one section of a document to another using custom navigational aids such as links.

One benefit of placing a document online is that you can convert traditional cross-references into links, which users can use to jump directly to the referenced section or file. For example, you can make each item under the Contents list into a link that jumps to its corresponding section in the document. You can also use links to add interactivity to traditional book elements such as glossaries and indexes.

First you'll add some navigational tools to the Page Navigation toolbar.

1   With your pointer anywhere in the Page Navigation toolbar, right-click (Windows) or Control-click (Mac OS) and choose Show All Tools.

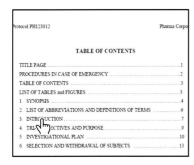

Now you'll try out an existing link.

2   Click the First Page button (⌃) in the Page Navigation toolbar to return to the first page and then click the Next Page button (⬇) twice to move to the Table of Contents page (page 3).

3   Move the pointer over the "3. Introduction" heading in the Table of Contents. The Hand tool changes to a pointing finger, indicating the presence of a link. Click to follow the link.

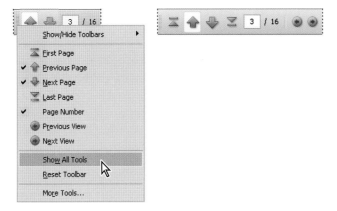

This entry links to the Introduction.

4   Click the Previous View button (●) to return to your previous view of the Contents.

You can click the Previous View button at any time to retrace your viewing path through a document. The Next View button reverses the action of your last Previous View.

In this section, you have learned how to page through a PDF document, change the magnification and page layout mode, and follow links.

Now you'll restore the default toolbar configuration.

5   Choose View > Toolbars > Reset Toolbars.

Searching PDF documents

You can quickly search through a PDF document, looking for a word or a phrase. If, for example, you didn't want to read through this Protocol document but simply wanted to find occurrences of the term *adverse event*, you can use either the Find feature or the Search feature to locate that information. The Find feature will look for a word or phrase in the active document. The Search feature will look for a word or phrase in one document, across a selection of documents, or in a PDF Portfolio. Both features search text, layers, form fields, and digital signatures.

First you'll run a simple Find operation on the open document.

1   In the Find textbox on the toolbar, enter the word or phrase you want to locate. We typed in **adverse event**.

To see the options available with the Find feature, click the arrow to the right of the textbox. You can use these options to refine your search, looking for whole words only or specifying uppercase or lowercase letters, and you can also include bookmarks and comments in the search. Options are in effect (on) when there is a check mark next to the name of the option.

2   Press Enter or Return to start the Find operation.

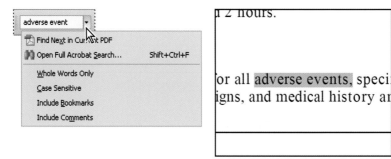

The first occurrence of *adverse event* is highlighted on page 5 of the document.

3 Click the Find Next button (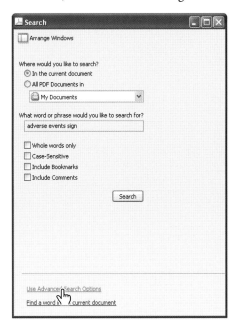) on the toolbar to find the next occurrence of the phrase.

Next you'll perform a more sophisticated search of the Protocol document using the Search feature. You'll search only the Protocol document, but the Search feature allows you to search all documents in a folder as well as all documents in a PDF Portfolio. You can even search non-PDF files in a PDF Portfolio.

4 Choose Edit > Search.

5 To search only the open document, select the In The Current Document option.

In this search, we'd like to find references to adverse events that are significant.

6 In the Search text box, enter **adverse events sign**.

7 Click the Use Advanced Search Options link at the bottom of the Search pane.

8 For Return Results Containing, choose Match Any of the Words from the pop-up menu. This ensures that the search will show all results for "adverse," "events," and derivatives of "sign."

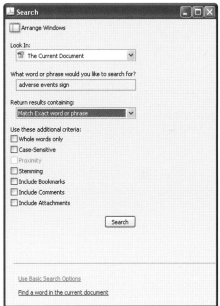

9 Click Search.

10 The search results are displayed in the Search pane.

11 Click on any search result to go to the page that contains that information.

▶ Tip: You have additional options available in the Search preferences. To check your Search preferences choose Edit > Preferences (Windows) or Acrobat > Preferences (Mac OS), and select Search in the left pane.

You can check any of the other search results in the Search pane by clicking them.

12 When you're finished, click the Close button at the top of the Search pane.

The Search feature searches object data and image XIF (extended image file format) metadata. When you search multiple PDF documents, Acrobat also looks at the document properties and XMP metadata. If any of your PDF documents have attachments, you can include those attachments in the search also. If you include a PDF index in your search, Acrobat searches indexed structure tags. To search an encrypted document, you must first open the document.

Printing PDF documents

When you print Adobe PDF documents, you'll find that many of the options in the Acrobat Print dialog box are the same as those found in the Print dialog boxes of other popular applications. For example, the Acrobat Print dialog box, lets you print the current view, a page, an entire file, or a range of pages within a PDF file. (On Windows, you can also access the Print dialog box by choosing Print from the context menu.)

Here's how you can print noncontiguous pages or portions of pages in Acrobat.

1 In the Protocol1.pdf or Protocol.pdf document, click the Pages button in the navigation pane, if necessary, to open the Pages panel. Then, click the thumbnails that correspond with the pages you want to print. You can Ctrl-click (Windows) or Command-click (Mac OS) page thumbnails to select contiguous or non-contiguous pages.

2 If you have a printer attached to your system and if it is turned on, choose File > Print. Make sure the name of the printer attached to your system is displayed. If you have selected pages in the Pages panel, the Selected Pages option will be selected automatically in the Print dialog box.

3 Click OK or Print to print your selected pages. Click Cancel to abort the printing operation.

If you have an Internet connection and a web browser installed on your system, you can click Printing Tips in the Print dialog box to go to the Adobe website for the latest troubleshooting help on printing.

4 Click the Pages button to close the navigation pane.

5 Choose File > Close to close your Protocol document.

For information on printing comments, see Lesson 9, "Using Acrobat in a Review Cycle."

If your printer supports duplex printing, you can print booklets and brochures as described in "Print a booklet" in the Adobe Acrobat Help.

If your PDF file contains odd-sized pages, you can use the Page Scaling options in the Print dialog box to reduce, enlarge, or divide pages. The Fit to Printable Area option scales each page to fit the printer page size. Pages in the PDF file are magnified or reduced as necessary. The Tiling options print oversize pages on several pages that can be assembled to reproduce the oversize image.

Filling out PDF forms

PDF forms can be interactive or noninteractive. Interactive PDF forms have built-in form fields and they behave in very much the same way as most forms that you encounter on the web or that are sent to you electronically. You enter data using the Acrobat Select tool or Hand tool. Depending on the settings applied by the person who created the form, users of Adobe Reader may or may not be able to save a copy of the completed form before they return it.

Noninteractive PDF forms (or flat forms) are forms that have been scanned to create a facsimile of a form. These forms do not contain actual form fields; they contain only the images of form fields. Traditionally you would print out these forms, fill them out by hand or using a typewriter, and then mail or fax the hard copy. With Acrobat you can fill out these noninteractive or flat forms online using the Acrobat Typewriter tool.

In this section, you'll fill in a noninteractive or flat form.

For information on creating interactive forms, see Lesson 10, "Working with Forms in Acrobat."

1   Choose File > Open, and navigate to the Lesson06 folder. Select the FlatForm.pdf file and click Open.

2   Move your pointer over some of the supposed form fields. Notice that the Hand tool does not change shape. You cannot add information to this form using the Hand tool.

3   Choose Tools > Typewriter > Show Typewriter toolbar.

4   Move your pointer over the tools in this toolbar and take a moment to read the tool tips. You can use these tools to increase or decrease the size of the text you enter, or increase or decrease the space between lines of type that you enter.

5   Select the Typewriter tool ( ). The pointer icon changes.

6 Position the pointer over the Name field and click to establish an insertion point. Then type in your name. We typed in **John Doe**.

You can fill in more of the form if you wish. When you're finished, you'll try resetting the form to clear the data.

7 Select the Hand tool, and click the Reset button at the bottom of the form.

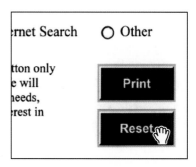

The reset button doesn't work and neither does the Submit button, because these are only images of buttons. (This is a noninteractive form.) To submit this form, you would have to save it as a PDF file and email it to the supplier. Alternatively you could print out the completed form and fax or mail a hard copy to the supplier.

8 Choose File > Save As, and save a copy of the form in the Lesson06 folder using the file name **FlatForm_complete.pdf**.

You can open the saved file if you wish to verify that all your data was saved.

9 Click the close button to close the Typewriter tool.

10 Choose File > Close to close the order form.

With Acrobat 9, it is easy to fill out most forms and submit the data electronically or manually.

About flexibility, accessibility, and structure

The accessibility and flexibility of your Adobe PDF files determine how easily vision- and motion-impaired users and users of hand-held devices can access, reflow, and if you allow it, reuse the content of your files. You control the accessibility and flexibility of your Adobe PDF files through the amount of structure you build into the source file and how you create the Adobe PDF file.

In this section of the lesson, you'll look at what constitutes flexible and accessible documents. First, you'll examine a tagged PDF document and see how easy it is to reflow the document and extract content.

By making your PDF documents more accessible to users, you can broaden your readership and better meet government standards for accessibility. Accessibility in Acrobat falls into two categories:

- Accessibility features that help authors create accessible documents from new or existing PDF documents. These features include simple methods for checking accessibility and adding tags to PDF documents. (See "Looking at accessible documents" in this lesson.) With Acrobat Pro and Pro Extended, you can also correct accessibility and reading-order problems in PDF files by editing the PDF file structure.

- Accessibility features that help readers who have motion or vision limitations to navigate and view PDF documents more easily. Many of these features can be adjusted by using a wizard, the Accessibility Setup Assistant.

For Adobe PDF files to be flexible and accessible, they must have structure, and Adobe PDF files support three levels of structure—tagged, structured, and unstructured. Tagged PDF files have the most structure. Structured PDF files have some structure, but are not as flexible or accessible as tagged PDF files. Unstructured PDF files have no structure. (As you will see later in this lesson, you can add limited structure to unstructured files.) The more structure a file has, the more efficiently and reliably its content can be reused.

Structure is built into a document when the creator of the document defines headers and columns, adds navigation aids such as bookmarks, and adds alternate text descriptions for graphics, for example. In many cases, documents are automatically given logical structure and tags when they are converted to Adobe PDF.

When you create Adobe PDF from Microsoft Office files or from files created in later versions of Adobe FrameMaker, InDesign, or PageMaker, or when you create Adobe PDF using Web Capture, the resulting PDF files are tagged automatically.

In summary, the greatest amount of built-in structure is obtained when you create a document that has defined structure and convert that document to give tagged PDF files.

In Acrobat Pro or Pro Extended, if your PDF documents don't reflow well, you can correct most problems using the Content panel in the navigation pane or the TouchUp Reading Order tool. However, this is not as easy as creating a well-structured document in the first place. For an in-depth guide to creating accessible PDF documents, visit the Adobe website at http://access.adobe.com.

Looking at accessible documents

In this section, you'll examine a tagged PDF file.

Working with a tagged Adobe PDF file

First you'll look at the accessibility and flexibility of a tagged PDF file that was created from a Word file on Windows.

1 Open Acrobat 9, and choose File > Open, and open the Tag_Wines.pdf file in the Lesson06 folder.

2 Choose File > Save As, and save the file as **Tag_Wines1.pdf** in the Lesson06 folder.

Checking for accessibility

It's always a good idea to check the accessibility of any Adobe PDF document before you distribute it to users, and the Acrobat Quick Check feature tells you right away if your document has the information necessary to make it accessible. At the same time, it checks for protection settings that would prohibit access.

1 Choose Advanced > Accessibility > Quick Check.

The message box indicates that the document Tag_Wines1.pdf has no accessibility issues.

2 Click OK to close the message box.

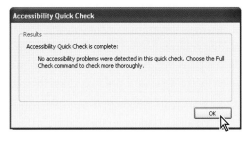

You can add security to your PDF files and still make them accessible. The 128-bit encryption offered by Acrobat 9 prevents users from copying and pasting text from a PDF file while still supporting assistive technology. You can also use the Enable Text Access For Screen Reader Devices For The Visually Impaired option to modify security settings on older PDF documents (Acrobat 3 and later) to make them accessible without compromising security. This option is in the Password Security Settings dialog box.

Now you'll take a quick look at how flexible a tagged PDF file is. First you'll reflow the PDF file and then you'll save the contents of the PDF file as accessible text.

Reflowing a flexible PDF file

First you'll adjust the size of your document window to mimic the smaller screen of a hand-held device.

1 Choose View > Zoom > Actual Size to display the document at 100%.

2 Resize the Acrobat window to about 50% of the full-screen display. In Windows, click the Maximize/Restore Down button if the window is currently maximized; if the window isn't maximized, drag a corner of the application window to reduce it. In Mac OS, resize the document pane by dragging a corner.

Your goal is to resize the Acrobat window so that the ends of the sentences in the document pane are cut off.

3 Choose View > Zoom > Reflow.

The content of the document is reflowed to accommodate the smaller document screen, and you can now read an entire line of text without using the horizontal scroll bar.

When you reflow text, artifacts such as page numbers and page headers often drop out because they are no longer relevant to the page display. Text is reflowed one page at a time, and you cannot save the document in the reflowed state.

Now you'll examine how the display changes when you change the magnification.

4 Click the arrow next to the magnification box on the toolbar, and choose 400% from the menu.

5 Scroll down the page to see how the text reflows. Again, because the text is reflowed, you don't have to use the horizontal scroll bar to move back and forth across the page to read the enlarged text. The text is automatically contained within the document pane.

Awards

As of the beginning of the year, Chamberg

6 When you've finished viewing the reflowed text, maximize the Acrobat document window and close your file.

Acrobat also allows you to save the contents of a tagged document in a different file format for reuse in another application. For example, if you save this file as accessible text, you'll see that even the contents of the table are saved in an easily usable format.

With Acrobat you can even make some unstructured documents more readily accessible to all types of users. You can add tags to a PDF document using the Advanced > Accessibility > Add Tags To Document command in Acrobat Standard, Acrobat Pro, and Pro Extended. However, you can only correct tagging and order errors in Acrobat Pro and Pro Extended. In the next section, you'll view the results of adding tags.

Making files flexible and accessible

Some tagged Adobe PDF documents may not contain all the information necessary to make the document contents fully flexible or accessible. For example, your file may not contain alternate text for figures, language properties for portions of the text that use a different language than the default language for the document, as well as expansion text for abbreviations. (Designating the appropriate language for different text elements ensures that the correct characters are used when you reuse the document for another purpose, that the word can be pronounced correctly when read out loud, and that the document will be spell-checked with the correct dictionary.)

You can add alternate text and multiple languages using the Tags panel. (If only one language is required, it is easier to choose the language in the Document Properties dialog box.) You can also add alternate text using the TouchUp Reading Order tool.

Now you'll look at the accessibility of a page of a user guide. This document was designed to be printed, so no attempt was made to make it accessible.

1   Choose File > Open, and open the AI_UGEx.pdf file in the Lesson06 folder.

2   Choose Advanced > Accessibility > Quick Check. The message box indicates that the document has no logical structure. Click OK to clear the message box.

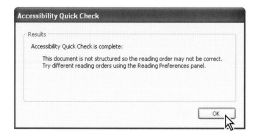

Now you'll see how this page reflows.

3   Choose View > Zoom > Actual Size to display the document at 100%.

4   Reduce the size of the document pane: In Windows, click the Maximize/ Restore Down button if the window is maximized; if it isn't, drag a corner of the window. In Mac OS, drag a corner of the document pane to resize it. We made our Acrobat window small enough that the width of a full page could not be displayed on the screen (at 100%).

5   Choose View > Zoom > Reflow.

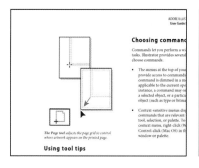 

The text reflows well, despite the lack of structure.

6   Choose View > Zoom > Fit Page. Resize the Acrobat window to best fit your needs.

In this section of the lesson, you'll improve the flexibility and accessibility of the page. First you'll add tags to as many elements as possible using Acrobat.

7 Choose Advanced > Accessibility > Add Tags To Document.

In Acrobat Pro and Pro Extended, a Recognition Report is displayed in the navigation pane. Leave this pane open.

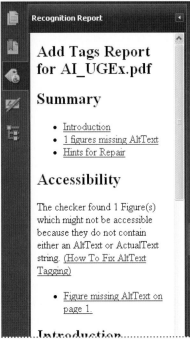

8 If you are using Acrobat Pro or Pro Extended, leave the file open. If you are using Acrobat Standard, choose File > Close to close your work. The remainder of this lesson is for Acrobat Pro and Pro Extended users.

When you add tags to a document, Acrobat adds a logical tree structure to the document that determines the order in which page content is reflowed and read by screen readers and the Read Out Loud feature. On relatively simple pages, the Add Tags To Document command can work well. On more complex pages—pages that contain irregularly shaped columns, bulleted lists, text that spans columns, and son on—the Add Tags To Document command may not be sufficient.

To correctly tag these more complex pages you need to use the TouchUp Reading Order tool.

Adding tags

While Acrobat can track the structure of most page elements and tag them appropriately, pages with complex layouts or unusual elements may not always result in successfully tagged PDF documents and may require editing. When you tag a PDF file using Acrobat, Acrobat returns a Recognition Report in the Navigation pane that lists pages where problems were encountered and suggestions for fixing them.

It's a good idea to check these items in the PDF document to determine what corrections, if any, need to be made. Use the report to navigate to the problem areas of your PDF document by clicking the links for each error. Then use the TouchUp Reading Order tool to correct the problem.

▶ **Tip:** The Recognition Report is a temporary file and can't be saved. The Full Check feature generates an accessibility report that can be saved.

Adding Alt Text (alternate text)

Non-text elements in your document, such as figures and multimedia elements, won't be recognized by a screen reader or Read Out Loud feature unless they are accompanied by alternate text. When you reviewed the Recognition Report, you noticed that the figure is missing Alt Text. You'll add alternate text now. First though, you'll close the Recognition Report.

1 Click the Hide button or Close button to close the Recognition Report.

2 Choose Tools > Advanced Editing > TouchUp Reading Order Tool. Then right-click (Windows) or Control-click (Mac OS) on the figure in the document pane, and choose Edit Alternate Text from the menu. In the Alternate Text dialog box, enter the text you want the Screen Reader to use. We entered: **Figure shows Hand tool being used to drag the artboard across the Illustrator window**. Then click OK.

▶ **Tip:** If the Show Tables And Figures option is selected in the TouchUp Reading Order dialog box, the alt text will be displayed in a label in the document pane.

3 To check your alternate text, choose View > Read Out Loud > Activate Read Out Loud. Then choose View > Read Out Loud > Read This Page Only. You'll hear your alternate text. To stop the reading, press Shift+Ctrl+E (Windows) or Shift+Command+E (Mac OS).

Notice that both the alternate text and the caption are read. If you want only the alternate text to be read, combine the figure and caption elements using the TouchUp Reading Order dialog box.

4 Choose File > Close to close your work without saving your changes, and click the close button to close the TouchUp Reading Order dialog box. Select the Hand tool.

For an in-depth guide to creating accessible PDF documents, visit the Adobe website at http://access.adobe.com.

Using the Acrobat accessibility features

Many people with vision and motor impairments use computers, and Acrobat has a number of features that make it easier for these users to work with Adobe PDF documents. These features include:

- Automatic scrolling.

- Keyboard shortcuts.

- Support for several screen-reader applications, including the text-to-speech engines built into Windows and Mac OS platforms.

- Enhanced onscreen viewing.

Acrobat 9 offers improved viewing of XFA Forms in Acrobat or Adobe Reader. And improved screen reader support allows easier integration of third-party screen readers.

Using the Accessibility Setup Assistant

Both Acrobat 9 and Adobe Reader have an Accessibility Setup Assistant that launches automatically the first time the software detects a screen reader, screen magnifier, or other assistive technology on your system. (You can also launch the Assistant manually at any time by choosing Advanced > Accessibility > Setup Assistant.) This Assistant walks you through setting the options that control how PDF documents appear onscreen. This Assistant also allows you to set the option that sends print output to a Braille printer.

A full explanation of the options that can be set in the Accessibility Setup Assistant is available in the Adobe Acrobat 9 Help. The options available depend on the type of assistive technology you have on your system, and the first panel of the Accessibility Setup Assistant requires you to identify the type of assistive technology that you are using:

- Select Set Options For Screen Readers if you use a device that reads text and sends output to a Braille printer.

- Select Set Options For Screen Magnifiers if you use a device that makes text appear larger on the screen.

- Select Set All Accessibility Options if you use a combination of assistive devices.

- Select Use Recommended Settings And Skip Setup to use the Adobe-recommended settings for users with limited accessibility. (Note that the preferred settings for users with assistive technology installed are not the same as the default Acrobat settings for users who are not using assistive technology.)

In addition to the options you can set using the Accessibility Setup Assistant, you can set a number of options in the Acrobat or Adobe Reader preferences that control automatic scrolling, reading out loud settings, and reading order. You may want to use some of these options even if you don't have assistive technology on your system. For example, you can set your Multimedia preferences to show available descriptions for video and audio attachments.

If you opened the Accessibility Setup Assistant, click Cancel to exit the dialog box without making any changes.

About automatic scrolling

When you're reading a long document, the Acrobat automatic scrolling feature saves a lot of keystroke and mouse actions. You can control the speed of the scrolling, scroll backward and forward, and exit automatic scrolling with a single keystroke.

Now you'll test the automatic scroll feature.

1   Choose File > Open, and open the Protocol.pdf file. If necessary, resize your Acrobat window to fill your desktop and select the Hand tool ( ).

2   Choose View > Automatically Scroll.

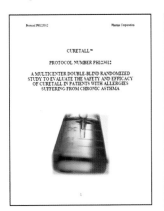

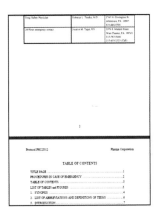

3   You can set the rate of scrolling using the number keys on your keyboard. The higher the number, the faster the rate of scrolling. Try pressing 9 and then 1, for example, to change rates of scrolling. To exit automatic scrolling, press the Esc key.

About keyboard shortcuts

Before keyboard shortcuts are available, you may have to change your General preferences (see Lesson 2, "Looking at the Work Area").

For most common commands and tools, the keyboard shortcut is displayed next to the command or tool name if you have the preferences set to use single-key accelerators. A list of the keyboard shortcuts is available in the Adobe Acrobat 9 Help.

You can also use the keyboard to control Acrobat within Microsoft Internet Explorer in Windows. If the focus is on the web browser, any keyboard shortcuts you use act according to the web browser settings for navigation and selection. Pressing the Tab key shifts the focus from the browser to the Acrobat document and application, so navigation and command keystrokes function normally. Pressing Ctrl + Tab shifts the focus from the document back to the web browser.

Changing background color

Now you'll experiment with changing the color of the background. Note that these changes affect only the onscreen display on your own system; they do not affect the printed document, nor are they saved with the document for display on systems other than your own.

1   Choose Edit > Preferences (Windows) or Acrobat > Preferences (Mac OS), and select Accessibility in the left pane.

2   Select the Replace Document Colors option.

3   Select Custom Color.

4   Click the Page Background color square to open the color tab.

5   You can select a color from the color picker or you can select a custom color. We chose pale gray.

6   Click OK to apply your changes.

7   When you are finished, you can leave your background color as it is, or return it to white.

You can change the background color of form fields and the color of form fields displayed when your pointer moves over them in the Forms preferences. You can change the background color for full-screen presentations in the Full Screen preferences. You can change the underline color used in the spell check feature to identify misspelled words in the Spelling preferences.

Smoothing text

Acrobat allows you to smooth text, line art, and images to improve onscreen readability, especially with larger text sizes. If you use a laptop or if you have an LCD screen, you can also choose a Smooth Text option to optimize your display quality. These options are set in the Page Display preferences.

Magnifying bookmark text

You can increase the text size used in bookmark labels.

1   If necessary, click the Bookmarks button to display the Bookmarks panel.

2   Choose Text Size > Large from the Options menu of the Bookmarks panel.

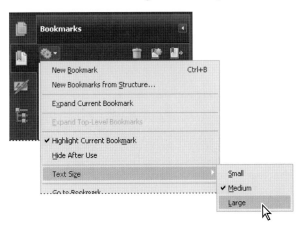

3   Restore your bookmark text size to medium.

You should experiment with screen display options and other accessibility controls to find a combination that best suits your needs.

4   When you are finished, choose File > Close. You need not save your work.

Setting screen reader and reading out loud preferences

After you have installed your screen reader or similar application and set it up to work with Acrobat, you can set the screen reader preferences in Acrobat. You set these preferences in the same panel in which you set the Read Out Loud feature preferences that control the volume, pitch, and speed of the speech; the nature of the voice; and the reading order preferences.

Newer systems (both Windows and Mac OS platforms) have built-in text-to-speech engines. Although the Read Out Loud feature can read the text of a PDF file out loud, it is not a screen reader. Not all systems support the Read Out Loud feature.

In this section, you'll look at the preferences that affect how Adobe PDF documents are read out loud. Unless you have text-to-speech software on your system, you do not need to set these preferences.

1 Choose File > Open, and open the Tag_Wines.pdf file.

2 If your system has text-to-speech software, choose View > Read Out Loud > Activate Read Out Loud. (You may not need to activate the Read Out Loud function, depending on how much of the lesson you completed.)

3 After you have activated the Read Out Loud feature, choose View > Read Out Loud > Read This Page Only. You will hear the currently displayed page read. To stop the reading, press Shift+Ctrl+E (Windows) or Shift+Command+E (Mac OS).

You can experiment with the following reading options.

4 Choose Edit > Preferences (Windows) or Acrobat > Preferences (Mac OS), and select Reading in the left pane.

You can control the volume, pitch, speed, and voice used. If you use the default voice, you cannot change the pitch and speed of delivery.

If your system has limited memory, you may wish to reduce the number of pages before data is delivered by page-by-page. The default value is 50 pages.

5 You need to click OK in the Preferences dialog box to apply any changes that you make. Or you can click Cancel to exit the Preferences dialog box without making any changes.

6 To test your settings, choose View > Read Out Loud > Read This Page Only.

7 To stop the reading, press Shift+Ctrl+E (Windows) or Shift+Command+E (Mac OS).

8 When you are finished, choose File > Close. You need not save your work. Then quit Acrobat.

Review questions

1 Name several ways in which you can move to a different page.

2 Name several ways in which you can change the view magnification.

3 How do you check whether or not a file is accessible?

4 Where do you turn keyboard shortcuts on or off?

Review answers

1 You can move to a different page by clicking the Previous Page or Next Page button in the Page Navigation toolbar; dragging the scroll box in the scroll bar; entering a page number in the page box in the Page Navigation toolbar; or clicking a bookmark, page thumbnail, or link that jumps to a different page.

2 You can change the view magnification by choosing View > Zoom > Actual Size, Fit Page, or Fit Width; marquee-zooming; choosing a preset magnification from the magnification menu in the Select & Zoom toolbar; or entering a specific percentage in the magnification box.

3 Choose Advanced > Accessibility > Quick Check.

4 You turn keyboard shortcuts on or off in the General preferences, using the Use Single-Key Accelerators to Access Tools option.

7 ENHANCING AND EDITING PDF DOCUMENTS

Lesson Overview

In this lesson, you'll do the following:

- Use page thumbnails to rearrange pages in a document and navigate through a document.

- Rotate, crop, and delete pages.

- Insert pages into a document.

- Work with links and bookmarks.

- Renumber pages in a document.

- Copy text from a document.

- Copy images from a document.

- Create an image file from a PDF file.

 This lesson will take approximately 45 minutes to complete. Copy the Lesson07 folder onto your hard drive if you haven't already done so.

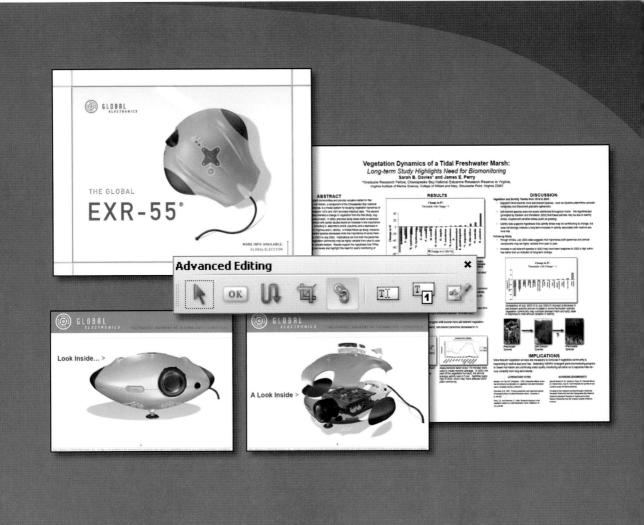

Looking at the work file

You'll work with a presentation for the fictitious company Global Electronics. The presentation has been designed both for print and for online viewing. Because this online presentation is in the developmental phase, it contains a number of mistakes. In the first part of this lesson, you'll use Acrobat to correct the problems in this PDF document.

1 Start Acrobat.

2 Choose File > Open. Select GE_Presentation.pdf, located in the Lesson07 folder, and click Open. Then choose File > Save As, rename the file **GE_Presentation1.pdf**, and save it in the Lesson07 folder.

Notice that the document opens with the Bookmarks panel open and that bookmarks have already been created. Bookmarks are links that are generated automatically from the table-of-contents entries of documents created by most desktop publishing programs or from formatted headings in applications such as Microsoft Word. While these automatically generated bookmarks are usually adequate to navigate through a document, you can also set bookmarks to direct readers to specific sections in your document. You can also set the appearance of bookmarks and add actions to them.

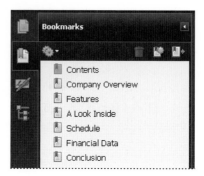

3 Use the Next Page button (⬇) to page through the presentation.

Notice that the bookmark icon that corresponds to the page that you are viewing is highlighted as you move through the pages. (There are a couple of bookmark errors that you'll correct later.)

4 With the Hand tool (🖑) or the Select tool (I𝕜) selected, click the icon for the Contents bookmark to return to the first page of the presentation, which functions as the table of contents.

5 In the document pane, move the pointer over the items listed under Contents. Notice that the items in the list have already been linked, as shown by the hand changing to a pointing finger.

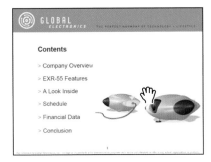 

6 Click the Company Overview entry in the document pane to follow its link. (Be sure to click the entry in the table of contents, not the bookmark in the Bookmarks panel.)

Notice that the page number on the page displayed in the document pane is 2, whereas the page number in the toolbar shows the page as being page 4 of 7. Clearly the page is out of order.

7 Choose View > Go To > Previous View to return to the table of contents.

Now you'll use page thumbnails to get a clearer picture of what's wrong with the organization of the presentation and correct it.

But first, because you'll be doing a lot of paging through the presentation, you'll add more tools to the Page Navigation toolbar.

8 Right-click (Windows) or Control-click (Mac OS) anywhere in the Page Navigation toolbar area, and choose Show All Tools from the context menu.

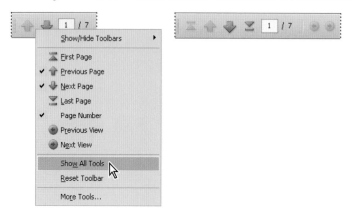

Moving pages with page thumbnails

Page thumbnails offer convenient previews of your pages. You can use them for navigation. They are especially useful if you are looking for a page that has a distinctive appearance. You can also drag them in the Pages panel to change the pagination in the document pane, which is what you'll do now.

1 Click the Pages button (▤) in the navigation pane to see thumbnails of each page.

First you'll widen the Pages panel so that you can see all the thumbnails without having to scroll.

2 Move your pointer over the margin between the navigation pane and the document pane. When the pointer changes shape, drag to the right to widen the navigation pane. Adjust the width of the navigation pane so that you have two columns of page thumbnails.

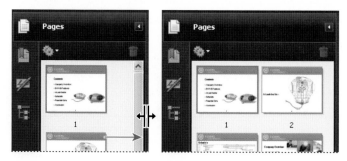

Now you'll move two pages of the presentation that were incorrectly placed. As you noticed earlier, the Company Overview page is out of place. It should be the first page after the Contents page. Also the EXR-55 Features page should follow the Company Overview page (based on the table of contents). You'll move both pages together.

3   Click the page 4 thumbnail to select it.

4   Ctrl-click (Windows) or Command-click (Mac OS) the page 5 thumbnail to add it to the selection.

5   Drag the selected thumbnail images up until the insertion bar appears to the right of the page 1 thumbnail. The page 1 thumbnail represents the Contents page.

6   Release the mouse button to insert the page thumbnails at their new position.

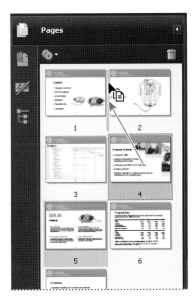 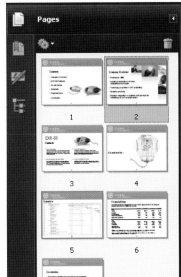

The Company Overview page now follows the Contents page, and the EXR-55 Features page follows the Company Overview page.

7   To check the sequence of pages, click the First Page button (⬚) on the Page Navigation toolbar to go to the first page of the presentation, and then use the Next Page button (⬇) to page through the presentation.

8   When you're satisfied that the pages are in the correct order, choose File > Save to save your work.

Editing Adobe PDF pages

If you look at the first page of the presentation (page 1 of 7), you'll notice that the first page, the Contents page, is rather plain. To make the presentation more attractive, we've created a new title page for you.

Rotating a page

You'll open a title page for the presentation, and then rotate and crop the new page to match the rest of the presentation.

1 Choose File > Open, navigate to the Lesson07 folder, and select the Front.pdf file. Click Open.

2 Click the Pages button to open the Pages panel, and click the Options button (⚙) at the top of the Pages panel. Choose Rotate Pages.

▶ **Tip:** If you want to rotate all the pages in a file for viewing purposes only, choose View > Rotate View > Clockwise or Counterclockwise. When you close the file, the pages revert to their original rotation.

3 For Direction, choose Clockwise 90 degrees. Because you are only rotating one page, you can use the default settings for everything else in this dialog box. Click OK.

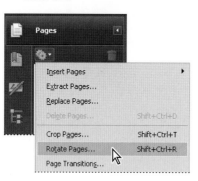
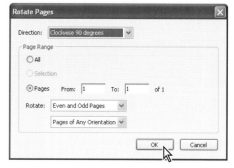

Inserting a page from another file

Now you'll use page thumbnails to insert the title page at the beginning of the presentation.

Because you'll be tiling windows vertically (stacking windows side-by-side) in this part of the lesson, you may prefer to adjust the width of the Pages panel to display the page thumbnails in one column. If you need help adjusting the width of the Pages panel, see "Moving pages with page thumbnails" earlier in this lesson.

1 Choose Window > Tile > Vertically to arrange the two document windows side-by-side.

You can insert pages by dragging page thumbnails between Page panels.

2   Select the page thumbnail for the title page in the Pages panel of the Front.pdf window, and drag the page thumbnail into the Pages panel for the GE_Presentation1.pdf window. When the insertion bar appears

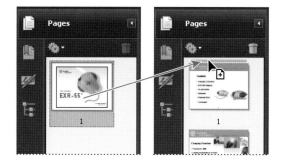

to the left of the page 1 thumbnail, release the mouse button. (If you have a single row of thumbnails, the insertion bar appears above the page 1 thumbnail.)

The title page is inserted into the presentation in the correct location.

3   In the Front.pdf document window, choose File > Close, and close the Front.pdf file without saving any changes. Resize the GE_Presentation1.pdf window to fill the document window or screen.

4   Choose File > Save to save your work.

View the page thumbnails in the Pages panel. Although the new title page appears to be the same size as the other pages in the book, the image area is smaller. The image has a significant white margin around it.

Cropping a page

You'll use the Crop Pages dialog box to enter dimensions for the imported page so that it matches the other pages in the document. You'll temporarily change the page units from inches to points, which will give you more control over the crop operation.

1   With the page 1 thumbnail still selected in the Pages panel, click the Options button at the top of the Pages panel and choose Crop Pages.

The Crop Pages dialog box lets you specify the units and margins for cropping the page.

2   Make sure that CropBox is selected from the pop-up menu.

3   Select Points from the Units menu.

If you change the value for Units here, the change is temporary; if you change the value in the Units & Guides preferences, the change remains in effect until changed again.

4 For Margin Controls, use the up and down arrows to enter the following values. You can tab to move from one entry to the next.
(If you type in the new values instead of using the up and down keys, be careful not to press Enter or Return after the last entry or you will execute the crop action automatically.)

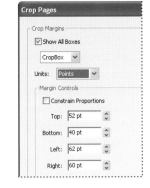

- Top: **52**

- Bottom: **40**

- Left: **62**

- Right: **60**

5 Click in the preview area. A line representing the crop location appears both in the preview in the dialog box and in the document. You may need to drag the Crop Pages dialog box out of the way to view the crop line in the document. You can drag the dialog box by its title bar.

6 If needed, use the up and down arrows next to the margin values again to fine-tune the location of the crop line so that the crop lines align with the edges of the title border.

7 For Page Range, make sure that you are cropping only the selected page, page 1 of the document, and click OK.

8 Choose File > Save to save the GE_Presentation1.pdf file.

You can also use the Crop tool (⛏) to crop the page. Choose Tools > Advanced Editing > Crop Tool. Drag in the document pane to define the crop area, and then double-click in the crop area to open the Crop Pages dialog box. Because Acrobat automatically enters your top, bottom, right, and left crop margins when you use this method, all you have to do is fine-tune the settings.

Now you'll check the links on the Contents page of your presentation to make sure that online viewers navigate to the correct pages.

9 Type **2** in the page number text box on the toolbar to select the page number, and press Enter or Return to return to the Contents page.

10 On the Contents page in the document pane, click each link in turn. (You must have the Hand tool or the Select tool selected.) Use the Previous View button (⬅) to return to the Contents page each time. Notice that the Schedule link takes you to the wrong page and that the Financial link is not working.

Editing links

Now you'll correct the broken links.

1 Click the page thumbnail for page 2 to return to the Contents page if necessary.

2 Scroll down the page thumbnails in the Pages panel and notice that the Financial Data page is page 7 in the presentation. You'll use this information to set the link correctly.

3 Choose Tools > Advanced Editing > Show Advanced Editing Toolbar to display the Advanced Editing toolbar.

4 Select the Link tool (🔗). Notice that all the links on the page in the document pane are outlined in black when the Link tool is active.

5 Move the pointer over the broken Financial Data link in the document pane. The link is selected when blue handles appear on the link box. Right-click (Windows) or Control-click (Mac OS) in the link box, and choose Properties from the context menu.

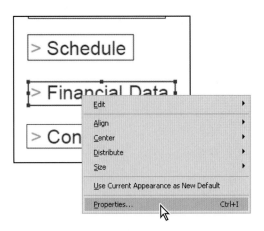

6 Click the Actions tab in the Link Properties dialog box to set the correct destination for the link.

7 Choose Go To A Page View from the Select Action menu, and click Add.

8 Use the scroll bar on the right of the document pane to move to page 7. When the page preview box shows page 7, click Set Link in the dialog box.

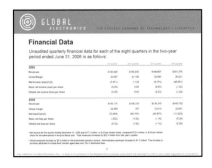

9 In the Link Properties dialog box, click OK to apply your changes to the link.

10 Select the Hand tool (✋) and test your link. When you are finished, click the Previous View button (◉) to return to the Contents page.

Earlier in this lesson, you noticed that the Schedule link incorrectly took you to the A Look Inside page.

11 Follow the same procedure you used above to correct the Schedule link, except you'll edit the existing link to go to page 6 rather than page 5.

12 When you are finished, click the Previous View button to return to the Contents page.

13 Choose File > Save to save your work.

14 Choose Tools > Advanced Editing > Hide Advanced Editing Toolbar to close the toolbar.

Inserting one PDF file into another PDF file

In Acrobat, you can insert or replace a page, a specified range of pages, or all pages from one PDF document into another. Earlier in this lesson, you used page thumbnails to insert a page from one PDF document into another. Now you'll replace the place holder page with a two-page file (Look_Inside.pdf).

1 With the Hand tool selected (👋), click the Bookmarks button in the navigation pane to display the bookmarks.

Although the bookmark "A Look Inside" appears in the list, the presentation contains only a placeholder image for the product details. You'll replace this placeholder page with the product details pages from another document and then fix the bookmark.

2 Drag in the scroll bar in the document pane to go to page 5 (5 of 8) in the document, or click the A Look Inside bookmark icon in the Bookmarks panel.

3 Choose Document > Insert Pages > From File (Windows) or Document > Insert Pages (Mac OS).

4 In the Select File To Insert dialog box, select Look_Inside.pdf in the Lesson07 folder, and click Select.

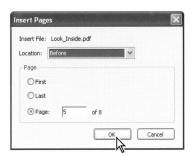

5 In the Insert Pages dialog box, for Location, choose Before.

6 Make sure that Page is selected and that the Page text box contains **5**. Then click OK.

The product detail pages are inserted where they belong.

7 Page through the document to verify that the pages have been inserted in the correct location.

 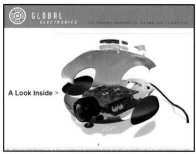

8 Choose File > Save to save your work.

You'll need to delete the placeholder page, but first you'll add a bookmark for the title page that you added and then update the link for the A Look Inside bookmark.

Adding multimedia files

With Acrobat 9 Pro Extended, you can easily transform your PDF files into exciting multidimensional communication tools by inserting video, audio, and Flash applications that will run cross-platform with just Acrobat or Reader 9.

The new Multimedia features on the Tasks toolbar, in the Tools menu, and on the Multimedia toolbar in Acrobat Pro Extended let you convert video and sound files to FLV files that ensure high-quality viewing and compatibility across computer platforms. Most multimedia file types (including ASF, ASX, AVI, MOV, MP4, MPEG, MPG, QT, WFM, mp3, WAV, M4V, and MPEG4) are converted to FLV format. (FLV and H.264 files can be placed without encoding and so can be placed using Acrobat Pro.)

For more information, see Lesson 11, "Creating Multimedia Presentations."

Working with bookmarks

A bookmark is simply a link represented by text in the Bookmarks panel. While bookmarks that are created automatically by many authoring programs are generally linked to headings in the text or to figure captions, you can also add your own bookmarks in Acrobat to create a custom outline of a document or to open other documents.

Additionally you can use electronic bookmarks as you would paper bookmarks—to mark a place in a document that you want to highlight or return to later.

Adding a bookmark

First, you'll add a bookmark for the front cover of the presentation.

1   Click the First Page button (▣) to display the front cover of the presentation, and make sure that the Single Page button (▣) is selected. A bookmark always displays a page at the magnification set when the bookmark was created.

2   In the Bookmarks panel, click the New Bookmark icon (▣). A new, untitled bookmark is added below whatever bookmark was selected or at the bottom of the list of bookmarks.

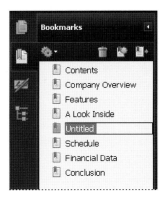

3   In the text box of the new bookmark, type in the bookmark label that you want. We typed in **Title Page**. Click anywhere in the Bookmarks panel to move the focus from the text box to the bookmark.

Now you'll move the bookmark into the correct location in the bookmark hierarchy.

4   Drag the bookmark icon directly up and above the Contents bookmark. Release the bookmark when you see an arrow and dotted line above the Contents bookmark.

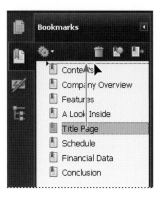 

5   Choose File > Save to save your work.

Test your new bookmark by selecting another bookmark to change the document window view and then selecting the Title Page bookmark again.

Changing a bookmark destination

1   In the Bookmarks panel, click the A Look Inside bookmark icon. The document pane displays the placeholder page.

2   Click the Previous Page button (⬆) twice to go to page 5 (5 of 10) of the document, which is the page you want the bookmark to link to—the first page of the product details that you added.

3   Click the Options button at the top of the Bookmarks panel, and choose Set Bookmark Destination from the menu. Click Yes to the confirmation message to update the bookmark destination.

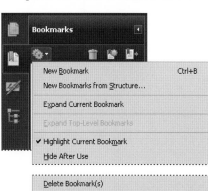 

4 Choose File > Save to save the GE_Presentation1.pdf file.

Other ways of creating bookmarks

You can add your own custom bookmarks and links to any PDF document using the tools in Acrobat. Here are some different methods for adding new bookmarks.

Using keyboard shortcuts

You can create a bookmark using the keyboard shortcut for the New Bookmarks command. (Many Acrobat commands can be executed using keyboard shortcuts.)

1 To create a new bookmark using a keyboard shortcut, press Ctrl+B (Windows) or Command+B (Mac OS), and then name the bookmark. Click outside the bookmark to deselect it.

2 In the document window, navigate to the page that the bookmark should be linked to.

3 With the newly created bookmark selected in the Bookmarks panel, choose Set Bookmark Destination from the Options menu in the Bookmarks panel.

Automatically setting the correct link

You can create, name, and automatically link a bookmark by selecting text in the document pane.

1 Select the Select tool in the toolbar.

2 Move the I-beam into the document page, and drag to highlight the text that you want to use as your bookmark.

Be sure to have the magnification of the page at the required level. Whatever magnification is used will be inherited by the bookmark.

3 Click the New Bookmark icon at the top of the Bookmarks panel. A new bookmark is created in the bookmarks list, and the highlighted text from the document pane is used as the bookmark name. By default, the new bookmark links to the current page view displayed in the document window.

Moving bookmarks

After creating a bookmark, you can easily drag it to its proper place in the Bookmarks panel. You can move individual bookmarks or groups of bookmarks up and down in the Bookmarks list and you can nest bookmarks.

You'll nest the Company Overview, Features, A Look Inside, Schedule, Financial Data, and Conclusion bookmarks under the Contents bookmark.

1   Ctrl-click (Windows) or Command-click (Mac OS) the Company Overview, Features, A Look Inside, Schedule, Financial Data, and Conclusion bookmarks to select them all.

2   Position the pointer on one of the selected bookmarks, hold down the mouse button, and drag the bookmarks up and under the Contents bookmark. When the arrow is below and to the right of the Contents bookmark button, release the mouse button.

 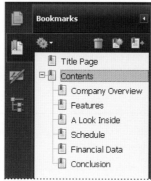

3   Choose File > Save to save your work.

Deleting a page

Now you'll delete the placeholder page from the presentation.

1   Scroll through the document to page 7 of 10.

2   Choose Document > Delete Pages.

3 Make sure that you are deleting page 7 to 7 of the presentation. Click OK. Click Yes to clear the confirmation box.

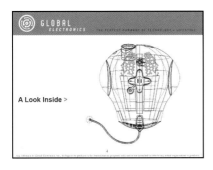 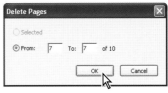

The page is deleted from the GE_Presentation1.pdf file.

4 Choose File > Save, and save your work.

You can page through the presentation to check that the placeholder page has been deleted from the book.

Renumbering pages

You may have noticed that the page numbers on the document pages do not always match the page numbers that appear below the page thumbnails and on the toolbar. Acrobat automatically numbers pages with Arabic numerals, starting with page 1 for the first page in the document, and so on.

1 Click the Pages button in the navigation pane to display the page thumbnails.

2 Click the page 1 thumbnail to go to the title page.

You'll renumber the first page of the document—the title page—using lowercase roman numerals.

3 Click the Options button at the top of the Pages panel, and choose Number Pages.

4 For Pages, select From and enter pages from **1** to **1**. For Numbering, select Begin New Section, choose "i, ii, iii" from the Style menu, and enter **1** in the Start text box. Click OK.

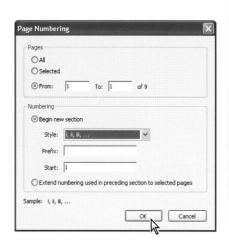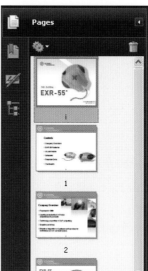

5 Choose View > Go To > Page. Enter **1**, and click OK.

▶ **Tip:** You can physically add page numbers to the pages of your Adobe PDF document using the Add Headers & Footers command. You can also add Bates numbering.

Notice that the number 1 in the page number text box is now assigned to the Contents page of the presentation.

6 Choose View > Toolbars > Reset Toolbars.

7 When you are finished, close the file. You do not need to save your work.

Setting up presentations

Generally, when you make a presentation to a group of people, you want the document to take over the entire screen, hiding distractions such as the menu bar, toolbars, and other window controls.

You can set up any PDF file to display in Full Screen mode, and you can set a variety of transition effects to play as you move between pages. You can even set the speed at which pages "turn." You can also convert presentations that you've prepared in other programs, such as PowerPoint, to Adobe PDF, preserving many of the authoring program's special effects. For more information, see Lesson 11, "Creating Multimedia Presentations."

Editing and extracting text and images

In this section of the lesson, you'll work with a display poster created to summarize a research project on wetland vegetation patterns. You'll copy text and images from the poster to use in a different project.

You'll start by opening a PDF version of the poster you're going to extract text and images from.

Choose File > Open. Select FreshWater.pdf in the Lesson07 folder, and click Open. Then choose File > Save As, rename the file **FreshWater1.pdf**, and save it in the Lesson07 folder.

To make sure that readers see the entire poster, the poster has been set to open in the Fit Page view and with the navigation pane closed.

Editing text

You use the TouchUp Text tool to make last-minute corrections to text in a PDF document. You can edit text and change text attributes such as spacing, point size, and color. In order to add or replace text, you must have a licensed copy of the font installed on your system; however, you can change text attributes if the font is embedded in the PDF file.

You'll use the TouchUp Text tool to change the color of a heading.

1 Choose Tools > Advanced Editing, and select the TouchUp Text tool (▦).

Acrobat may take a moment to load the system fonts. A bounding box then encloses the text that can be edited. (On Mac OS, you may need to create an insertion point in the document before you see the bounding box.)

2 Drag through the first line of the poster title, "Vegetation Dynamics of a Tidal Freshwater Marsh." Right-click (Windows) or Control-click (Mac OS), and choose Properties from the context menu. If necessary, click OK to clear the warning message because you're just going to change font color.

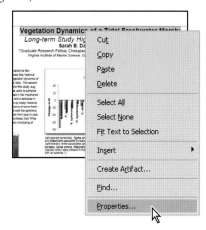

3 In the Text tab of the TouchUp Properties dialog box, click the Fill box, and choose a color for the line of text. (We used terracotta.)

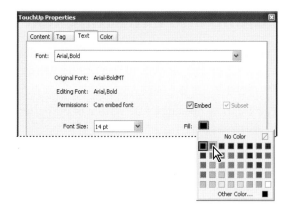

4 Click Close to close the dialog box, and click outside the text selection in the document pane to view the result.

You can experiment with changing other text attributes, such as the font size, and with adding color to other headings. To reopen the TouchUp Properties dialog box (with the TouchUp Text tool still selected), select the text that you want to edit, right-click (Windows) or Control-click (Mac OS), and choose Properties from the context menu.

5 When you are finished, select the Hand tool, and choose File > Save to save the file in the Lesson07 folder.

Copying tables

You can select and copy a table to the clipboard. You can also save it to a file that can then be loaded or imported to another application. If you have a CSV-compliant application on your system, such as Microsoft Excel, you can open the selected table directly in the application. You can click a table in a tagged PDF document to select the entire table.

Note: You can also export from PDF into XML for easier import into Microsoft Excel.

To copy a table using the Select tool:

1   Select the Select tool.

2   Hold the pointer over the table. If the pointer becomes the table icon, click in the table to select the entire table; if not, drag a box around the rows and columns to be copied.

3   Do one of the following:

   •   To copy the table to an open document in another authoring application, Ctrl-click (Windows) or Control-click (Mac OS) the table, and choose Copy As Table. Then paste the table into the open document.

   •   To copy the table to a file, Ctrl-click (Windows) or Control-click (Mac OS) the table, and choose Save As Table. Name the table, select a location and the file format, and click Save.

   •   To copy the table directly to a spreadsheet, Ctrl-click (Windows), and choose Open Table In Spreadsheet. Your CSV-compliant application, such as Excel, opens to a new spreadsheet displaying the imported table.

   •   To copy a table in RTF, drag the selected table into an open document in the target application.

Copying text and images from a PDF file

Even if you no longer have access to the source file for your poster, you can reuse the text and images in other applications. For example, you might want to add some of the text or images to a web page. You can copy the text out of the PDF file in rich text format or as accessible text so you can import it into a different authoring application for reuse. You can save images in the file in JPEG, TIF, or PNG format.

If you want to reuse only small amounts of text or one or two images, you can copy and paste text from a PDF file and copy images to the clipboard or to an image format file using the Select tool. (If the Copy, Cut, and Paste commands are unavailable, the creator of the PDF may have set restrictions on editing the content of the document.)

Copying all the text

The Export command allows you to export your PDF file directly to one of several common formats, including Microsoft Word. In this part of the lesson, you'll use the Export command to convert your poster as accessible text.

1 Choose File > Export > Text > Text (Accessible).

2 In the Save As dialog box, make sure that Text (Accessible) (*.txt) is specified for Save As Type (Windows) or Format (Mac OS). Click Save to complete the export of text. The file is saved as FreshWater1.txt in the Lesson07 folder.

If you want to import content into an Excel file, use the File > Export > XML command to get the best results.

3 Minimize the Acrobat window, and open the text file (FreshWater1.txt) using a text editing or authoring application, such as Microsoft Word. Notice that all the text is copied and that much of the spacing and formatting is retained to simplify re-use of the text.

4 Close the text file and the authoring application when you are finished, and maximize the Acrobat window.

You can use this process to convert your PDF files to any of the formats listed in the Export menu. If you want to use the same settings every time you convert PDFs to a particular format, specify those settings in the Convert From PDF preferences. Choose Edit > Preferences (Windows) or Acrobat > Preferences (Mac OS), and select Convert From PDF from the left pane. Select a file format from the list and click Edit Settings. (Click the Default button at any time to revert to the default settings.)

Saving in RTF format

Acrobat 9 adds two options for saving the content of a PDF file into rich text format.

1   Choose File > Save As.

2   In the Save As dialog box, select Rich Text Format (*.rtf) for Save As Type (Windows) or Format (Mac OS), and click Settings.

The Retain Flowing Text option retains as many layout elements as possible while retaining text flow.

The Retain Page Layout option gives preference to retaining the layout.

Copying and pasting small amounts of text

As you saw in the prior section, copying all the text from a PDF file for use in another application is very easy. And it's equally easy to copy and paste a word, sentence, or paragraph into a document in another application using the Select tool.

1   In Acrobat, in the FreshWater1.pdf file, click the Select tool (📖) on the Select & Zoom toolbar and move the pointer over the text that you want to copy. Notice that the pointer changes when it is in the text-selection mode.

2   Drag through the text that you want to copy. We copied the text of the abstract.

3   Right-click (Windows) or Control-click (Mac OS), and choose Copy.

Note that the Copy With Formatting option, which preserves the column layout, appears only if the document is tagged.

4   Minimize the Acrobat window, open a new or existing document in an authoring application such as a text editor or Microsoft Word, and then choose Edit > Paste.

Your text is copied into the document in your authoring application. You can edit and format the text as you wish. If a font copied from a PDF document is not available on the system displaying the copied text, the font cannot be preserved. A substitute font will be used.

5   Close your document and authoring application (such as Word) when you are finished, and maximize the Acrobat window.

Note: If you're unable to select text in a PDF file, the text may be part of an image. You can convert image text to text that can be selected by choosing Document > OCR Text Recognition > Recognize Text Using OCR.

Copying individual images

You can also copy individual images for use in another application using the Snapshot tool or the Select tool.

1 In the Acrobat document pane, click outside any text that you selected in the previous section of the lesson to deselect the text.

First you'll add the Snapshot tool to the Select & Zoom toolbar.

2 Choose View > Toolbars > More Tools. In the More Tools dialog box, scroll down to the Select & Zoom Toolbar and select the Snapshot tool. Click OK to add the tool to the toolbar.

3 Select the Snapshot tool (📷) on the toolbar. Move the pointer over the map at the bottom of the first column in the document window.

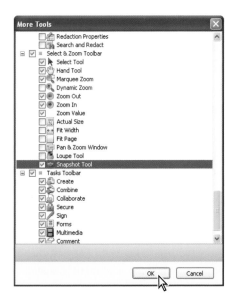

The Snapshot tool allows you to copy both text and images. However, the resulting image is in bitmap format and any text is not editable.

4 Marquee-drag to enclose the map image at the bottom of the page. The image is copied to your clipboard. Click OK to clear the message box.

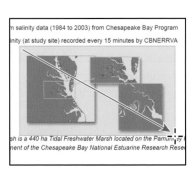

If you click anywhere on the page instead of dragging a marquee with the Snapshot tool selected, the entire page is copied to the clipboard.

In addition to copying the image to your clipboard, you can do the following:

- You can right-click (Windows) or Control-click (Mac OS) on the highlighted image, and copy the image for pasting into another application, print the image directly, or create a link from the image.

- You can click the Create button in the Tasks toolbar and choose the PDF From Clipboard or PDF From Clipboard Image command to paste the image into an untitled PDF file.

5 Click the Create button on the Tasks toolbar, and choose PDF From Clipboard (Windows) or PDF From Clipboard Image (Mac OS) to create a new page showing the copied map.

6 When you're finished, close any open files other than Freshwater1.pdf, and close any applications other than Acrobat.

You can export all the images in a PDF file to JPEG, PNG, TIFF, or JPEG2000 format by choosing Advanced > Document Processing > Export All Images. Each image is saved in a separate file.

The JPEG file format allows you to save a lot of data in a small file space. Unfortunately, you lose image quality each time you re-save a JPEG file. TIFF is an excellent file format for preserving image quality, but TIFF files are very large. Consider editing your images in TIFF format and then saving the final images in JPEG format.

Editing images using the TouchUp Object tool

You use the TouchUp Object tool to make last-minute corrections to images and objects in an Adobe PDF document. For major revisions, use your original authoring application, and then regenerate the PDF document.

The TouchUp Object tool is only available in Acrobat Pro and Acrobat Pro Extended.

You can use the TouchUp Object tool context menu to perform some editing tasks on images without starting an external editing application. To open the context menu, right-click (Windows) or Control-click (Mac OS) the text using the TouchUp Object tool. Using the TouchUp Object tool can change how a document reflows and can affect accessibility. For example, changing the location of an object affects the order in which that object (or its alternate text) is read by a screen reader.

To edit an image or object with the TouchUp Object tool:

1 Choose Tools > Advanced Editing, and select the TouchUp Object tool (✐).

2   Select an object, such as the set of three images in the third column, right-click (Windows) or Control-click (Mac OS) the image or object, and then choose a command.

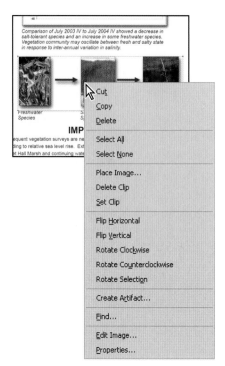

- Delete Clip deletes objects that are clipping the selected object. For example, if you scale text and the resulting characters are clipped, selecting this option shows you the complete characters.

- Create Artifact removes the object from the reading order so it isn't read by a screen reader or the Read Out Loud command.

- Edit Image, which appears when a bitmap image is selected, opens an editing program such as Adobe Photoshop.

- Edit Object, which appears when a vector object is selected, opens an editing program such as Adobe Illustrator.

- Properties allows you to edit properties for the content, tag, and text, such as adding alternative text to an image to make it accessible.

3   Click outside the menu to exit the process without making a selection.

Converting PDF pages to image format files

Earlier in this lesson, you copied the text and images in the poster for re-use in other applications, but you may also want to have an image of the poster. You can easily create a TIFF version of the poster by choosing File > Export > Image. To extract all the art in image file format, choose Advanced > Document Processing > Export All Images. In this case, each piece of art is saved in a separate file.

You can export raster images but not vector objects.

When you are finished, close all open files and exit Acrobat.

Review questions

1 How can you change the order of pages in a PDF document?

2 How do you insert an entire PDF file into another PDF file?

3 What kinds of text attributes can you change from within Acrobat?

4 How do you copy text from a PDF file?

5 How can you copy photographs or images from a PDF file?

Review answers

1 You can change the page order by selecting the page thumbnails corresponding to the pages you want to move, and dragging them to their new locations in the Pages panel.

2 To insert all the pages from a PDF file before or after any page in another PDF file, choose Document > Insert Pages, and select the file you wish to insert. If you want to combine two PDF files—that is, add one file to the beginning or end of another PDF file—you can use the Merge Files Into A Single PDF command.

3 You can use the TouchUp Text tool to change text formatting—font, size, color, letter spacing, and alignment—or to change the text itself.

4 If you're copying a couple of words or sentences, use the Select tool to copy and paste the text into another application. If you want to copy all the text from a PDF document, use the Export command and save the PDF file in a text format.

5 You can copy photographs or images from a PDF file in several ways:

- You can copy an image using the Select tool.

- You can copy an image using the Snapshot tool.

- You can save each image in a PDF file to an image format by choosing Advanced > Document Processing >Export All Images.

8 ADDING SIGNATURES AND SECURITY

Lesson Overview

In this lesson, you'll do the following:

- Create a digital ID that uses an image.

- Digitally sign documents.

- Apply password protection to a file to restrict who can open it, and apply a password to limit printing and changing of the file.

- Certify a document.

 This lesson will take approximately 45 minutes to complete. Copy the Lesson08 folder onto your hard drive if you haven't already done so.

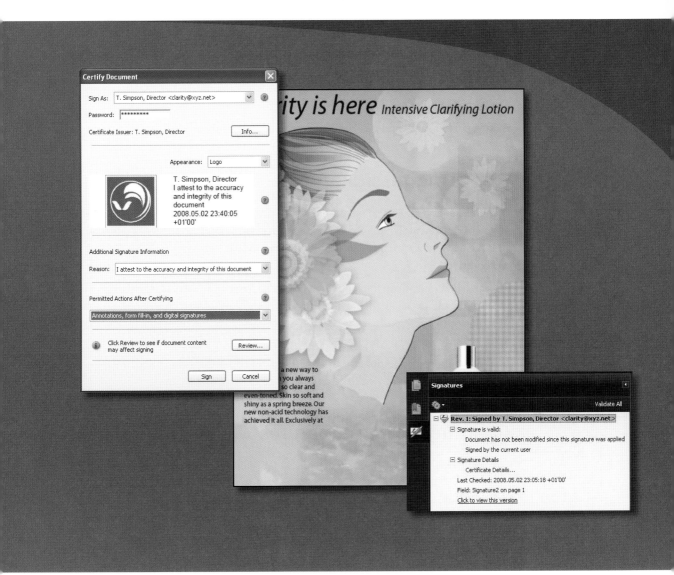

Getting started

Acrobat 9 gives you all the tools you need to sign a PDF document to indicate your approval or certify a PDF document to approve its contents. Acrobat also provides the tools you need to secure your PDF documents. You can use passwords to restrict users from opening, printing, and editing PDF documents. You can use a certificate to encrypt PDF documents so that only an approved list of users can open them. If you want to save security settings for later use, you can create a security policy that stores security settings. You can also permanently remove sensitive content from your PDF documents using the Redaction feature (see Lesson 12, "Using the Legal Features").

First you'll look at digital IDs and how to create and use them.

About digital signatures

A digital signature, like a conventional handwritten signature, identifies the person signing a document. Unlike a handwritten signature, a digital signature is difficult to forge because it contains encrypted information that is unique to the signer and easily verified.

To sign a document, you must obtain a digital ID from a third-party provider or create a digital ID (self-signed digital ID) for yourself in Acrobat. The digital ID contains a private key that is used to add the digital signature and a certificate that you share with those who need to validate your signature.

For information about Adobe security partners that offer third-party digital IDs and other security solutions, visit the Adobe website at www.adobe.com.

Creating digital signatures

For this lesson, you'll use a self-signed digital ID, which is often adequate for signing documents within a corporate environment. You can set the appearance of your digital signature, select your preferred digital signature signing method, and determine how digital signatures are verified in the Security preferences. You should also set your preferences to optimize Acrobat for validating signatures before you open a signed document.

1   Start Acrobat.

2   Choose Edit > Preferences (Windows) or Acrobat > Preferences (Mac OS), and select Security in the left pane. You may need to scroll down the list.

Adding images to your digital signatures

First you'll add the company logo to your signature block.

1 In the Preferences dialog box, click New to open the Configure Signature Appearance dialog box. This is where you can personalize your digital signature by adding a graphic to your signature. For the moment, the Preview pane shows the default digital signature appearance, which is text-based.

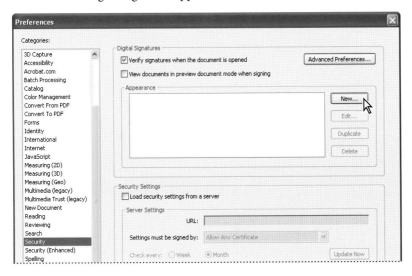

First you'll name the appearance of your signature and then add your corporate logo to the signature block.

2 In the Title text box, enter a name for the appearance of your signature. We entered **Logo** because we're going to add our corporate logo to the signature line. You should use a name that is easy to associate with the contents of the signature appearance. You can create several digital signatures for yourself.

3 In the Configure Graphic section of the dialog box, select the Imported Graphic option, and click File.

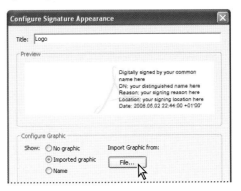

4 In the Select Picture dialog box, click Browse, and select the Clarity_Logo.pdf file in the Lesson08 folder. (Supported file types are listed in the Files Of Type (Windows) or Show (Mac OS) menu.) Click Select, and then click OK to return to the Configure Signature Appearance dialog box.

Now you'll specify the information to be included in the text block of your signature. You'll include your name, the reason for signing the document, and the date.

5 In the Configure Text area of the Configure Signature Appearance dialog box, leave Name, Date, and Reason selected. Deselect all the other options.

6 When you're happy with the preview of your signature block, click OK.

7 In the Preferences dialog box, select View Documents In Preview Document Mode When Signing.

8 Click Advanced Preferences, and click the Creation tab. Select the Show Reasons When Signing option, and click OK.

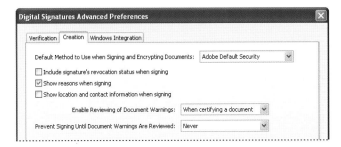

Signing in Preview Document mode

Use the Preview Document mode when you want to analyze a document for content that may alter the appearance of the document after you sign it. Such content may include transparency, scripts, fonts, and other dynamic content that can alter a document's appearance. The Preview Document mode suppresses this dynamic content, allowing you to view and sign the document in a static and secure state.

When you view a PDF in Preview Document mode, a document message bar lets you know whether the PDF complies with the PDF/SigQ Level A or Level B specification. Level A indicates that the document contains no dynamic content that can alter its appearance. Level B indicates that the document contains dynamic content that can be suppressed during signing. If the document doesn't comply with Level A or B, you may want to refrain from signing the document and contact the document author about the problem.

You can use Preview Document mode to check the integrity of a document at any time.

Acrobat automatically runs the Document Integrity Checker, which checks for Qualified Signatures conformance, before entering the signature preview mode.

You opt to use the Preview Document mode in the Security preferences.

Selecting a signing method

Now you'll specify a default signing method.

1 Click the Advanced Preferences button in the Security preferences dialog box again.

In the Verification tab of the Digital Signatures Advanced Preferences dialog box, notice that the Require Certificate Revocation Checking To Succeed Whenever Possible During Signatures Verification option is selected. This ensures that certificates are always checked against a list of excluded certificates during validation.

2 Make sure that the option to verify signatures using the document-specified method when a document is opened is selected. You'll be prompted if you don't have the necessary software when you try to open a document.

Also in the Verification tab is a pop-up menu allowing you to choose the default method for verifying signatures. This menu is dimmed unless you change the method used for verification by selecting a different radio button. You set the default method to be used when signing and encrypting documents in the Creation tab.

3 Click the Creation tab and check that Adobe Default Security is selected for the Default Method To Use When Signing And Encrypting Documents option.

On Windows, you also have a Windows Integration tab where you can specify whether identities from Windows Certificates can be imported and whether all root certificates in the Windows Certificates can be trusted. We recommend that you leave the defaults in this tab.

4 Click OK, and click OK again to close the Preferences dialog box.

Opening the work file

In this part of the lesson, you'll send an advertisement for Clarity skin lotion to the advertising agency for finalization. You've reviewed the document and made required changes, and now you'll sign the revised advertisement electronically.

Signing a document electronically offers several advantages, not least of which is that you can email the signed document rather than having to fax it or send it by courier. Although digitally signing a document doesn't necessarily prevent people from changing the document, it does allow you to track any changes made after the signature is added and revert to the signed version if necessary. (You can prevent users from changing your document by applying appropriate security to the document, as you'll see later in this lesson.)

- Choose File > Open. Select Lotion.pdf in the Lesson08 folder, and click Open. Then choose File > Save As, rename the file **Lotion1.pdf**, and save it in the Lesson08 folder.

Creating digital IDs

A digital ID is like a driver's license or passport. It proves your identity to people with whom you communicate electronically. A digital ID usually contains your name and email address, the name of the company that issued your digital ID, a serial number, and an expiration date.

A digital ID lets you create a digital signature or decrypt a PDF document that has been encrypted. You can create more than one digital ID to reflect different roles in your life. For this section of the lesson, you'll create a digital ID for T. Simpson, Director of Advertising.

1 Choose Advanced > Security Settings.

2 In the Security Settings dialog box, select Digital IDs in the left pane. Then click the Add ID button ().

You'll create a self-signed digital ID. With a self-signed ID, you share your signature information with other users using a public certificate. (A certificate is a confirmation of your digital ID and contains information used to protect data.) While this method is adequate for most unofficial exchanges, a more secure approach is to obtain a digital ID from a third-party provider.

3 In the Add Digital ID dialog box, select A New Digital ID I Want To Create Now. Click Next.

If you're working in Mac OS, skip to step 5. If you're working in Windows, you'll choose where to store your digital ID. The PKCS#12 Digital ID File option stores the information in a file that you can share with others. A Windows Default Certificate Digital ID is stored in the Windows Certificate Store. Because you want to easily share your digital ID with colleagues, you'll use the PKCS#12 option.

4 Make sure that New PKCS#12 Digital File ID is selected, and click Next.

Now you'll enter your personal information.

5 Enter the name you want to appear in the Signatures tab and in any signature field that you complete, and enter a corporate or organization name (if necessary) and an email address. We entered **T. Simpson, Director,** for the name, **Clarity** for the Organization Name, and **clarity@xyz.net** for the email address. Make sure that you select a Country/Region. We used the default **US - United States**.

6 Choose a Key Algorithm to set the level of security. We chose the default **1024-bit RSA**. Although 2048-bit RSA offers more security protection, it is not as universally compatible as 1024-bit RSA.

Now you'll specify what the encryption applies to. You can use the digital ID to control digital signatures, data encryption (security), or both. When you encrypt a PDF document, you specify a list of recipients from your Trusted Identities, and you define the recipient's level of access to the file—for example, whether the recipients can edit, copy, or print the files. You can also encrypt documents using security policies.

For this lesson, you'll choose digital signatures.

7 From the Use Digital ID For menu, choose Digital Signatures, and then click Next.

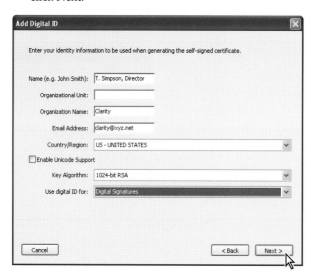

Now you'll save and safeguard your information.

8   If you want to change the location where your information is stored, click the Browse button and locate the required folder. For this lesson, you'll use the default. Now you must set a password. We used Lotion123 as the password. Reenter your password to confirm it. Remember that the password is case-sensitive. Be sure to make a note of your password and keep it in a safe place. You cannot use or access your digital ID without this password. (Your password may not contain double quotation marks or the characters ! @ # $ % ^ & * , | \ ; < > _ .)

9   Click Finish to save the digital ID file in the Security folder.

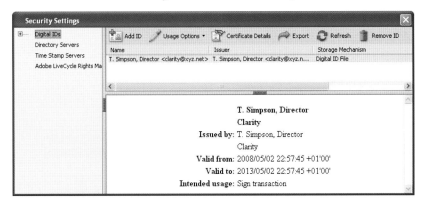

Your new digital ID appears in the Security Settings dialog box. In Windows, select the digital ID to see its details. In Mac OS, double-click it to view the certificate details. When you've finished checking your digital ID, click Close to close the dialog box.

Sharing certificates with others

Your digital ID includes a certificate that others require to validate your digital signature and to encrypt documents for you. If you know that others will need your certificate, you can send it in advance to avoid delays when exchanging secure documents. Businesses that use certificates to identify participants in secure work-flows often store certificates on a directory server that participants can search to expand their list of trusted identities.

If you use a third-party security method, you usually don't need to share your certificate with others. Third-party providers may validate identities using other methods, or these validation methods may be integrated with Acrobat. See the documentation for the third-party provider.

When you receive a certificate from someone, their name is added to your list of trusted identities as a contact. Contacts are usually associated with one or more certificates and can be edited, removed, or reassociated with another certificate. If you trust a contact, you can set your trust settings to trust all digital signatures and certified documents created with their certificate.

You can also import certificates from a certificate store, such as the Windows certificate store. A certificate store may contain numerous certificates issued by different certification authorities.

Now you'll sign the advertisement and return it to the agency.

Signing the advertisement

Because you want the advertising agency to know that the changes to this advertisement are approved and you want them to be sure that no additional changes have been made since the time you approved it, you'll create a visible signature field and sign the document.

1 Click the Sign button (✎) on the Tasks toolbar, and choose Place Signature from the menu.

2 Acrobat reminds you that you need to create a signature field. Click OK to close the alert box, and drag to create a signature field. We dragged a signature field in the area below the headline.

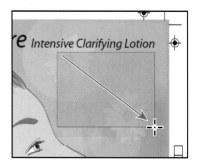

Acrobat automatically switches into the Preview mode, which analyzes the document for content that may alter the document's appearance and then suppresses that content, allowing you to view and sign the document in a static and secure state.

3   In the preview toolbar, click Sign Document.

4   In the Sign document dialog box, enter the password associated with the ID in the Sign As text box. We entered Lotion123.

5   For Appearance, select Logo.

6   If you wish, you can add a reason for signing the document from the pop-up menu.

7   Click Sign to apply your signature, and click Save to save the signed file.

The recipient of the signed document will need your signer's certificate to validate the digital signature.

Modifying signed documents

Now you'll add a comment to the signed document to see how the digital signature information changes. But first you'll look at the signatures panel to see what a valid signature looks like.

1 Click the Signatures button in the navigation pane to display the Signatures panel. If necessary, drag the right margin of the Signatures panel so that you can see all the signature information. Expand the signature line, and expand both the Signature Is Valid and the Signature Details entries.

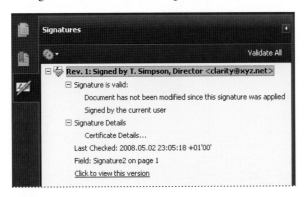

Now you'll add a note to the advertisement and see how the addition changes the digital signature.

2 Choose Tools > Comment & Markup > Sticky Note (💬).

3 Click anywhere on the document page to add a note. We added a note saying, **Good work.**

The signature status is changed by the addition of a note. If necessary, expand the signature again to see the status.

As soon as you add the note, that fact is recorded in the Signature panel.

Now you'll validate the signature.

4   Right-click (Windows) or
    Control-click (Mac OS) on
    the signature box in the
    document pane, and choose
    Validate Signature.

▶ **Tip:** Use the
Signature panel to
review the change
history of a document
or to track changes
when a document is
signed using multiple
digital signature IDs.

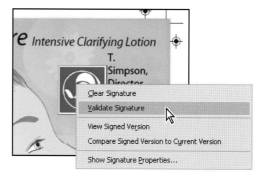

5   The alert box explains that although the signature is valid, a change has been
    made. Click Close to close the warning box.

▶ **Tip:** Right-click
(Windows) or Control-
click (Mac OS) on
the signature box in
the document pane,
and choose Show
Signature Properties to
resolve any issues with
the signature.

6   Right-click (Windows)
    or Control-click (Mac
    OS) on the signature
    box in the document
    pane, and choose View
    Signed Version.

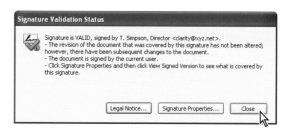

The View Signed Version option allows you to recover your unchanged file. If a
document has signatures on multiple versions of the document, for example, you
can view any previously signed version of the document by selecting the signature in
the Signatures tab and then choosing View Signed Version from the Options menu.

7   Close both files. You do not need to save your work.

About security

You can secure a PDF using any of the following security methods:

- Add passwords and set security options to restrict opening, editing, and printing PDFs.

- Encrypt a document so that only a specified set of users has access to it.

- Save the PDF as a certified document. Certifying a PDF adds a (visible or invisible) certifying signature that lets the document author restrict changes to the document.

- Apply server-based security policies to PDFs (for example, using Adobe LiveCycle Rights Management). Server-based security policies are especially useful if you want others to have access to PDFs for a limited time.

You can also use security envelopes to protect your PDF documents in transit as outlined in the "Exploring on your own" section at the end of this lesson.

In the next part of the lesson, you'll add password protection to a file and you'll certify a document to approve its contents.

Securing PDFs in FIPS mode (Windows)

Acrobat and Reader (version 8.1 and later) provide a FIPS mode to restrict data protection to Federal Information Processing Standard (FIPS) 140-2 approved algorithms using the RSA BSAFE Crypto-C 2.1 encryption module.

The following options are not available in FIPS mode:

- Applying password-based security policies to documents. You can use public key certificates or Adobe LiveCycle Rights Management to secure the document, but you cannot use password encryption to secure the document.

- Creating self-signed certificates. In FIPS mode, you cannot create self-signed certificates. In FIPS mode, you can open and view documents that are protected with non-FIPS compliant algorithms, but you cannot save any changes to the document using password security. To apply security policies to the document, use either public key certificates or LiveCycle Rights Management.

Looking at security settings

As you have seen, you can digitally sign a document or certify a document to attest to the contents of the document at the time of signing or certification. There are times, however, when you simply want to restrict access to a document. You can do this by adding security to your Adobe PDF files.

When you open a document that has restricted access or some type of security applied to it, you'll see a Security Settings button (🔒) to the left of the document window.

1 Choose File > Open, and open the Secure_Survey.pdf file in the Lesson08 folder.

2 Click the Sign button (✎) on the Tasks toolbar, and notice that the commands are dimmed.

3 Choose Tools > Comment & Markup, and again notice that the commenting and text mark-up tools are unavailable.

4 Click the Security Settings icon (🔒) in the navigation pane to view the security setting. Click the Permission Details link to view more detail.

The dialog box lists the actions that are allowed and those that are not allowed. As you read down the list, you'll see that signing and commenting are not allowed, which is why the related tools are dimmed.

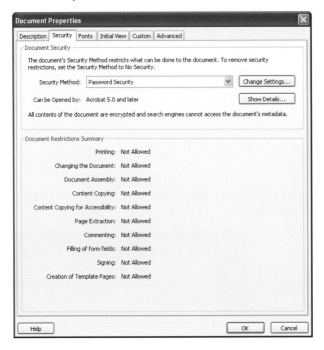

5   When you have finished reviewing the information, click Cancel to close the Document Properties dialog box.

6   Choose File > Close to close the Secure_Survey.pdf file.

Adding security to PDF files

You can add security to your Adobe PDF files when you first create them or after the fact. You can even add security to files that you receive from someone else, unless the creator of the document has limited who can change security settings.

In this part of the lesson, you'll add password protection to limit who can open your document and who can change the security settings.

Adding passwords

You can add two kinds of passwords to protect your Adobe PDF documents. You can add a Document Open password so that only users who have the password can open the document, and you can add a Permissions password so that only users who have the password can change the permissions for the document.

You'll add protection to your logo file so that no one can change the contents of the logo file and so that unauthorized users can't open and use the file.

1 Choose File > Open, and open the SBR_Logo.pdf file.

2 Choose File > Save As, name the file **SBR_Logo1.pdf,** and save it in the Lesson08 folder.

3 Click the Secure task button (🔒), and choose Show Security Properties.

No security at all has been applied to this file. You'll first choose the type of security to add.

4 From the Security Method menu, choose Password Security. The Password Security Settings dialog box opens automatically.

First you'll set the compatibility level.

The default compatibility level is compatibility with Acrobat 7.0 or later. If you're sure that all your users have Acrobat 7.0 or later, this compatibility level is the preferred setting. If you think that some of your users may still be running earlier versions of Acrobat, then you should select an earlier version. Be aware, however, that this may use a lower encryption level.

5 Select your compatibility level from the Compatibility menu. We used Acrobat 7.0 And Later.

6 Select the Require A Password To Open The Document option, and then type in your password. We typed in **SBRLogo**.

You'll share this password with anyone that you want to be able to open the document. Remember that passwords are case-sensitive.

Now you'll add a second password that controls who is allowed to change printing, editing, and security settings for the file.

7 Under Permissions, select Restrict Editing And Printing Of The Document, and type in a second password. We typed in **SBRPres**. Your open password and permissions password can't be the same.

8 From the Printing Allowed menu, choose whether to allow printing at all, printing at low resolution, or printing at high resolution. We chose Low Resolution (150 dpi).

> ▶ **Tip:** Always record your passwords in a secure location. If you forget your password, you can't recover it from the document. You might also want to store an unprotected copy of the document in a secure location.

9 From the Changes Allowed menu, choose the type of changes you will allow users to make. We chose Commenting, Filling In Form Fields, And Signing Existing Signature Fields to allow users to comment on the logo.

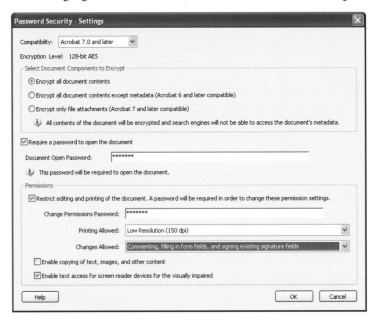

10 Click OK to apply your changes.

11 In the first dialog box, re-enter the Open Password. We entered **SBRLogo**. Then click OK, and click OK again to clear the alert box.

12 In the second dialog box, re-enter the Permissions Password. We entered **SBRPres**. Then click OK, and click OK again to clear the alert box.

Notice that the actions available to users don't appear to have changed. But if you click the Show Details button, you'll see the limitations applied.

13 Click OK to exit the Document Properties dialog box.

14 Click File > Save to save your work and apply the security changes.

15 Choose File > Close to close the SBR_Logo1.pdf file.

Now you'll check the security that you've added to your file.

Opening password-protected files

1 Choose File > Open and re-open the SBR_Logo1.pdf file in the Lesson08 folder.

You're prompted to enter the required password to open the file.

2 We entered **SBRLogo**, and clicked OK.

Notice that "(SECURED)" has been appended to the filename at the top of your display.

Now you'll test the Permissions Password.

3 Click the Secure task button (🔒), and choose Show Security Properties from the menu.

4 In the Document Properties dialog box, try changing the Security Method from Password Security to No Security.

Acrobat prompts you to enter the Permissions password.

5 We entered **SBRPres** and clicked OK and then OK again.

All restrictions are now removed from the file.

6 Click OK to close the Document Properties dialog box.

7 Choose File > Close, and close the file without saving the changes.

Certifying PDF files

Earlier in this lesson, you signed a PDF document to signify that you had approved the content and requested changes. You can also certify the contents of a PDF document. Certifying a document rather than signing it is useful if you want the user to be able to make approved changes to a document. When you certify a document and a user makes approved changes, the certification is still valid. You can certify forms, for example, to guarantee that the content is valid when the user receives the form. You, as the creator of the form, can specify what tasks the user can perform. For example, you can specify that readers can fill in the form fields without invalidating the document. However, if a user tries to add or remove a form field or a page, the certification will be invalidated.

▶ **Tip:** Before you distribute a document that you intend others to sign or fill in, you should enable usage rights for Adobe Reader users (choose Advanced > Extend Features In Adobe Reader).

Now you'll certify a form to be sent to clients of a winery, asking them to estimate their purchases. By certifying the form, you are sure that the client fills out the form as you designed it, with no additions or deletions to the form fields.

1 Choose File > Open, and open the Final_Survey.pdf file in the Lesson08 folder.

For information on the Forms message bar, see Lesson 10, "Working with Forms in Acrobat."

2 Choose File > Properties, and click the Security tab.

The information in the Document Properties dialog box shows that no security and no restrictions have been applied to the document.

3 Click Cancel to close the Document Properties dialog box without making any changes.

4 Choose Advanced > Sign & Certify > Certify With Visible Signature.

5 Click Drag New Signature Rectangle. Click OK, and click OK again.

You'll use the digital ID that you created earlier in the lesson to certify the file.

6 Drag anywhere in the document to create a signature field. We created a signature field in the top right, next to the logo. Then click the Sign Document button on the document message bar.

7 In the Certify Document dialog box, if you have created more than one digital ID, select the digital ID to use. We selected T. Simpson, Director.

8 Enter your password. We entered **Lotion123**.

9 For Appearance, select Logo.

10 Choose a reason for signing the document. We chose to certify that we attested to the accuracy and integrity of the document.

11 From the Permitted Changes After Certifying menu, choose Annotations, Form Fill-In, And Digital Signatures.

12 Click Sign to complete the certification process.

13 Save your file as **Final_Survey_Cert.pdf**.

14 Click the Signatures button to open the Signatures panel and review which actions the certification allows. You may need to expand the entries in the panel.

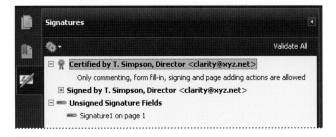

1▶ **Tip:** Whenever you open a certified document, you'll see a Certification icon at the left of the message bar. You can click on this icon at any time to see certification information for the document.

15 When you've finished reviewing the certification information, click the close button to close the Signatures panel.

234**192** LESSON 8   Adding Signatures and Security

Signing certified documents

Now you'll sign the document that you just certified to verify that filling in a signature field doesn't invalidate the certification.

1 With the Hand tool selected, click in the Approved Signature box at the bottom of the document. Click Continue to clear the message box. Then click the Sign Document button on the document message bar.

2 In the dialog box, if you have more than one digital ID defined, select your digital ID. We selected T. Simpson, Director.

3 Enter your password. We entered **Lotion123**.

4 Leave the other values, click Sign, and save the file in the Lesson08 folder using the same file name.

5 Click the Signatures button in the navigation pane, and expand the certification entry marked with the blue ribbon icon.

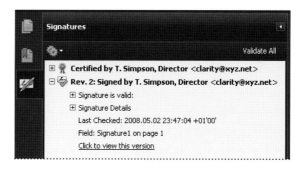

Notice that the certification is still valid even though a signature has been added.

6 Choose File > Close.

Exploring on your own: Using security envelopes

In Acrobat you can attach files to a PDF document and encrypt only the file attachments. In this case, the PDF document in which the file attachments are embedded functions as a security envelope. Anyone can open the security envelope and view the cover page and even a list of contents, but the attachments can only be opened as defined by the security you apply. When the attachments are opened and saved, they are identical to the original. No encryption is applied.

Suppose that you want to send a copy of the lotion advertisement to a satellite office. The advertisement is confidential at this point, so you want to be sure that no unauthorized person intercepts and opens it. To ensure this, you'll create a security envelope, attach the advertisement to it, and apply security. You'll use the wizard to walk you through the process; however, you can also create security envelopes manually.

1 On Windows in Acrobat, click the Secure button on the Tasks toolbar, and choose Create Security Envelope or choose Advanced > Security > Create Security Envelope. On Mac OS, choose Advanced > Security > Create Security Envelope.

2 In the Create Security Envelope dialog box, click the Add File To Send button. In the Files To Enclose dialog box, browse to select the file or files to add. We added the Lotion.pdf file in the Lesson08 folder. Note that you can add non-PDF files and that you can add more than one file. (Use Ctrl-click or Command-click to add multiple files from the same location, or add files one at a time if the files are located in different folders.) Click Open to add the files.

If you want to experiment with adding non-PDF files, try adding some of the lesson files from the Lesson03 folder.

The file or files you have added are displayed in the Currently Selected Files window. You can delete any file by selecting it and clicking Remove Selected Files.

3 Click Next.

4 In the Available Templates panel, select the template you want to use, and then click Next. We chose the eEnvelope with a date stamp. Click Next.

5 On Windows, for the delivery method, we elected to have the wizard email the completed envelope immediately. Click Next and then click Yes to clear the message box.

6 In the Security Policy dialog box, first select Show All Policies. The policies available to you are listed. Select a policy. We chose Encrypt With Password. Click Next.

7 Complete the Identity panel if you haven't already established an identity.

8 Click Finish.

Now you'll choose your security settings.

9 In the Password Security Settings dialog box, we chose to use the default setting for the compatibility level and the document contents to encrypt, and we chose to set a password requirement for opening the documents.

10 Click OK, and if you set a password requirement, you'll be asked to re-enter the password.

After you complete this process, Acrobat will launch your default email program and create an email with the security envelope attached. Send the email to yourself to see what the finished product looks like. (On Mac OS you need to save, close, and reopen the file before Acrobat launches the email program.)

11 When you are finished, close any open files and close Acrobat.

Review questions

1 Where do you change the appearance of your digital signature?

2 How many digital signatures can you create?

3 Why would you want to apply password protection to a PDF file?

4 When would you apply permissions protection?

Review answers

1 You change the appearance of your digital signature in the Configure Signature Appearance dialog box. You can access this dialog box from the Security Preferences dialog box. You can also change the appearance of your digital signature in the Sign Document dialog box during the signing process.

2 You can have numerous digital signatures. You can create different digital signatures for the different identities that you use. You can have personal signatures, corporate signatures, family signatures, etc.

3 If you have a confidential document that you don't want others to read, you can apply password protection. Only users with whom you share your password will be able to open the document.

4 Permissions protection limits how a user can use or reuse the contents of your Adobe PDF file. For example, you can specify that users cannot print the contents of your file, or copy and paste the contents of your file. Permission protection allows you to share the content of your file without losing control over how it is used.

9 USING ACROBAT IN A REVIEW CYCLE

Lesson Overview

In this lesson, you'll do the following:

- Discover multiple ways to use Acrobat in a document review process.

- Annotate a PDF file with the Acrobat commenting and markup tools.

- View, reply to, summarize, and print document comments.

- Initiate a shared review.

- Initiate live collaboration.

- Learn how to host an online meeting with Adobe ConnectNow.

 This lesson will take approximately 60 minutes to complete. Copy the Lesson09 folder onto your hard drive if you haven't already done so.

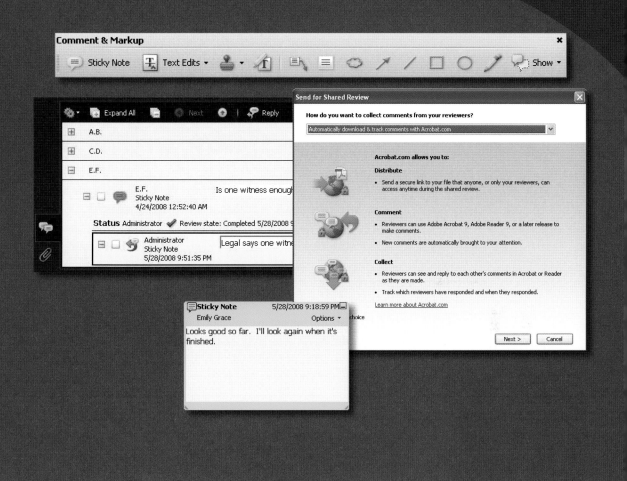

About the review process

There are several ways to use Acrobat in a document review process. No matter which method you use, the workflow contains some core elements: the review initiator invites participants and makes the document available to them; reviewers comment; and the initiator gathers and works with those comments.

You can share any PDF document by email, on a network server, or on a website, and ask individuals to comment on it using Acrobat Standard, Acrobat Pro, or Acrobat Pro Extended. If you post it or email it manually, you'll need to keep track of returned comments and merge them on your own. If you're requesting feedback from only one or two other people, this might be the most efficient way for you to work. For most reviews, however, you can gather comments more efficiently using a managed review process. Additionally, in a shared review or live collaboration, reviewers can see and respond to each other's comments.

When you initiate an email-based review in Acrobat, a wizard helps you send the PDF file as an email attachment, track responses, and manage the comments you receive. Anyone with Acrobat 6 or later can add comments to the PDF file. If you are using Acrobat 9 Pro or Pro Extended, you can also enable reviewers using Adobe Reader 7 and later to add comments.

When you initiate a shared review in Acrobat, a wizard helps you post the PDF file to a network folder, WebDAV folder, SharePoint workspace, or Acrobat.com, a free secure web-based service. Through the wizard, you email invitations to reviewers, who then access the shared document, add comments, and read others' comments using Acrobat 9. You can set a deadline for the review, after which no reviewers can publish additional comments. If you're using Acrobat 9 Pro or Pro Extended, you can also enable Adobe Reader 9 users to review your document.

Using Acrobat 9, you can also initiate live collaboration. Through live collaboration, you hold a virtual meeting specifically connected to a single document. You or other participants can simultaneously move the document on all participants' screens at once, so that you are all literally on the same page.

Getting started

In this lesson, you'll add comments to a PDF document, view and manage comments, and initiate a shared review. By definition, collaboration requires you to work with other people. Therefore, many of the exercises in this lesson will be more meaningful if you work through them with one or more colleagues or friends. However, if you are working independently, you can complete the exercises using alternative email addresses, which are available free through websites such as Gmail.com and Yahoo.com. (See the legal agreements on email websites to determine how you may use their email addresses).

Adding comments to a PDF document

Unless a document includes security features, you can add comments to any PDF file. In most cases, you'll use the commenting features to provide feedback to a document's author, but you may also find them useful to write notes to yourself as you're reading documents. Acrobat includes several commenting tools, and you'll recognize some of them from the physical world. For example, the Sticky Note and Highlight Text tools are electronic versions of the physical tools you may have on your desk.

In this exercise, you'll use some of the commenting tools to provide feedback on a medical trial protocol document.

About the commenting tools

Acrobat provides several commenting and markup tools, designed for different commenting tasks. Most comments include two parts: the markup or icon that appears on the page, and a text message that appears in a pop-up note when you select the comment. (For detailed information about using each tool, see Adobe Acrobat 9 Help.)

- **Sticky Note tool** (≡) – Create sticky notes, just as you would in the physical world. Click wherever you want the note to appear. Sticky notes are great when you want to make overall comments about a document or a section of a document, rather than commenting on a particular phrase or sentence.

- **Text Edits tool** (⊞) – Indicate which text should be deleted, inserted, or replaced using this tool. Your comments don't affect the text in the PDF document, but they make your intention clear.

- **Stamp tool** (⬙) – Use a virtual rubber stamp to approve a document, mark it confidential, or perform several other common stamping tasks. You can create custom stamps for your own purposes, as well.

- **Highlight Text tool** (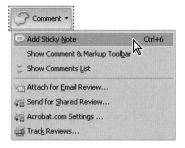) – Highlight the text you want to comment on, and then type your comment.

- **Callout tool** (🖹) – Specify the area you're commenting on without obscuring it. Callout markups have three parts: a text box, a knee line, and an end-point line. Drag handles to resize each part and position it exactly where you want it.

- **Text Box tool** (≡) – Create a box that contains text, positioned anywhere on the page, and at any size. It remains visible on the page, rather than closing like a pop-up note.

- **Cloud** (☁), **Arrow** (↗), **Line** (╱), **Rectangle** (▢), **Oval** (◯), **and Pencil**(✎) **tools** – Use the drawing tools to emphasize areas on the page or communicate your thoughts artistically, especially when reviewing graphical documents.

▶**Tip:** To create a custom stamp, choose Tools > Comment & Markup > Stamps > Show Stamps Palette. Click Import, select the file you want to use, and then follow the onscreen instructions.

Adding sticky notes

You can attach a sticky note anywhere in a document. Because notes can easily be moved, they are best suited to comments about the overall content or layout of a document, rather than specific phrasing. You'll add a sticky note on the first page of this document.

1 In Acrobat, choose File > Open.

2 Navigate to the Lesson09 folder, and double-click the Curetall_Protocol.pdf file.

3 Choose Comment > Add Sticky Note from the Tasks toolbar.

💬 Comment ▾
🗨 Add Sticky Note   Ctrl+6
Show Comment & Markup Toolbar
✍ Show Comments List
🗐 Attach for Email Review…
🗐 Send for Shared Review…
🗐 Acrobat.com Settings …
🗐 Track Reviews…

A sticky note opens. The log-in name for Acrobat automatically appears on the note, as well as the date and time.

4   Type **Looks good so far. I'll look again when it's finished.**

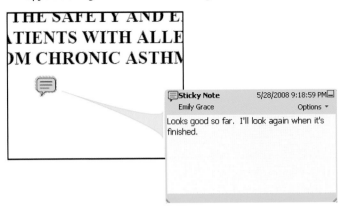

5   Click Options in the Sticky Note dialog box, and choose Properties from the pop-up menu.

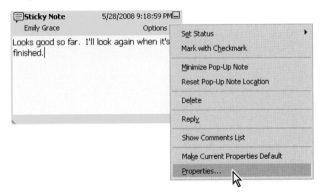

6   Click the Appearance tab, and then click the Color swatch.

7   Select a blue swatch. The sticky note changes color automatically.

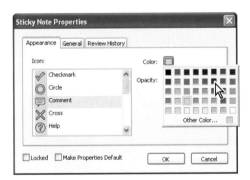

8 Click the General tab.

9 In the Author box, type **Reviewer A**.

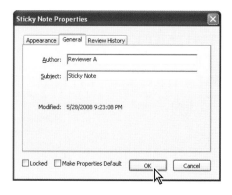

You can change the name attached to a comment. You may want to do that, for example, if you are using someone else's computer.

10 Click OK.

The blue sticky note is still open on the page. You can leave it open or click the close icon in the upper-right corner to close it. To reopen it, just double-click the sticky note icon.

Emphasizing text

Use the Highlight Text tool to emphasize specific text in a document. After highlighting the text, you can add a message, as well. You'll make a comment using the Highlight Text tool in this document.

1 Scroll to page 2 in the document.

2 Choose Comment > Show Comment & Markup Toolbar from the Tasks toolbar. The Comment & Markup toolbar contains all the commenting and markup tools.

3 Click the Highlight Text tool ( ) in the toolbar.

4 Drag the cursor over "Jocelyn M. Taget, RN" on the first line of the table. The text is highlighted in yellow.

5 Double-click the highlighted text. A comment message box opens.

6 Type **Double-check contact info.**

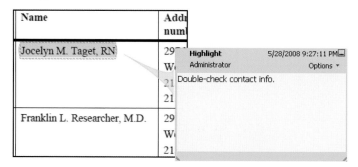

7 Click the close icon in the upper-right corner of the message box to close it.

Marking up documents with the Text Edits tool

You can clearly communicate which text should be deleted, inserted, or replaced using the Text Edits tool. You'll suggest some text changes to the protocol document.

1 Scroll to page 3 of the protocol document.

2 Click the Text Edits tool (📝) in the toolbar, and click OK in the informational dialog box that appears.

3 Select the word "Patients" in the title of the study (in the fourth cell of the table).

4 Type **patients** to replace it.

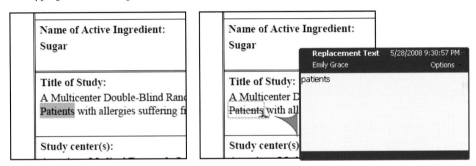

A Replacement Text dialog box appears, with the text "patients" in it, and the original text is crossed out. An insertion point icon appears in the original text.

5 Click the close button in the Replacement Text dialog box.

6 Click an insertion point after "Evaluation of tolerability and evaluation of long-term" in the Objective section of the table.

7 Type **efficacy** to insert text.

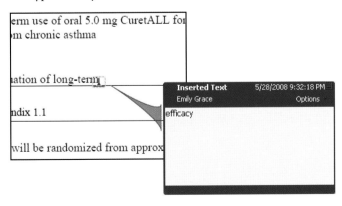

The Inserted Text dialog box opens, with the word "efficacy" in it. An insertion point icon appears in the original text.

8 Click the close button in the Inserted Text dialog box.

9 Go to page 10 in the document.

10 Under "Potential Risks and Benefits" toward the bottom of the page, select the words "based on studies to date."

11 Press the Delete or Backspace key on your keyboard.

Chemical Structure of CuretAll	Chemical Structure of CuretAll
ical studies (Appendices 2.1 through 2.12) indica retALL for the indications stated.	ical studies (Appendices 2.1 through 2.12) indica retALL for the indications stated.
risks to humans based on studies to date. There i rom chronic asthma who are also suffering from a	risks to humans based on studies to date. There i rom chronic asthma who are also suffering from a
age, Dosage Regimen and Treatment Periods	age, Dosage Regimen and Treatment Periods
port the premise that a 5mg tablet taken orally up osage to study subjects.	port the premise that a 5mg tablet taken orally up osage to study subjects.

▶ **Tip:** To check the spelling in your comments, choose Edit > Check Spelling > In Comments, Fields, & Editable Text. (If the PDF file is open in a browser, click Spell Check in the Edit toolbar.)

A red line appears through the text, indicating deletion.

12 Close the Comment & Markup toolbar.

13 Close the document. You can save changes or close without saving changes.

Working with comments

You can view comments on the page, in a list, or in a summary. You can import, export, and print comments. And you can reply to comments if you're participating in a shared review or will be returning the PDF file to a reviewer in an email-based review. In this lesson, you'll import comments from reviewers, sort comments, show and hide comments, and change their status.

Importing comments

If you use a managed shared review process, comments are imported automatically. However, if you're using an email-based review process or collecting comments informally, you can import comments manually. You'll import comments from three reviewers into a draft for an informed consent form.

1 In Acrobat, choose File > Open.

2 In the Lesson09 folder, double-click the Curetall_Informed_Consent.pdf file.

3 Choose Comments > Import Comments.

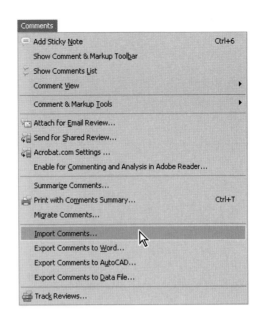

4 Navigate to the Lesson09/Comments folder.

5 Shift-click to select the following files:

- Curetall Informed Consent_ab.pdf
- Curetall Informed Consent_cd.pdf
- Curetall Informed Consent_ef.fdf

6 Click Select.

Two of the documents are PDF files with comments included; the FDF file is a data file that contains comments that a reviewer exported.

Acrobat imports the comments and displays them in the comment list.

▶ **Tip:** As a reviewer, you can export comments to a data file (named with an .fdf extension) to reduce file size, especially if you're submitting comments by email. To export comments, choose Comments > Export Comments To Data File.

Viewing comments

The comments list appeared at the bottom of the Acrobat window when you imported comments. You can open it at any time by choosing Comments > Show Comments List. The comments list includes every comment in the document, with the comment author's name, the type of comment, and the comment itself.

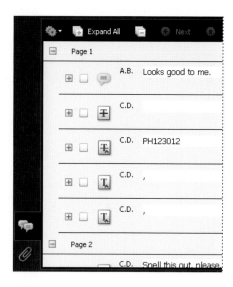

1   Scroll through the comment list. By default, comments are listed in the order they appear in the document, and you can expand or contract the set of comments for any page.

2   Click the minus sign next to Page 1 to contract the page 1 comments.

3   In the Comments List tool bar, choose Sort By > Author. Click OK in the informational dialog box that appears.

Acrobat rearranges the comments so that they are categorized by comment author instead of page number.

4   Click the plus sign next to C.D. to expand the comments by this author.

5   Click the last comment by C.D., an inserted comma. When you click the comment, Acrobat moves the page to the comment location so that you can see it in context. Click the plus sign next to the comment to see its properties, including the type of comment and the date and time it was entered.

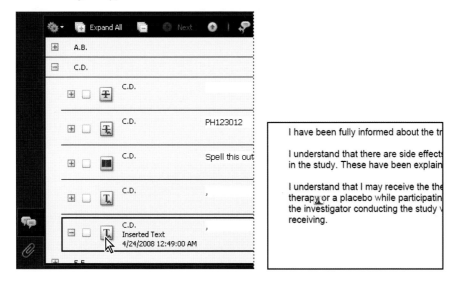

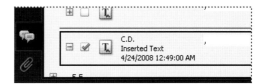

6   Click the box next to the comment by C.D. so that it has a check mark in it. Click OK in the informational dialog box that appears.

You can add check marks to indicate that you've read a comment, replied to it, discussed it with someone, or anything else that is meaningful to you.

7   Choose Show > Show By Checked State > Unchecked from the Comments List toolbar. Click OK in the informational dialog box that appears.

8 Expand the comments by C.D. again. The comment you checked is no longer listed, but it remains in the document. You can use the Show commands to declutter the comment list and focus on the comments you want to work with, whether you want to see only text edits, comments by a particular reviewer, or comments that meet other criteria.

Tip: If there isn't room to display the button names in the Comments toolbar, Acrobat displays only the icons. To see the button names, expand or maximize the application window.

9 Choose Show > Show All Comments. Click OK in the informational dialog box that appears.

10 Expand the comments by C.D. again. All the comments are listed again.

11 Click the plus sign next to E.F. to expand the comments.

12 Select the comment by the author E.F.

13 Choose Set Status > Review > Completed in the Comments List toolbar.

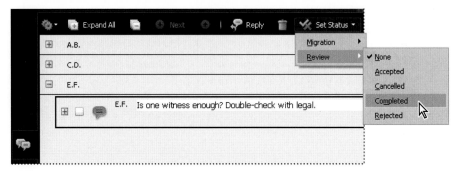

You can set the status of each comment for your own records and to show reviewers how their comments were handled.

14 With E.F.'s comment still selected, click Reply in the Comments List toolbar. A reply box opens in the comment list, with your name next to it.

Note: The reviewer will see your reply only if you are using a shared review process or if you email a saved copy of the PDF file to the reviewer.

15 Type **Legal says one witness is fine, per Janet**.

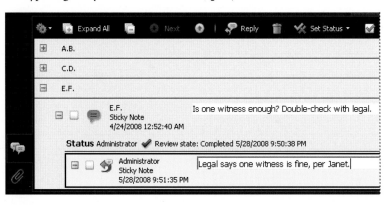

16 Close the document without saving your changes.

Initiating a shared review

In a shared review, all participants can view and respond to each other's comments. It's a great way to let reviewers resolve conflicting opinions, identify areas for research, and develop creative solutions during the review process. You can host a shared review on a network folder, WebDAV folder, SharePoint workspace, or Acrobat.com, a new free web service. For this exercise, you'll use Acrobat.com to host a shared review. You'll need to invite at least one other person to participate. If you are working on your own, you may want to create an alternative email address using a free web service such as Gmail or Yahoo.

Inviting reviewers

You'll use the Send For Shared Review wizard to invite reviewers to participate in a shared review of a document.

1   Decide who you will invite to participate in a shared review, and make sure you have their email addresses. If you are working on this lesson alone, create an alternative email address that you can send an invitation to.

2   Choose File > Open.

3   Navigate to the Lesson09 folder, and double-click the Aquo_market_summary. pdf file.

4   Choose Comments > Send For Shared Review.

5   Select Automatically Download & Track Comments With Acrobat.com from the pop-up menu at the top of the Send For Shared Review dialog box.

6   Click Next.

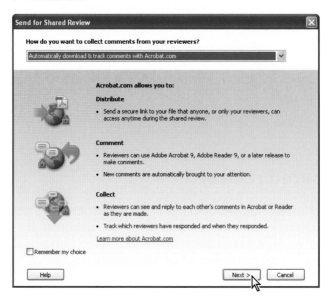

● **Note:** When you create an Adobe ID, you'll receive an email confirmation. Reply to that email within three days to verify your Adobe ID. You do not need to interrupt the shared review workflow to confirm the Adobe ID, though.

7   If you are prompted for your Adobe ID and password, enter them, and then click Sign In. If you don't have an Adobe ID, click Create Adobe ID and then complete the form online. Read the services agreement, and then select I Have Read And Agreed To the Following. Then click Next. Click Agree if the Acrobat. com Services Agreement dialog box appears.

Acrobat.com authenticates your Adobe ID if you signed in or have previously signed in, or creates your Adobe ID if you required a new one.

8   Enter the email addresses for people you want to invite.

9   Customize the message that will be sent to participants, or accept the default message.

10 Select Open Access from the Access Level menu, so that anyone who has the URL can participate.

The Limit Access option restricts access to the participants you invite.

11 Click Send.

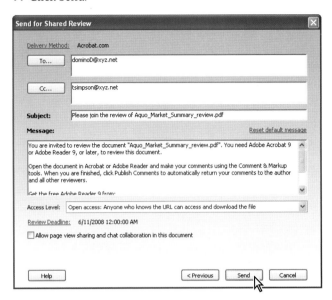

The Acrobat.com server sends invitation email messages with a link to the document on Acrobat.com. Acrobat saves your document to Acrobat.com and to your local hard drive.

12 Close the document.

About Acrobat.com

Acrobat.com is a new secure web-based service with many free features. Though it's called Acrobat.com, it's not actually part of the Acrobat application. In fact, you can share files of any format there, not just PDF files. To access Acrobat.com, type www.acrobat.com in your web browser, or choose Collaborate > Go To Acrobat.com on the Tasks toolbar. To access the free features, such as file sharing, you need only a free Adobe ID. For more information about Acrobat.com, visit www.acrobat.com.

Participating in a shared review

You or your colleague will participate in the shared review, adding comments for others to view.

1 If you're working alone, open the email invitation you sent to an alternative email address. If you're working with a colleague or friend, ask them to open the email invitation you sent and follow the steps below.

2 Click the URL to go to Acrobat.com.

3 If prompted, log into Acrobat.com with an Adobe ID or as a guest.

4 Click Download in the upper-right corner of the Acrobat.com window, and then click Open or double-click the downloaded file to open the PDF file in Acrobat.

5 If a Shared Review dialog box appears, click Connect; if the Welcome To Shared Review dialog box appears, click OK.

6 Add several comments to the PDF file using the commenting tools.

7 Click Publish Comments in the document message bar to save comments to the server.

8 Close the document. You do not need to save your changes.

Tracking review comments

You can keep track of reviewers' comments and reply to comments yourself from within Acrobat. You'll open the review PDF file and check for new comments.

1 In Acrobat, choose File > Open.

2 Navigate to the Lesson09 folder, and double-click the Aquo_Market_Summary_ Review.pdf file.

3 Click Connect in the Shared Review dialog box and OK in the Welcome to Shared Review window if one appears.

Acrobat saved a review version of your document when you sent it for shared review.

4 In the document message bar, click Check For New Comments.

Acrobat reports the new comments and displays them.

5 Double-click a comment icon, and click Options in the comment message box.

6 Choose Reply.

7 Type a reply to the reviewer.

8 Click Publish Comments in the document message bar.

Acrobat publishes your reply to the server.

9 Choose Comments > Track Reviews.

Tracker opens.

10 Select the Aquo_market_summary_review.pdf file on the left. Tracker displays the list of reviewers you invited to participate and how many comments each reviewer has made. It also lists the deadline for the review, and lets you send email reminders to reviewers or add more participants. You can also change the deadline.

11 Close the document.

▶ **Tip:** To see what's changed between two versions of a PDF document, choose Document > Compare Documents, specify the document, and select the type of document. Acrobat highlights changes on screen.

Starting an email-based review

In an email-based review, you send out a tracked copy of the PDF document, so that you can easily merge the comments you receive. To start an email-based review, choose Comments > Attach For Email Review. Enter information in the Identity Setup dialog box, if the information isn't already available to Acrobat. Specify the PDF to include in the review, and then click Next. The PDF file you specify becomes the master file; you'll merge comments you receive from reviewers into this file. Type the email addresses of your reviewers or choose them from your email application's address book. Customize the email invitation, and then click Send Invitation. Reviewers receive the PDF file as an attachment. When they open the attachment, Acrobat presents commenting tools and a PDF file with reviewing instructions.

After you receive comments from reviewers, open the attached file in email. The Merge Comments dialog box opens. Select Yes to open the master copy of the PDF file and merge all comments into it, and then be sure to save the master PDF.

Exploring on your own: Initiating live collaboration

You can invite others to review a PDF with you live in an online session. In a Collaborate Live session, you can share pages, including magnification, so that everyone sees the same part of the document. You can use the live chat window to communicate your thoughts about the document. Though Acrobat is required to initiate a Collaborate Live session, participants can use either Acrobat 9 or Adobe Reader 9.

In this exercise, you'll discuss the market summary document with a colleague. If you are working alone, use an alternative email address.

1 In Acrobat, choose File > Open. Open the Aquo_Market_Summary.pdf file again.

2 Choose File > Collaborate > Send & Collaborate Live.

3 Click Next in the introductory screen.

4 If prompted, enter your Adobe ID and password, and click Sign In. If you don't have an Adobe ID, create one, and click Next to continue.

Acrobat.com authenticates your Adobe ID.

5 Enter the email addresses for the people you want to invite to participate in the live collaboration. Insert a semicolon or a return between each email address.

6 Customize the email subject and message if you want to.

7 Make sure Store File On Acrobat.com And Send A Link To Recipients is deselected for this exercise.

When this option is deselected, Acrobat sends the file as an attachment to the recipients.

8 Click Send.

Acrobat sends the email invitations. When it has sent the invitations, the Collaborate Live navigation panel opens in the document.

9 Ask your colleague to open the PDF attachment in the email invitation. If you're working alone, check your email and open the PDF attachment.

When a participant opens the PDF attachment, the Collaborate Live navigation panel opens.

10 Ask participants to sign in as guests. If you're working alone, sign in as a guest in the second copy of the document.

11 Click the Start Page Sharing button to start sharing pages with each other. Click OK in any message boxes that appear, alerting you that everyone will be viewing the same page, and that you can share a page view of the document.

12 Type chat messages in the box at the bottom of the pane. Click the color box if you want to use a different color for your chat text.

13 To share your screen in an Adobe ConnectNow meeting, choose Share My Screen from the Options menu.

14 When you have finished with your Collaborate Live session, choose Disable Chat & Page Sharing In All Copies from the Options menu in the Collaborate Live navigation panel. Click OK if a warning message appears.

15 Close the document and quit Acrobat.

Hosting an Adobe ConnectNow meeting

Adobe ConnectNow is a personal web-conference tool that you can use to conduct real-time meetings on your desktop. You launch it from Acrobat, and meeting attendees join by logging into a web-based meeting space room from their own computers. You can share your desktop, use live chat, share online whiteboards, and work with many other collaboration features.

To start a meeting, choose File > Collaborate > Share My Screen. Enter your Adobe ID and password, or create one if you don't have one. Once you're in the meeting room, invite participants. For more information about Adobe ConnectNow, choose Help > Adobe ConnectNow Help within the meeting room.

Review questions

1 How do you add comments to a PDF document?

2 How can you consolidate comments made by several reviewers on the same document?

3 What is the difference between an email-based review process and a shared review process?

Review answers

1 You can add comments to a PDF using any of the commenting and markup tools in Acrobat. Click Comment on the Tasks toolbar, and then choose Show Comment & Markup Toolbar to see all the tools available. To use a tool, click it, and then either click on the page or select the text or other objects you want to comment on.

2 Open the original PDF file that you sent out for review, and then choose Comments > Import Comments. Select the PDF or FDF files that reviewers returned to you, and click Select. Acrobat imports all the comments into the original document.

3 In an email-based review process, each reviewer receives the PDF document through email, makes comments, and returns the PDF document through email; reviewers do not see each other's comments.

In a shared review process, you post the PDF document to a central server or folder, and then invite reviewers to make their comments. When reviewers publish comments, they can be seen by all other reviewers, so everyone can respond to each other. You can also enforce a deadline more easily with a shared review process, as commenting tools are no longer available to reviewers after the deadline.

10 WORKING WITH FORMS IN ACROBAT

Lesson Overview

In this lesson you'll do the following:

- Create an interactive PDF form.

- Add form fields, including text, radio buttons, and action buttons.

- Distribute a form.

- Track a form to determine its status.

- Learn how to collect and compile form data.

- Validate and calculate form data.

 This lesson will take approximately 60 minutes to complete. Copy the Lesson10 folder onto your hard drive if you haven't already done so.

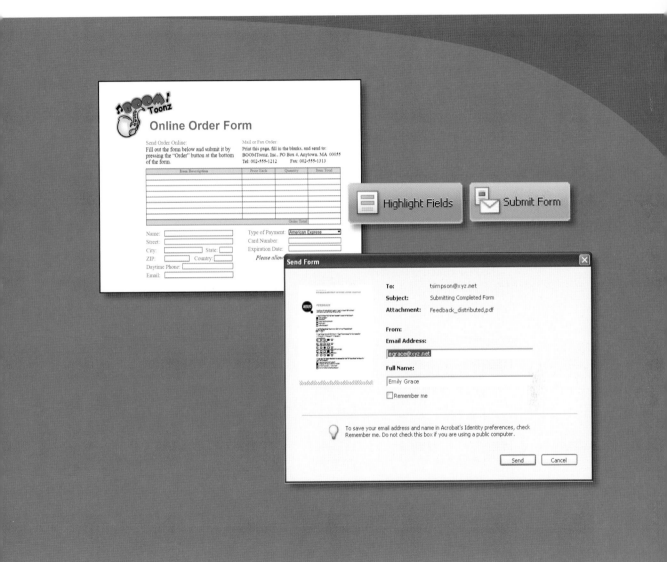

Getting started

In this lesson, you'll prepare a feedback form for the IT department of a fictitious drink manufacturing company. You'll convert an existing PDF document into an interactive form, and use the form tools in Acrobat 9 to add form fields that users can complete online. Then, you'll distribute the form, track it, and collect and analyze the data, all using tools within Acrobat.

Converting PDF files to interactive PDF forms

With Acrobat, you can create interactive PDF forms from documents you've created in other applications, such as Microsoft Word or Adobe InDesign, or scanned in from existing paper forms. You will start by opening a flat form that has already been converted to PDF. You will then use the forms tools to convert it to an interactive form.

1 Start Acrobat.

2 Choose File > Open, and navigate to the Lesson10 folder. Open the Feedback.pdf file.

The PDF contains the text for the form, but Acrobat doesn't recognize any form fields in the document yet.

3 Choose Forms > Start Form Wizard.

4 Select An Existing Electronic Document (Windows) or Start With a PDF Document (Mac OS), and then click Next.

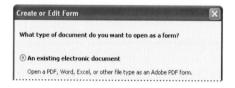

5 Select Use The Current Document, and then click Next.

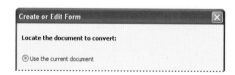

The Form Wizard analyzes the document and adds interactive form fields. When it has finished, the wizard prompts you to inspect the document to ensure that it added form fields appropriately, and to add fields manually where necessary.

6 Click OK to close the Welcome To Form Editing Mode dialog box.

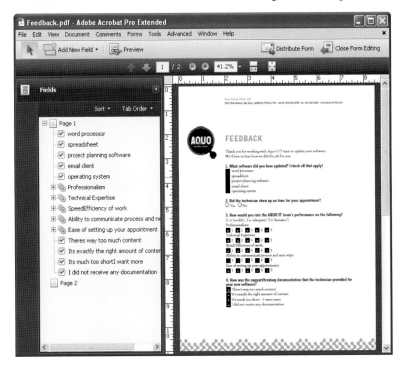

Acrobat lists the form fields added by the wizard in the Fields pane on the left. The Form Editing toolbar includes buttons for working with forms.

LiveCycle Designer

Adobe LiveCycle Designer ES is a stand-alone application included with Adobe Acrobat Pro or Acrobat Pro Extended for Windows. Use Designer ES when you want to extend the basic form capabilities in Acrobat. For example, a Designer ES form can include fields that let you easily add graphics to a form, and you can create dynamic forms that adapt to accommodate varying amounts of data or user interaction.

You must use LiveCycle Designer to edit any forms that were opened and saved in LiveCycle Designer, even if the form was originally created in Acrobat.

For in-depth information about using LiveCycle Designer, see *Creating Dynamic Forms with LiveCycle Designer* by Adobe Press.

Adding form fields

● **Note:** If a document has been password-protected to prevent editing, you must know the password to add or edit fields. Once a form has been enabled for Adobe Reader, so that Reader users can save the completed form, no one can edit it.

You can use the form tools in Acrobat to add form fields to any document. Because you've used the wizard to convert a document to an interactive PDF form, you're already in Form Editing mode. You can access this mode at any time by choosing Forms > Add Or Edit Fields.

Each form field has a name, which should be unique and descriptive; you'll use this name when you collect and analyze data, but it does not appear on the form the user sees. You can add tool tips and labels to help users understand how to complete form fields.

Adding a text field

The wizard found most of the form fields in the document, but it missed a couple of fields on the second page. You'll add a text field for an email address. Text fields enable users to enter information, such as their name or telephone number, on a form.

1   If you are not in Form Editing mode, choose Forms > Add Or Edit Fields.

2   Scroll to the second page of the PDF form.

3   Select Text Field from the Add New Field menu. Your cursor becomes a crosshair, attached to a text box.

4   Click to the right of "Email address (optional):" to place the text field.

5   Type **email address** in the Field Name box. Do not select the Required Field option because this is an optional field.

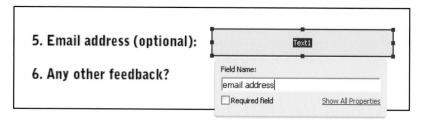

6 Drag the right edge of the text field to make it longer.

Adding a multiline text field

The next field is for additional feedback. Someone completing the form could type just a few words or several lines. You'll create a text field that supports multiple lines.

1 Select Text Field from the Add New Field list.

2 Click below "6. Any other feedback?" to add a text field.

3 Type **other feedback** in the Field Name box. This is another optional field, so do not select Required Field.

4 Drag the lower-right blue handle to increase the size of the box for multiple lines of text.

5 Double-click the text field to edit its properties.

6 In the Text Field Properties dialog box, click the Options tab.

7 Select Multi-line and Scroll Long Text.

8 Select Limit Of _ Characters, and type **750** for the limit.

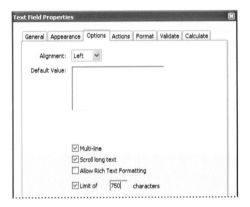

9 Click Close.

10 Click Preview. If it isn't already selected, click Highlight Fields to see how the field will appear to users.

Specifying an answer format

You can use special formatting to restrict the type of data that is entered into a text field, or to automatically convert data into a specific format. For example, you can set a zip code field to accept only numbers, or a date field to accept only a specific date format. And you can restrict numerical entries to numbers within a certain range.

To restrict the format for a text field, open its properties. Click the Format tab, select the format category, and then select the appropriate option for your field.

Adding radio buttons

The second question on the feedback form requires a yes or no answer. You'll create radio buttons for that question. Radio buttons let the user select one—and only one—option from a set of options.

1 If you're in Preview mode, click Edit Layout to return to Form Editing mode.

2 Go to page 1 of the form.

3 Select Radio Button from the Add New Field menu.

4 Click on the circle next to the word "Yes" after question 2.

● **Note:** All radio buttons in a set need to have the same name.

5 Type **on time** in the Radio Group Name box.

6 Select Required Field.

7 Verify that the Button Value is Yes.

8 Click Add Another Button To Group at the bottom of the dialog box. Your cursor becomes a box again.

9 Click on the circle next to "No."

10 Type **No** in the Button Value box.

11 Click Preview. Click Yes, and then click No. Notice that you can select only one radio button at a time.

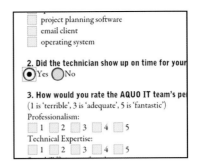

Adding an action button

Buttons let users perform an action, such as playing a movie file, going to a different page, or submitting a form. You'll create a reset button that will clear the form fields so the user can start over.

1 Click Edit Layout to return to Forms Editing mode.

2 Select Button from the Add New Field menu.

3 Click in the upper-left corner of the form to create the button.

4 Type **Reset** in the Field Name box, and then click Show All Properties.

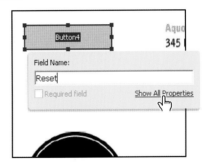

5 Click the Options tab.

6 Type **Start over** in the Label box.

The field name is used to collect and analyze data, but does not appear on the form itself. The label, however, appears in the field when the user is completing the form.

7 Click the Actions tab.

8 Select Mouse Up from the Select Trigger menu, and then select Reset A Form from the Select Action menu. Click Add.

When the user clicks the button and releases the mouse (Mouse Up), the form will reset.

9 Click OK in the Reset a Form dialog box to reset the selected fields. By default, all form fields are selected.

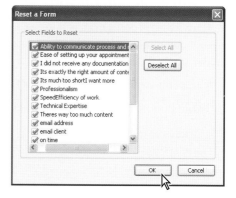

10 Click the Appearance tab.

11 Click the Border Color swatch and select a blue color, then click the Fill Color swatch and select gray.

12 Choose Beveled from the Line Style menu.

The button will appear with a gray background and blue outline, and the beveled line will make it appear to be three-dimensional.

13 Click Close to close the Button Properties dialog box.

14 Click Preview. Select options for a few questions, and then click the Start Over button you created. The fields reset.

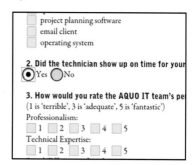

15 Choose File > Save. If the Save As dialog box appears, save the file with the same name.

Types of form fields

You can include the following types of fields in a PDF form you create in Acrobat:

- **Barcodes** encode the input from selected fields and display it as a visual pattern that can be interpreted by decoding software or hardware (available separately).

- **Buttons** initiate an action on the user's computer, such as opening a file, playing a sound, or submitting data to a web server. You can customize buttons with images, text, and visual changes triggered by moving or clicking a mouse.

- **Check boxes** present yes-or-no choices for individual items. If the form contains multiple check boxes, the user can typically select as few or as many of these as wanted.

- **Combo boxes** let the user either choose an item from a pop-up menu or type in a value.

- **Digital signatures** let the user electronically sign a PDF document with a digital signature.

- **List boxes** display a list of options the user can select. You can set a form field property that enables the user to Shift-click or Control-click to select multiple items on the list.

- **Radio buttons** present a group of choices from which the user can select only one item. All radio buttons with the same name work together as a group.

- **Text fields** let the user type in text, such as name, address, email address, or phone number.

Tip: When you fill out a PDF form, you can press the Tab key to move to the next field. As the form author, you can set the tab order. To see the current tab order, make sure you're in Form Editing mode, and then choose Tab Order > Show Tab Numbers in the Fields pane; to change the tab order, select an option from the Tab Order menu.

Distributing forms

After you have designed and created your form, you can distribute it in several different ways. In this lesson, you'll send the feedback form to yourself, if you have an email account, and then collect the response in email. You'll use the tools in Acrobat 9 to distribute the form, but first you'll enable Adobe Reader users to save a completed form.

1 If you're in Form Editing mode, click Close Form Editing.

2 Choose Advanced > Extend Features In Adobe Reader.

3 Read the information in the dialog box, and then click Save Now.

4 In the Save As dialog box, click Save to save the form with the same name.

5 Click Yes or Replace to replace the existing file.

Note: You cannot edit a form or any other PDF document after you have enabled rights for Reader in it. Enable a form just before distributing it.

Ordinarily, Adobe Reader users cannot save PDF forms that they have filled out. When you use the Extend Features In Adobe Reader command, however, Acrobat saves the form as a Reader-enabled PDF file, so that people using Adobe Reader can save the completed form.

6 Choose Forms > Distribute Form.

7 Click Save if you are prompted to save, and click Yes if you are prompted to clear the form before distributing it.

8 In the Distribute Form dialog box, choose Manually Collect Responses In My Email Inbox, and then click Next.

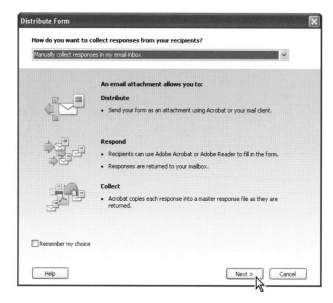

9 Select Send It Automatically Using Adobe Acrobat, and then click Next.

10 If prompted, enter or verify your email address, name, title, and organization name, and then click Next. If you've entered that information previously, Acrobat uses the information it has stored.

11 Type your email address in the To box. Make sure Collect Name & Email From Recipients To Provide Optimal Tracking is selected. Then click Send.

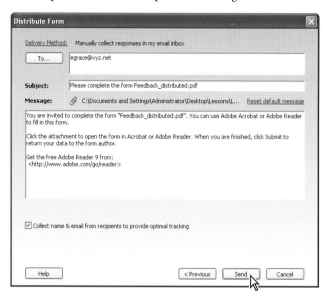

Note: You can customize the subject line and email message that accompanies your form, and you can send the form to multiple people at once. For the purposes of this lesson, however, you are sending the form only to yourself with the default message and subject line.

Acrobat opens your default email application and sends the message with the attached form. Depending on the security settings in your email application, you may need to approve the message before it can be sent.

Acrobat opens Tracker to help you manage the form that you have distributed. Tracker lets you view and edit the location of the response file, track which recipients have responded, add more recipients, email all recipients, and view the responses for a form. You can open Tracker at any time by choosing Forms > Track Forms.

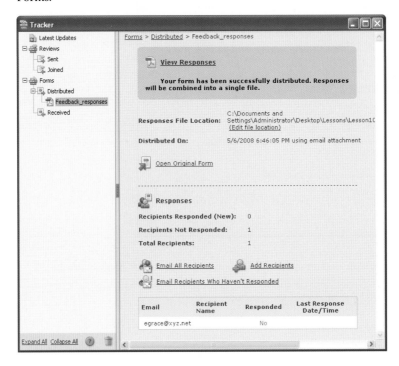

12 Check your email, and open the invitation to complete the form.

13 Open the attached PDF form. It opens in Acrobat, and a document message bar appears above the form.

● **Note:** If form recipients are using older versions of Acrobat or Reader, the document message bar may not be visible or may contain different information.

The document message bar displays information about the form. If the form does not contain a Submit Form button, one is included in the document message bar. Additionally, the document message bar informs Reader users about their usage rights for the form, and it specifies whether a form is certified or contains signature fields.

Options for distributing forms

There are several ways to get your forms to the people who need to fill them out. You can simply post a form on a website, for example, or send it directly from your email application. To take advantage of Acrobat form management tools to track, collect, and analyze data, use one of these options:

- Host your form on Acrobat.com, and send recipients a secure link to it. From Acrobat, you can create your own user account on Acrobat.com, and then use Acrobat.com to upload and share most document types.

- Send the form as an email attachment, and manually collect responses in your email inbox.

- Send the form using a network folder or a Windows server running Microsoft SharePoint services. You can automatically collect responses on the internal server.

To distribute a form using any of these methods, choose Forms > Distribute Form, and then follow the online instructions. To learn more about distributing forms, see Acrobat Help.

Collecting form data

Electronic forms aren't simply more convenient for users; they also make it easier for you to track, collect, and review form data. When you distribute a form, Acrobat automatically creates a PDF Portfolio for collecting the form data. By default, this file is saved in the same folder as the original form and is named [filename]_responses.

You'll complete the form and submit it, and then collect the form data.

1 Complete the form you opened and select options for each question, as if you were the recipient. Type a few words in the multiline field for number 6. Then click Submit Form.

2 In the Send Form dialog box, verify the email address and name you're using to send the data, and then click Send.

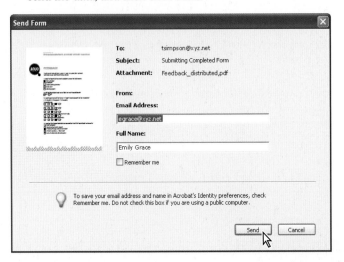

Note: Depending on the security settings in your email application, you may need to approve the message before it is sent.

3 In the Select Email Client dialog box, select Desktop Email Application if you use an application such as Microsoft Outlook, Eudora, or Mail. Select Internet Email if you use an Internet email service such as Yahoo or Hotmail. (You must send the file manually from an Internet email service.) Click OK.

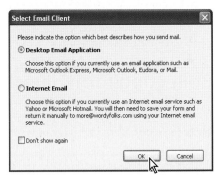

If you receive a message about sending the email, click OK. Depending on settings in your email application, you may need to send the message manually.

4 Check your email. The completed form arrives in a message with the subject line "Submitting Completed Form." Double-click the attachment in that message.

5 Select Add to An Existing Responses File, and accept the default filename. Then, click OK.

Acrobat compiles the data in the response file that was created when you used the Distribute Form wizard to send out the form.

6 Click Get Started at the bottom of the PDF Portfolio welcome screen.

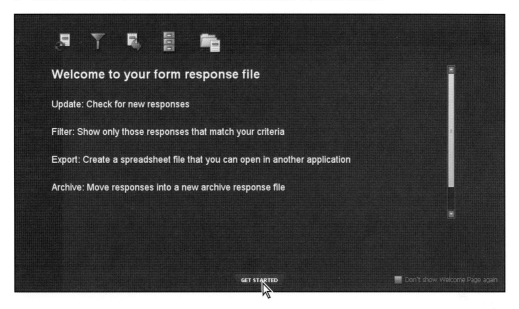

Form data you've collected is listed in the PDF Portfolio. Each response is listed as a separate component. You can use the PDF Portfolio to filter, export, and archive data.

Note: You can add multiple form responses to the responses file at once. Click Add, and then navigate to the responses you want to include.

Working with form data

Once your data has been compiled, you can view each response, filter responses according to specific questions, export the data to a CSV or XML file for use in a spreadsheet or database, or archive the data for access later. You'll filter the data from the feedback form and then export it to a CSV file.

1 Click Filter on the left side of the PDF Portfolio.

2 Scroll down the Select Field Name menu, and choose Other Feedback.

3 Select Is Not Blank from the next menu.

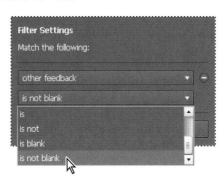

The form you completed is listed because it contains data in the Other Feedback field.

4 Select Is Blank from the second menu.

The form you completed disappears because it no longer matches the filter criteria. You can add filters to sort responses based on as many criteria as you like.

5 Select Is Not Blank again, so that your form reappears.

6 Click Done at the bottom of the Filters pane.

7 Click the Home button to return to the main PDF Portfolio window.

8 Select the response.

Note: You can select all the responses in your PDF Portfolio, or only specific responses.

9 Choose Export > Export Selected on the left side of the PDF Portfolio.

10 Select CSV as the file type, and click Save.

Acrobat creates a comma-separated data file that contains the data from the selected responses. You can open a CSV file in Microsoft Excel or another spreadsheet or database application.

11 Close any open PDF files and Tracker.

Exploring on your own: Calculating and validating numeric fields

Acrobat offers many ways to ensure that users fill out your forms correctly. You can experiment with creating fields that will allow the user to enter only information of a specific type. You can also create fields that automatically calculate values based on entries in other fields.

Validating numeric fields

To ensure that correct information is entered into form fields, use the Acrobat field validation feature. For example, if a response needs to be a number with a value between 10 and 20, restrict entries to numbers within this range. Here, you'll limit the price of instruments on an order form to no more than $1,000.

1 Choose File > Open, navigate to the Lesson10 folder, and open the Order_Start.pdf file.

2 Choose Forms > Add Or Edit Fields.

3 Double-click the Price.0 field (the first cell in the "Price Each" column).

4 In the Text Field Properties dialog box, click the Format tab and set the following values:

- For Select Format Category, choose Number.

- For Decimal Places, choose 2 to allow cents to be entered.

- For Separator Style, choose 1,234.56 (the default).

- For Currency Symbol, choose Dollar ($).

Now you'll specify a validation check on the data entered in this field.

5 Click the Validate tab, then select Field Value Is In Range. In the range fields, type **0** in the From box and **1000** in the To box. Click Close.

6 Click Preview. Then type **2000** in the field you just created, and press Enter or Return. A message warns you that the entry you have tried to make is unacceptable.

Calculating numeric fields

In addition to verifying and formatting form data, you can use Acrobat to calculate values used in form fields. For your PDF order form, you will calculate the cost for each line item, based on the quantity that has been ordered. You will then have Acrobat calculate the total cost of all items that have been ordered.

1 If you're in Preview mode, click Edit Layout.

2 Double-click the first field in the Item Total column. The text field is labeled "Total.0."

3 In the Text Field Properties dialog box, click the Calculate tab and set the following values:

- Select the Value Is The option.

- For the value, choose Product (x). You'll be multiplying two fields.

- To select the fields to multiply, click Pick. In the Field Selection dialog box, select the boxes to the left of Price.0 and Quantity.0.

4 Click OK to close the Field Selection dialog box, and click Close to exit the Text Field Properties dialog box.

5 Click Preview, and then enter **1.50** for the price and **2** for the quantity in the first row, and press Enter or Return. The Item Total column displays $3.00.

6 Close any open files and quit Acrobat when you are finished.

Review questions

1 How can you convert an existing document into an interactive PDF form?

2 What is the difference between a radio button and a button?

3 How can you distribute a form to multiple recipients?

4 Where does Acrobat compile form responses?

Review answers

1 Open the document in Acrobat. Then, choose Forms > Start Form Wizard, and select your current document. Follow the onscreen instructions.

2 Radio buttons permit the user to select just one of a set of two or more options. Buttons trigger actions, such as playing a movie file, going to another page, or clearing form data.

3 You can post a form on Acrobat.com and then send an invitation to recipients, email the form to recipients, or post the form on an internal server. Choose Forms > Distribute Form to start the Distribute Form wizard.

4 When you use the Distribute Form wizard, Acrobat automatically creates a PDF Portfolio file for your responses. By default, the file is in the same folder as the original form, and the word "_responses" is appended to the name of the original form.

11 CREATING MULTIMEDIA PRESENTATIONS

Lesson Overview

In this lesson, you'll do the following:

- Add videos and Flash animations to PDF files.

- Learn how to add sounds to PDF documents.

- Set playback options for videos and Flash animations.

- Use an image file as a poster for a video or Flash animation.

- Control transitions and presentation timing using Full Screen mode

- Learn about adding widgets to your PDF files.

 This lesson will take approximately 60 minutes to complete. Copy the Lesson11 folder onto your hard drive if you haven't already done so.

Getting started

● **Note:** You need Acrobat 9 Pro or Pro Extended to add movies, sounds, Flash animations, and widgets to your presentations.

In this lesson, you'll create a presentation about a new environmental bottling campaign by Aquo, a fictitious drink manufacturer. You'll add video and animation files to three pages, and you'll control when the video or animation file plays and how it appears on the page. You'll assemble the pages into a presentation that will appear in Full Screen mode, complete with timed transitions.

1   Start Acrobat 9 Pro or Acrobat 9 Pro Extended.

2   To see what the finished file looks like, navigate to the Lesson11 folder and open the Aquo_presentation.pdf file. Click Yes if Acrobat warns you that the PDF file will open in Full Screen mode.

Acrobat menu bars and toolbars are hidden when you open this file because it is set to open in Full Screen mode. The pages turn on their own, but you can also use the right or left arrow keys on your keyboard to move forward or backward through the presentation. On the CEO bio page, click the headshot of the CEO to play a short video.

3   When you have finished examining the PDF file, stop the video and then press Esc or press Ctrl+L (Windows) or Command+L (Mac OS) to display menus and toolbars. You can keep this end file open for reference while you work on the exercise, or you can close the file by choosing File > Close.

Adding a video file to a PDF file (Acrobat Pro and Pro Extended)

● **Note:** In Acrobat 9 Pro, you can add FLV (Flash video) files or F4V (H.264 encoded video files). In Acrobat 9 Pro Extended, you can add videos in a much larger range of formats, and convert them into FLV files automatically.

In Acrobat 9 Pro or Pro Extended, you can add an FLV (Flash video) file to a PDF. The file is completely embedded within the PDF document, so anyone can view it using Adobe Reader 9; you do not need a QuickTime player or Flash player to view videos in the PDF file.

When you add a video file to a PDF, you can set launch behaviors and other options that determine how the video file appears and plays in the PDF document.

1   Choose File > Open.

2   Navigate to the Lesson11 folder, and double-click the Aquo_Bottle_Ad.pdf file.

3   Click the Multimedia button in the Tasks toolbar, and choose Video Tool.
The cursor becomes a crosshair.

4 Drag a box over the right half of the document. The Insert Video dialog box appears.

5 Click Browse (Windows) or Choose (Mac OS), and then navigate to the Lesson11 folder.

6 Select the Aquo_T03_Loop.flv file, and click Open. The Aquo_T03_Loop.flv file is a video file of the new Aquo bottle.

7 Select Show Advanced Options in the Insert Video dialog box.

8 Click the Launch Settings tab.

9 From the Enable When menu, choose The Page Containing The Content Is Opened. Make sure Retrieve Poster From Media is selected in the Poster Image section of the dialog box.

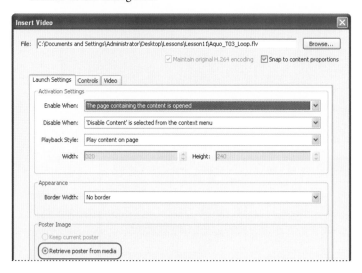

10 Click OK.

An image from the video file appears on the PDF page. A Play button automatically appears in the bottom-left corner of the video.

11 Click the Play button to play the video.

12 As the video plays, move the cursor over the video, and then away from the video. Playback controls appear at the bottom of the video when the cursor is over the video.

13 Stop the video, and then choose File > Save As. Name the file **Aquo_Bottle_ Anim.pdf,** and click Save.

14 Choose File > Close.

Adding a Flash animation
(Acrobat Pro and Pro Extended)

You can also add Flash animations (SWF files) to Adobe PDFs. You'll add an animated header to jazz up an ordinary document.

1   Choose File > Open.

2   In the Lesson11 folder, select the Aquo_FAQ.pdf file, and click Open.

3   Choose View > Toolbars > Multimedia.

Acrobat displays the Multimedia toolbar, which contains buttons for the 3D, Flash, Sound, and Video tools.

4   Select the Flash tool (🔳) in the Multimedia toolbar. The cursor turns into a cross-hair.

5   Drag a box across the top of the entire document. The Insert Flash dialog box opens.

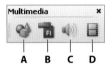

A. 3D tool **B.** Flash tool
C. Sound tool **D.** Video tool

▶ **Tip:** Use the 3D tool to place a three-dimensional file on a PDF page. To learn about working with 3D images in Acrobat, see Lesson 15, "Working with 3D in PDF Files."

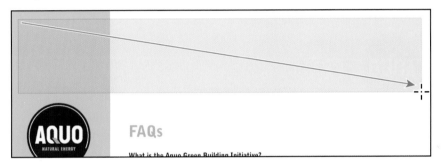

6   Click Browse or Choose, and navigate to the Lesson11 folder.

7   Select Aquo_Header.swf, and click Open.

8   Select Show Advanced Options in the Insert Flash dialog box.

9   Click the Launch Settings tab, and then choose The Page Containing The Content Is Visible from the Enable When menu.

10 Click OK. The header appears across the top of the document.

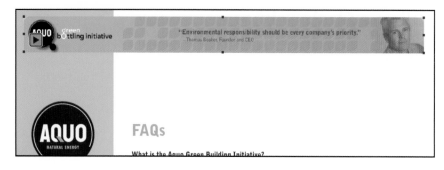

11 Select the Hand tool, and then move the cursor over the header. The header becomes a pointing finger to indicate that the object is interactive.

● **Note:** Though you've set the animation to play when the page becomes visible, you can also play it by clicking it.

12 Click the header to activate it. The animation plays, and continues to play.

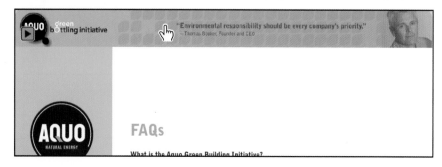

13 Select the Flash Tool in the Multimedia toolbar again, and double-click the header. The Edit Flash dialog box opens, with the same settings you saw in the Insert Flash dialog box.

14 Select the Launch Settings tab, and then choose The Page Containing The Content Is Not Visible from the Disable When menu. The animation will stop playing when the page is not visible.

15 Click OK.

16 Choose File > Save As. Name the file **Aquo_FAQ_Anim.pdf,** and click Save.

17 Choose File > Close.

Sound files

Adding sound files to a PDF document is similar to adding video and Flash animation files. Choose Multimedia > Sound Tool from the Tasks toolbar (or select the Sound Tool in the Multimedia toolbar), and then click where you want the sound to be placed.

Assigning a poster file for a video or animation (Acrobat Pro and Pro Extended)

By default, Acrobat displays the opening frame of a video or animation in the PDF document when the content is not playing. However, you can assign a separate image file to represent the video or animation. The image Acrobat displays is called the poster.

You'll add a new video to a biography of the CEO and assign an image for its poster.

Note: In Acrobat 9 Pro Extended, you can also assign a specific video or animation frame as the poster.

1 Open the Aquo_CEO.pdf file.

2 Select the Video tool (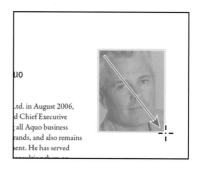) in the Multimedia toolbar.

3 Draw a box over the image on the right side of the page. You'll add a video of the company CEO talking about the initiative.

4 In the Insert Video dialog box, click Browse or Choose.

5 Select the CEO_Video.flv file in the Lesson11 folder, and click Open.

6 Select Show Advanced Options in the Insert Video dialog box.

7 Select the Launch Settings tab.

8 In the Poster Image area, select Create Poster From File, and then click Browse or Choose.

9 Select the Thomas_Booker_Small.jpg file in the Lesson11 folder, and click Open.

Note: You have not changed the activation settings because you want the video of the CEO to play only when the viewer clicks it.

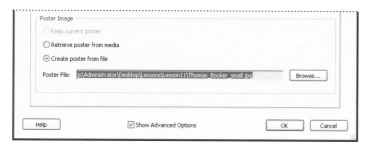

10 Select the Controls tab.

11 Choose Play, Stop, Seek, Mute, and Volume from the Skin menu.

The skin is the set of playback controls displayed with the video. Acrobat provides several skin options that determine the level of control you give viewers.

12 Make sure Auto-Hide Controls is selected.

When Auto-Hide is selected, the skin appears only when the cursor is moved over the video.

13 Click OK. The image of the CEO you selected as a poster appears where the video is placed on the page.

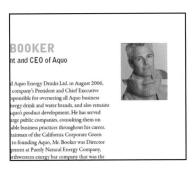

The poster has different dimensions than the original image, so you'll need to resize it.

14 Select the Video tool, and move the pointer over the image. Blue handles appear around the video poster

▶ **Tip:** Using the Shift key when resizing a video or animation file ensures that the image is adjusted proportionally.

15 Press the Shift key as you drag a corner of the poster to enlarge it so that it covers the original image. Drag the poster into position over the image. (The poster isn't the same size as the original image, but it should cover it completely.)

16 With the Video tool selected, double-click the poster. The Edit Video dialog box opens.

17 Click the Launch Settings tab.

18 Select Play Content In Floating Window from the Playback Style menu.

Acrobat can display video in a particular place on the page or in a floating window, depending on the option you choose here.

19 Click OK.

20 Select the Hand tool, and then click the video to activate it. You can drag the video around the screen by grabbing its border. When you move the cursor over the video, the playback controls, or *skin*, appears. Meanwhile, the video poster remains on the right side of the page.

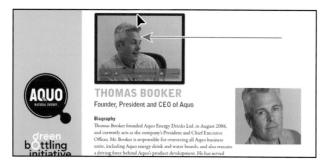

21 Stop the video, and then choose File > Save As. Name the file **Aquo_CEO_Anim.pdf,** and click Save.

22 Close the Multimedia toolbar, and then choose File > Close.

Creating a presentation

You can set up a PDF document to display as a presentation, in Full Screen mode, complete with transitions. If videos and animations are set to play when the page becomes visible, they'll begin playing when the viewer proceeds to that page, or when the page turns automatically. You'll combine the PDF files you've been working with to create a presentation.

Combining PDF files

You can easily combine multiple PDF files into a single PDF. The embedded multimedia objects you've added to your PDF documents are included in the new, merged file.

1 Choose File > Combine > Merge Files Into A Single PDF.

2 In the Combine Files dialog box, click Add Files, and then choose Add Files.

3 Select Aquo_Bottle_Anim.pdf, Aquo_FAQ_Anim.pdf, and Aquo_CEO_Anim.pdf, and then click Add Files. (Shift-click to select contiguous files; Ctrl-click or Command-click to select noncontiguous files.)

Note: If you already have a document open, Acrobat automatically includes it in the list. To delete a duplicate file, select it and click Remove.

4   Arrange the files so that the Aquo_Bottle_Anim.pdf file is first, followed by the Aquo_FAQ_Anim.pdf file, and then the Aquo_CEO_Anim.pdf file. To move a file up in the file order, select it and click Move Up. To move one down, select it and click Move Down.

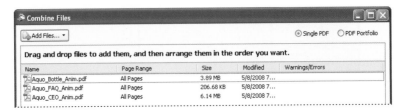

This is the order in which the files will appear in the final PDF presentation.

5   Click Combine Files. A progress bar appears while Acrobat merges the PDF files.

6   In the Save As dialog box, name the file **Aquo_Pres_Anim.pdf**, and click Save. Acrobat opens the presentation PDF file. The green bottle animation page is open, and the video plays.

7   Press the right arrow key on your keyboard to advance to the next page. As you move to that page, the header animation plays.

8   Press the right arrow key to advance to the final page. The CEO video does not play unless you click it, because you did not set it to play automatically.

Setting transitions

You can set Acrobat to automatically turn pages, and then apply a transition to determine how Acrobat displays each page turn. If you've worked with video editing applications, you'll recognize many of the transition styles. You'll set this presentation to automatically turn pages, and to fade the pages into each other.

1   Choose Advanced > Document Processing > Page Transitions.

2   In the Set Transitions dialog box, select Fade from the Transition menu, and Slow from the Speed menu.

The current page will slowly fade into the next page.

3 Select Auto Flip, and then type **10** in the Seconds box.

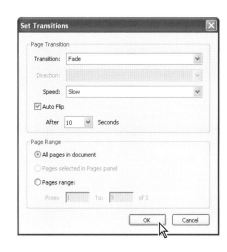

When Auto Flip is selected, the pages automatically turn after the number of seconds you enter. Ten seconds is enough time for the bottle video and the header animation to play. The presentation will stop on the last page, leaving it on the screen so that viewers have plenty of time to click the video of the CEO interview and play it in its entirety.

4 Select All Pages In Document.

5 Click OK.

Specifying Full Screen mode

Transitions work only in Full Screen mode, so to take advantage of the transition you've selected, you need to set your presentation to play in Full Screen mode.

1 Choose File > Properties.

2 Select the Initial View tab in the Document Properties dialog box.

3 In the Window Options area of the dialog box, select Open In Full Screen Mode.

4 Click OK.

5 Choose File > Save, and then choose File > Close.

6 Choose File > Open, select the Aquo_Pres_Anim.pdf file, and click Open.

7 If you see a Full Screen warning dialog box, click Yes.

Avoiding the Full Screen mode warning

By default, Acrobat warns you when a PDF file is set to be open in Full Screen mode, because it is possible for malicious programmers to create PDF files that appear to be other applications. If you click Remember My Choice For This Document, Acrobat will not show the warning again when you open the presentation on this computer. If you are presenting material on your own computer, you can change the preference so that Acrobat will not display the warning at the beginning of your presentation. To change the preference, choose Edit > Preferences (Windows) or Acrobat > Preferences (Mac OS), and then click Full Screen on the left. Deselect the Alert When Document Requests Full Screen option.

The presentation plays, moving from one page to the next with fade transitions between pages.

8　Click Esc to escape from Full Screen mode, and then close the file.

Working with widgets

In addition to Flash animations and videos, you can embed small Flash applications, called widgets, into your PDF document. For example, you could embed a calculator into a document someone would use to determine the cost of goods based on different circumstances. Or an RSS reader that lets your viewer link immediately to a relevant, current blog or news source on a related topic. Because widgets are SWF files, you can use the Flash tool to insert a widget into a document. To learn more about using widgets, see www.adobe.com.

Review questions

1 How can you add a video or animation to a document in Acrobat 9 Pro or Pro Extended?

2 Do recipients of your presentation need special viewing software to play videos or animations?

3 How can you create a presentation with timed page transitions?

Review answers

1 To add a video or animation to a PDF document, click the Multimedia button in the Tasks toolbar, and then choose Video Tool (FLV file or H.264-encoded video) or Flash Tool (Flash animation). The cursor becomes a crosshair. Click or drag where you want to place the video or animation, and then set launch, skin, and other properties. (If you're using Acrobat 9 Pro Extended, you can embed other video formats, as well, and Acrobat can transcode them to FLV format automatically.)

2 No. Anyone can view embedded video or animation files in PDF documents created in Acrobat 9 Pro or Pro Extended, as long as they have Acrobat 9 or Adobe Reader 9. Because Acrobat 9 natively supports Flash technology, no additional software is needed.

3 To add page transitions to a PDF document, choose Advanced > Document Processing > Page Transitions. Then, select a page transition style. To turn the pages automatically, select Auto Flip, and specify how long each page should be displayed. Presentations must be viewed in Full Screen mode for transitions to take effect, so select Open In Full Screen Mode in the Initial View pane of the Document Properties dialog box.

12 USING THE LEGAL FEATURES

Lesson Overview

In this lesson, you'll do the following:

- Apply Bates numbering to a document.

- Apply redaction to eliminate privileged information prior to submitting documents in response to a discovery motion.

 This lesson will take approximately 30 minutes to complete. Copy the Lesson12 folder onto your hard drive if you haven't already done so.

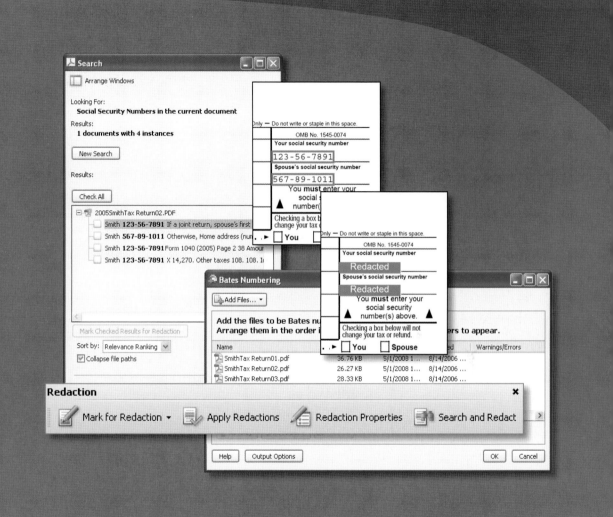

Acrobat 9 Pro and Pro Extended have new and improved features for the legal community:

- PDF Portfolios make it easy for you to collect documents for e-Briefs and case management. For information on PDF Portfolios, see Lesson 5, "Combining Files in PDF Portfolios."

- The Forms tools help you manage data collection within your firm as well as from clients and outside counsel. See Lesson 10, "Working with Forms in Acrobat."

- Improved scanning and optical character recognition facilitate conversion of paper documents to smaller, more searchable PDF files. See Lesson 3, "Creating Adobe PDF Files."

- The improved Compare tool allows you to more easily compare two versions of a document.

- New collaboration features allow you to share documents online so all participants can collaborate on the most current version of a document. You can even coordinate in real-time through web conferencing and screen-sharing. See Lesson 9, "Using Acrobat in a Review Cycle."

- The Split Document command allows you to split a large document easily and quickly into smaller documents based on file size to better meet court systems' upload requirements.

This lesson will focus on redaction and Bates Numbering.

About Bates numbering and redaction

Increasingly in the court systems and in law offices across the U.S., documents are processed electronically, usually as Adobe PDF. Acrobat 9 Pro and Pro Extended offer several features designed specifically to enhance the workflow in this environment.

- The Bates numbering feature allows you to automatically apply Bates numbering (as a header or footer) to any document or to documents in a PDF Portfolio. (If the PDF Portfolio contains non-PDF files, Acrobat will convert the files to PDF and add Bates numbering.) You can add custom prefixes and suffixes, as well as a date stamp. And you can specify that the numbering is always applied outside the text or image area on the document page.

- The redaction feature allows you to search a PDF document and automatically and permanently redact images, privileged or confidential words, phrases, or character strings (numbers and letters). You can search for patterns, such as patterns associated with phone numbers or social security numbers.

- You can also use the Examine Document command to inspect PDFs for metadata (such as the name of the document author), annotations, attachments, hidden data, form fields, hidden layers, or bookmarks and remove some or all of the data. You can run the Examine Document command on single documents (Document > Examine Document) or on multiple documents (Advanced > Document Processing > Batch Processing).

Applying Bates numbering

In law offices, Bates numbering is routinely applied to each page of a document when the document is part of a legal case or process.

In this part of the lesson, you'll apply Bates numbering to several documents, adjusting the format of the numbering to avoid overlaying text in the body of the documents.

1   Open Acrobat, and choose Advanced > Document Processing > Bates Numbering > Add.

2   In the Bates Numbering dialog box, click Add Files to open the menu.

You can add Bates numbering to individual files or to the contents of folders, as well as to PDF Portfolios. If a folder contains files that Acrobat does not support for PDF conversion, those files are not added.

3   Select Add Files, navigate to the Lesson12 folder, and select the SmithTax Return01.pdf file. Ctrl-click (Windows) or Command-click (Mac OS) to add the following files to your selection:

- SmithTax Return02.pdf
- SmithTax Return03.pdf
- SmithTax Return04.pdf

You can also add files in formats other than PDF, but the files must be in a format that can be converted to PDF.

4   Click Add Files.

Note: Bates numbering cannot be applied to protected or encrypted files or to some forms.

Tip: If you need to add Bates numbering to paper documents, scan the paper document using the File > Create PDF > From Scanner command and then apply Bates numbering to the resulting PDF file.

5   If necessary, use the Move Up and Move Down buttons to arrange the files in the following order:

- SmithTax Return01.pdf

- SmithTax Return02.pdf

- SmithTax Return03.pdf

- SmithTax Return04.pdf

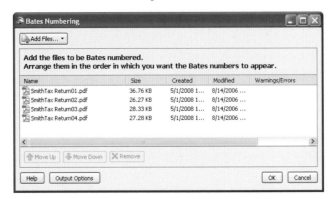

You set the name of your Bates numbered file, the save location, and the name of the Bates numbered file in the Output Options dialog box.

6   Click Output Options.

7   In the Output Options dialog box, specify where you would like to save the files. The default is to save the files to the same folder as the unnumbered document.

If you select Specific Folder, you are asked to browse to select a destination.

We selected the Same Folder As Originals option.

8   Under File Naming, select the Add To Original File Names option.

If you choose to keep the original file name, be sure to save the file in a different location from the original file; otherwise, you might overwrite the original file.

9   If you want to add a prefix or suffix to the file names, enter the data in the Insert Before and/or the Insert After text boxes. We typed **Bates** in the Insert After text box.

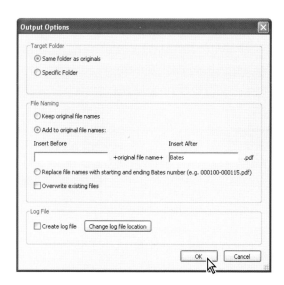

10 Deselect the Overwrite Existing Files option, and leave the other options unchanged.

11 Click OK to apply your options and return to the Bates Numbering dialog box.

12 Click OK.

Now you will define the style of the Bates numbering to be applied.

Defining Bates numbering

You define the font, color, type size and location of the Bates numbering in the Header And Footer dialog box. This is also where you opt to shrink the document contents to avoid overwriting content with the Bates numbering. Your Bates number can have 6 to 15 digits plus prefixes and suffixes.

First you'll specify the font and type size and color.

1   In the Add Header And Footer dialog box, specify your type size and color in the Font area. We chose Arial for the font and 10 for the type size. We toggled the underline on, and clicked the color swatch to select red for the page numbering.

2   The Margins area in the Add Header And Footer dialog box is where you specify the size of the blank margin around the image or text area of the page. This blank area is where the Bates numbering will be added in order to avoid overwriting text or images in the document. We chose to use the default values of 0.5 inches for the top and bottom margins and 1.0 inches for the left and right margins.

3 Click Appearance Options.

4 Select the Shrink Document To Avoid Overwriting The Document's Text And Graphics option. Click OK.

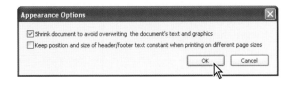

Now you'll choose where to place the Bates numbering—top left, center, or right (header), or bottom left, center, or right (footer).

5 Click in the text box where you want your Bates numbering to appear. We chose Right Header Text.

You specify the format of your Bates numbering sequence in the Bates Numbering Options dialog box. You can specify a prefix and/or suffix, as well as the number of digits in the numerical portion of the number.

6 Click Insert Bates Number, and enter your Bates numbering options. We specified **6** digits (15 is the maximum), with a prefix of **Smith** (for the client's name) and a suffix of **Jones** (for the principal lawyer's name). Since this is the first document in the package, we left the Start Number at 1. Click OK.

You can add the date as part of your Bates numbering, or you can add the date separately.

7 To add the date as part of the Bates numbering, click Page Number And Date Format.

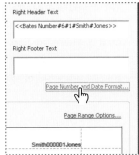

8 Choose a date format from the menu. We chose **mm/dd/yy**. Choose Bates Number from the Page Number Format menu. Leave the Start Page Number as 1. Click OK to return to the Add Header And Footer dialog box.

9 Click Insert Date to add the date to the Bates numbering formula. Your entry is previewed in the lower portion of the dialog box.

You can add space between the Bates number and the date by creating an insertion point in the Right Header Text box and pressing the space bar. You can also delete an entry or you can resequence the date and Bates numbering, putting the date first. Just drag over the date to highlight it, and then drag it to precede or follow the Bates number. You can even drag an entry to another of the text boxes. You can delete an entry by highlighting the entry and choosing Cut from the context menu.

Now you'll save your settings.

10 Click Save Settings, and name your settings **Smith_Jones.** Click OK.

If you need to number more documents at a future date, you can simply reuse the named settings.

11 When you are satisfied with the Bates numbering style, click OK to apply the Bates numbering across your target documents. Click OK to clear the message box.

12 Choose File > Open and open SmithTax Return01Bates.pdf. Bates numbering has been applied to this file as well as to SmithTax Return02Bates.pdf, SmithTax Return03Bates.pdf, and SmithTax Return04Bates.pdf.

13 Close any open documents.

If you need to add documents to the collection at a later date, add Bates numbering to the document or documents to be added as described above, setting the page number to follow sequentially after the last page number of the existing collection. For example, if the last page number in your collection is 6, then you would set the Bates numbering operation for the additional documents to start using the page number 7.

You add Bates numbering to files in a PDF Portfolio in the same way.

Editing Bates numbering

You cannot edit page numbering added with the Bates numbering feature. You can, however, delete Bates numbering and reapply a different Bates numbering formula.

Applying redaction

▶ **Tip:** Because redaction cannot be undone, you should always work on a copy or archive an unedited copy of the file for future use. It is recommended that you set your Documents preferences to automatically modify the file name when saving redactions.

Whenever the courts make documents public or law offices are required to produce documents that contain potentially confidential or privileged information, redaction may be applied to the documents to hide this information. To date, this has been a time-consuming manual process. With Acrobat Pro or Pro Extended, you can use the Redaction tool to automatically search for and permanently remove any privileged information. All you need to do is convert your electronic documents to Adobe PDF, or scan paper documents to PDF directly. You then use the Redaction tool to search for specific terms, such as names, telephone numbers, or account numbers, and permanently erase this information from a copy of your document. You can also search for common patterns. You can search a page or a page range. You can redact privileged or confidential information using the simple equivalent of a black marker, or you can add overlay text to the redaction, identifying the privilege asserted, applicable statutory or code citation, or other basis for the redaction.

First you'll look at an example of redaction.

1 In Acrobat, choose File > Open, navigate to the Lesson12 folder, and double-click SmithTax Return03.pdf.

Notice, in both Part I and Part II, that the description of the property has been redacted.

2 With the Hand tool (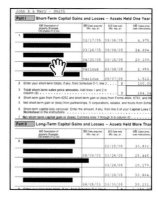) or Selection tool
   (![selection tool]), try to select the redaction. You cannot.
   Once redaction has been applied, it cannot
   be removed, nor can the material under the
   redaction mark be accessed in any way. For this
   reason, you should always save a file to which
   you've applied redaction under a new name. If
   you accidentally overwrite the original file, you
   cannot recover the redacted information.

3 Choose File > Close to close the tax return.

Now you'll redact identifying information—in this case, the two social security
numbers.

Changing the Documents preferences

First you'll change the Document preferences to make sure that you don't accidentally overwrite your original file with a redacted file.

1 In Acrobat, choose File > Open and navigate to the Lesson12 folder. Select the
   SmithTax Return01.pdf file, and click Open.

You'll set the Documents preferences to automatically modify a file name when you
save redaction markings and then you'll open the Redaction toolbar and set properties for the Redaction tool.

2 Choose Edit > Preferences (Windows) or Acrobat > Preferences (Mac OS), and
   select Documents in the left pane.

3 In the Examine Document section, select the Adjust Filename When Saving
   Applied Redaction Marks option. A checkmark appears in the box when this
   option is selected.

4 Type a prefix in the text box if
   you wish. We left it blank. By
   default, the suffix _Redacted
   will be add to a file name
   when redaction is applied.

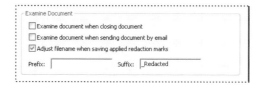

5 Click OK to apply the change.

Setting the Redaction tool properties

You access the Redaction Tool Properties dialog box from the Redaction toolbar.

1   To show the Redaction toolbar, choose Advanced > Redaction > Show Redaction Toolbar.

2   Dock the Redaction toolbar in the toolbar area. If you need help with the docking process, see Lesson 2, "Looking at the Work Area."

3   Select Redaction Properties ( ) in the Redaction toolbar to open the Redaction Tool Properties dialog box.

This is where you can change the color of the Redaction tool (the default is black) and add text to overlay the redaction mark if you wish. You also set the font size, color, and style used for the overlay text in this dialog box.

4   In the Redaction Tool Properties dialog box, click the color swatch next to the Redacted Area Fill Color label. Select a color for the redaction mark. We chose red.

5   Select the Use Overlay Text option. (The option is selected when a check mark is present.)

6   In the Overlay Text area, choose a font for the redaction text. We used the default font.

If you add overlay text, you can specify a font size or you can auto-size the text to fit the redaction area. We chose to auto-size the text by selecting the Auto-Size Text To Fit Redaction Region option.

7   For font color, we chose white. We deselected the Repeat Overlay Text option so that our redaction message will be displayed only once per redaction. We chose to center the redaction text.

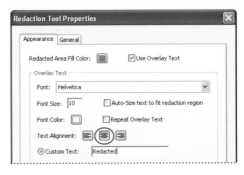

8   With the Custom Text option selected, we entered **Redacted** for the redaction text overlay.

If you want to indicate that information is redacted based on the U.S. Privacy Act or the U.S. Freedom of Information Act, select Redaction Code, and select the appropriate code set and code entry.

9   Click OK to apply your settings.

Searching text for redaction

You can use the search and redact feature to find a word, phrase, number, character string, or pattern and mark it for redaction. In this section you'll search for the social security numbers of your clients and redact them before producing the documents in a post-judgment discovery of assets.

1   Select the Search And Redact tool () in the Redaction toolbar. Click OK to clear the warning message.

2   In the Search pane, specify the document or folder you want to search. We selected In The Current Document.

If you want to search and redact across only the current page or across a page range in a document, choose Advanced > Redaction > Mark Page Range.

3   In the Search For section, select the Patterns option. Select an option from the menu. We selected Social Security Numbers. Click Search and Redact.

Use the Multiple Words or Phrases search option if you want to search for and redact more than one word or phrase at the same time, rather than running separate searches for each word or phrase.

The search panel shows the results.

4   Each occurrence of the search string is listed in the Search pane. Click on any entry to go to that occurrence in the document.

5   In the Search pane, we selected Check All to select all the occurrences of the social security number pattern listed in the Search pane.

6   To identify redaction candidates, click Mark Checked Results For Redaction in the Search pane to mark all the search results in the document pane. You can apply redaction after you have verified the marked redactions.

As you click each entry in the Search pane, the focus in the document pane moves to the entry marked for redaction. You can save and print out this copy if you want to have colleagues check the redaction process before applying the redaction. Be sure to choose the Document And Markups option (under Comments And Forms) in the Print dialog box in order to print the redaction markups.

7   When you are sure the redactions are correct and complete, click Apply Redactions (🖳) in the Redaction toolbar. Click OK to clear the message box. Click No to close the next message box. (This PDF file of the tax return was created by scanning a simple paper form. There is unlikely to be any information on hidden layers or in metadata and therefore no need to scan for additional information.)

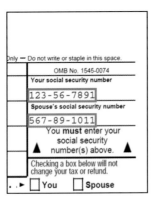
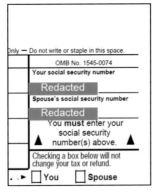

▶ **Tip:** If you cannot select text or graphics using the Mark For Redaction tool, you can still apply redaction by Control-dragging over the text or graphic and clicking the Apply Redaction button.

8   Choose File > Save, and save your file. Because of the change you made in your Document preferences earlier in the lesson, the suffix _Redacted is automatically applied to the file name. You can page through the file to review the redaction.

9   Close the Search pane and close your PDF file.

If you are working with a document that was created by scanning a paper document and converting the resulting file to PDF, you need to be aware that some text or graphics may be converted as images. Such text and graphics are not searchable unless you apply optical character recognition (OCR).

Creating PDF Portfolios

PDF Portfolios make it easy to assemble documents for e-Briefs and case management. You can assemble your Bates numbered and redacted documents in a PDF Portfolio that keeps each document separate for easy re-use. The documents in your PDF Portfolio retain their individual security settings and default views. Each file can be read, edited, formatted, and printed independently of the other files in the PDF Portfolio. Any changes that you make to documents in a PDF Portfolio are not made to the original document. The original document remains unchanged.

For information on working with PDF Portfolios, see Lesson 5, "Combining Files in PDF Portfolios."

Splitting documents

If your files are consolidated into a single, merged PDF file rather than assembled into a PDF Portfolio, you can use the Split Document command to separate out the original documents. You can also use this command to split up a document that is too large for court upload requirements.

1   Open your merged PDF file, and choose Document > Split Document.

2   In the Split Document dialog box, specify whether to split the document based on a number of pages, a maximum file size for each document created by the split, or top-level bookmarks.

3   Click the Output Options button to specify a target folder for the split files and your file naming preferences.

You cannot split documents to which you have applied security.

You can split multiple documents using the same criteria with the Apply To Multiple button in the Split Document dialog box.

Review questions

1   Can you remove redaction marks if you accidentally redact the wrong information?

2   How can you be sure that your Bates numbering doesn't overlap text or graphics in a document?

3   Can you edit Bates numbering after you have applied it to a document collection?

Review answers

1   No. Redaction is permanent. Always review the material marked for redaction carefully before applying redaction. And always save the redacted file under a different name to avoid overwriting the original file and losing it. Note, however, that if you haven't saved your document after applying redaction, you can select the redaction and remove it.

2   In the Add Header And Footer dialog box, click Appearance Options, and select the Shrink Document To Avoid Overwriting Document's Text And Graphics option.

3   No. You can only delete the current Bates numbering and reapply a different Bates numbering formula.

13 USING THE ENGINEERING AND TECHNICAL FEATURES

Lesson Overview

In this lesson, you'll do the following:

- Show, hide, and print layers created in an AutoCAD drawing.

- Work with the Acrobat measuring tools.

- Create a PDF file from a .dwg file.

- Look at the PDF mapping feature and Geospatial tools.

 This lesson will take approximately 45 minutes to complete. Copy the Lesson13 folder onto your hard drive if you haven't already done so.

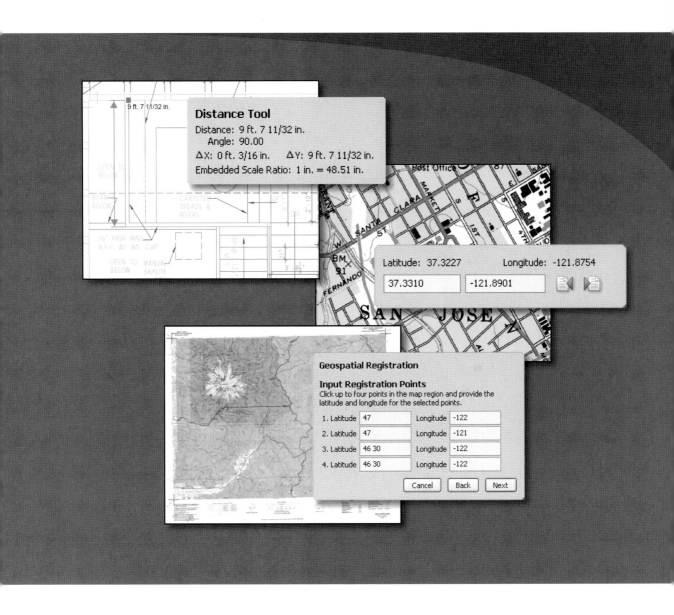

Distance Tool

Distance: 9 ft. 7 11/32 in.
Angle: 90.00
ΔX: 0 ft. 3/16 in.   ΔY: 9 ft. 7 11/32 in.
Embedded Scale Ratio: 1 in. = 48.51 in.

9 ft. 7 11/32 in.

Latitude: 37.3227   Longitude: -121.8754

37.3310   -121.8901

Geospatial Registration

Input Registration Points
Click up to four points in the map region and provide the
latitude and longitude for the selected points.

1. Latitude	47	Longitude	-122
2. Latitude	47	Longitude	-121
3. Latitude	46 30	Longitude	-122
4. Latitude	46 30	Longitude	-122

Cancel   Back   Next

Acrobat 9 offers enhanced tools and features for the engineering and technical market. Converting drawing files to PDF is simpler, faster, and produces smaller files. Measurement capabilities are improved. PDF Portfolios (Lesson 5) make it easier to work with design requirements, change orders, and close out materials. And enhancements to the forms feature make data collection from consultants and the field even easier (Lesson 10). A new PDF Maps feature allows you to create, view, and interact with PDF maps that contain geospatial coordinates.

All Acrobat 9 users can change the view state of layers. Only users of Acrobat Pro and Pro Extended can create PDF files containing layers.

All Acrobat 9 users can use the geospatial measurement and location tools and default views. Users of Acrobat 9 Pro and Pro Extended can create PDF maps, import map content, and export geospatial markups. Only users of Pro Extended can use the geospatial registration tool and 3D navigation feature.

Getting started

In this lesson, you'll first work on the architectural plans for a home remodeling project that involves adding a new master bedroom/bathroom suite to a private residence.

Working with layers

● **Note:** Permission to use this file is given by Arcadea Architecture, Boulder, Colorado (www.arcadea.com). The complexity of the drawings, labels, and layers has been significantly reduced for the purposes of this lesson.

Acrobat 9 is able to preserve layers from AutoCAD and other programs such as Microsoft Visio. These layers can be enabled or disabled for viewing and printing, making it easier to focus on the information in your file that is most relevant.

1   In Acrobat, choose File > Open. Navigate to the Lesson13 folder, select Remodel_Layers.pdf, and click Open.

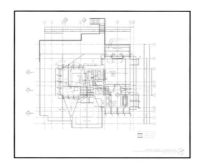

2   Choose File > Save As, and rename the file **Remodel_Layers1.pdf** and save it in the same folder.

Now you'll see the effect of showing and hiding layers.

3   Click the Layers button (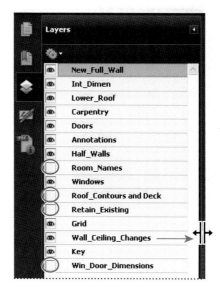) in the navigation pane, or choose View > Navigation Panels > Layers to open the Layers panel in the navigation pane.

4   The Layers panel lists the layers created when the AutoCAD file for the floorplan was converted to PDF. For this lesson, the number of layers has been reduced from the original architect's drawing and the layers have been relabeled for convenience.

5   In the Layers panel, click the Eye icon (⊙) located to the left of the layer name for each of the layers listed below:

- Room_Names
- Roof_Contours & Deck
- Retain_Existing
- Win_Door_Dimensions

If the Layers panel is too narrow for you to read the labels, you can drag the left margin of the pane to widen it.

Notice that all the text, lines, and other elements on these layers are now hidden from view. By default, layers that are not visible do not print. You can experiment with showing and hiding different layers.

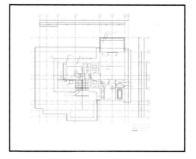

▶ **Tip:** You can add a layer to any PDF using the Import As Layer command in the Layers panel.

6 When you are finished, make sure each Eye icon is visible so that all layers are displayed again. Then click the Eye icon for the Grid layer to hide this layer.

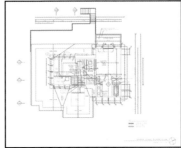

You also use the Layers panel to control which layers are visible when a document is opened and whether individual layers print.

7 Select the Marquee Zoom tool (🔍) and drag over the center of the drawing to better see the stairs.

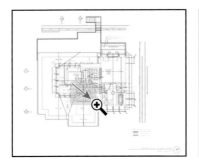

8 In the Layers panel, right-click or Control-click the name Carpentry and choose Properties.

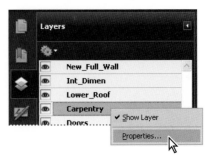

9 In the Layer Properties dialog box, for Default State, choose Off. For Print, choose Never Prints. Leave the other settings in this dialog box unchanged, and click OK.

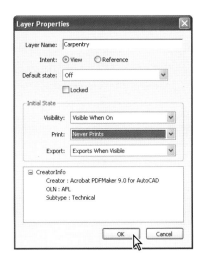

10 Choose File > Print, and in the Print dialog box, choose Current View. In the preview pane, you can see that the stairs will not print, even though they are visible on your monitor. Click Cancel to close the Print dialog box without printing the page.

If your computer is attached to a printer, you can experiment with printing the page with these settings applied versus with the default settings applied. You can also print to the Adobe PDF printer and view the results as a PDF file.

11 Select the Hand tool ( ), and click the Collapse button ( ) at the top right of the Layers panel to collapse the panel. Click the Single Page button ( ) to view the entire plan.

About PDF layers

Acrobat supports viewing, navigating, and printing layered content in PDFs created from applications such as InDesign, AutoCAD, and Visio.

You can control the display of layers using the default and initial state settings. For example, if your document contains a copyright notice, you can easily hide the layer containing that notice whenever the document is displayed onscreen while ensuring that the layer always prints.

You can rename and merge layers, change the properties of layers, and add actions to layers. You can also lock layers to prevent them from being hidden.

Acrobat does not allow you to author layers that change visibility based on the zoom level. However, you can highlight a portion of a layer that is especially important by creating a bookmark that magnifies or hides the layer using page actions. You can also add links that let users click a visible or invisible link to navigate to or zoom in on a layer.

To retain layers when you convert InDesign CS or later documents to PDF, make sure that Compatibility is set to Acrobat 6 (PDF 1.5) and that Create Acrobat Layers is selected in the Export PDF dialog box.

—From the Adobe Acrobat 9 Help

Using the Pan & Zoom tool

The Pan & Zoom tool makes it easy to focus on important portions of your documents. For example, if you need to make several measurements of the office in the master suite, you can use the Pan & Zoom tool to magnify the view.

First you'll add the tool to the Select & Zoom toolbar.

1 Right-click (Windows) or Control-click (Mac OS) anywhere on the Acrobat toolbar and choose More Tools. In the More Tools dialog box, scroll down to the Select & Zoom Toolbar, and select Pan & Zoom Window. Click OK to add the Pan & Zoom window to the toolbar.

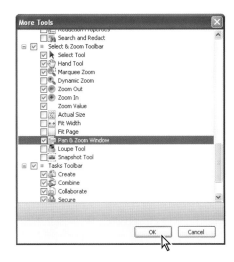

2 Click the Pan and Zoom button (🖼) to open the Pan & Zoom window. If necessary, drag the Pan & Zoom window to the side of the document pane or to a corner so that the architectural plans are also visible. You can resize the Pan & Zoom window by dragging any of the corners of the window.

3 Click the Zoom In or Zoom Out button in the Pan & Zoom window until the magnification in the document pane is 100%, and then drag the red box in the Pan & Zoom window until the office is centered in the document pane.

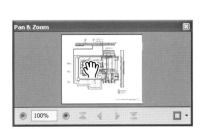
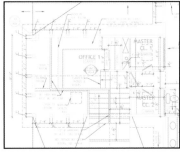

You can also resize the red box in the Pan & Zoom window by moving your pointer over a corner of the box until it changes to a double-headed arrow. Drag the arrow toward or away from the opposite corner to resize the box. As you make the box smaller or larger, the magnification in the document pane changes.

You will be measuring several items in the office area.

4 Click the Close button in the Pan and Zoom window to close it.

Using the 2D measuring tools

● **Note:** The measuring tools are available to Adobe Reader users only if the PDF creator enables measuring functionality.

You can use the enhanced 2D measuring tools in Acrobat 9 to measure heights, widths, and areas of objects in PDF documents.

Now you will add some measurements to this file, helping to clarify the size of some of the walls in the drawing.

First, though, you'll look at the Measuring preferences.

Setting the Measuring preferences

The Measuring preferences determine how data is measured.

1   Choose Edit > Preferences (Windows) or Acrobat > Preferences (Mac OS), and select Measuring (2D) in the left pane.

2   Click the Measuring Line Color box to change the color of the lines associated with the measuring tools. We chose orange.

3   Leave the Enable Measurement Markup option selected. This adds your measurement lines to the PDF. If you deselect this option, measurement lines disappear when you measure another object or select another tool.

4   Select the Use Default Label option.

5   From the Caption Style menu, choose Top to place the measurement above the measurement line. (This applies only to the Distance tool.)

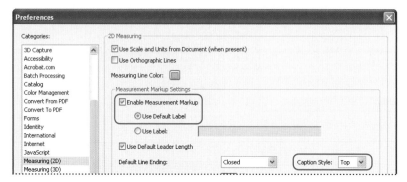

6   Leave the other settings at their default values and click OK to apply your changes.

Now you'll take some measurements.

Using the Distance tool

1 Choose View > Toolbars > Analysis to display the toolbar that contains the Measuring tool. You can leave the toolbar floating in the document pane or you can dock it in the toolbar area.

2 Select the Measuring tool (🖉), which opens the Measuring toolbar and Measurement Info panel.

The Measurement Info panel shows information about the measurement, such as delta values and scale ratio.

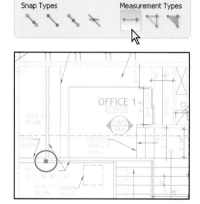

3 Select the Distance tool (↦) to measure the length of the half wall. Move the crosshair over the bottom edge of the half wall. A red square indicates when the cross-hair is aligned with the edge of the wall. When you see the red square, click to establish the beginning point of the measurement.

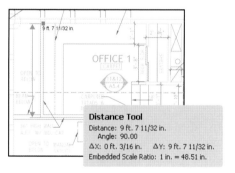

4 Shift-drag the pointer to the upper edge of the wall. Again a red square indicates when the cross-hair is aligned with the wall. Click to mark the endpoint of the measurement and add the label.

5 Right-Click (Windows) or Control-click (Mac OS), and choose Complete Measurement.

Use the Perimeter tool (⬖) to measure a set of distances between multiple points.

Use the Area tool (⬗) to measure the area within the line segments that you draw.

6 Choose File > Save to save your work.

Analysis ✕

A B C D

A. Object Data tool
B. Measuring tool
C. Geospatial Location tool
D. Geospatial Registration tool (Pro Extended only)

▶ **Tip:** You can delete a measurement by selecting the measurement in the document pane, right-clicking (Windows) or Control-clicking (Mac OS) and choosing Delete from the context menu.

Exporting measurements to spreadsheets

You can export any measurements that you make on the drawing to a spreadsheet.

1   With the Distance tool still selected, right-click or Control-click anywhere in the document pane, and choose Export Measurement Markup To Excel. For each measurement on your drawing, Acrobat will export the label, type of measurement, a value, and unit to a .csv file.

2   Save the exported data in the Lesson13 folder using the name **measure.csv**.

3   If you have Microsoft Excel installed, you can open the .csv file and review your measurements.

4   Close Microsoft Excel if necessary, and close the Analysis toolbar. Select the Hand tool to close the Measuring toolbar and Measurement Info panel.

5   Choose View > Toolbars > Reset Toolbars.

Using the Loupe tool

Before you go any further, you'll use the Loupe tool to see how accurate your measurement points were.

1   Choose View > Zoom > Fit Page.

2   Choose Tools > Select & Zoom > Loupe tool.

Use the Loupe tool (🔍) to view specific portions of your documents at a higher magnification while maintaining a separate zoom level in the document window. You can adjust the size of the Loupe Tool window and the blue box in the document pane by dragging the corners. You can also adjust the magnification in the Loupe Tool window and the size of the blue window using the slider.

3   Locate the upper edge of the half wall in the study and click once. The Loupe Tool window opens, showing a magnified view of this wall edge.

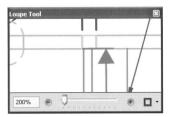

At this magnification, you see that the positioning of the measuring crosshairs is accurate.

4 With the Loupe tool still selected, place your pointer over the blue box in the document pane (not in the Loupe Tool window) and drag the rectangle to the lower edge of the wall. You can drag the rectangle anywhere in the document pane. You can also click anywhere in the document pane to position the blue box.

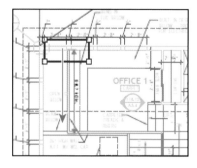
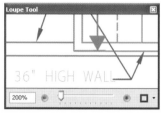

▶ **Tip:** You can choose Window > Split to view the same page in two different windows. You can use one window to display the entire page and one window to focus on a detail at an increased magnification. To remove the split, choose Window > Remove Split.

5 Click the close button to close the Loupe Tool window. Select the Hand tool.

6 Close the Remodel_Layers1.pdf file when you are finished. You do not need to save your changes.

Converting a drawing file to PDF (Acrobat Pro and Pro Extended)

1 In Acrobat, click the Create button on the Tasks toolbar, and choose PDF From File. In the Open dialog box, choose Autodesk AutoCAD for Files Of Type. Navigate to the Lesson13 folder, and select Remodel_Plan.dwg. Click Settings.

The Adobe PDF Settings For Autodesk AutoCAD Documents dialog box allows you to set a number of options, including how layers are treated.

● **Note:** Permission to use this file is given by Arcadea Architecture, Boulder, Colorado (www.arcadea.com).

2 In the Adobe PDF Settings For Autodesk AutoCAD Documents dialog box, select Last Active Layout for Layout Option. For Layer Option, select the Selected Layers option.

3 Click OK, and click Open.

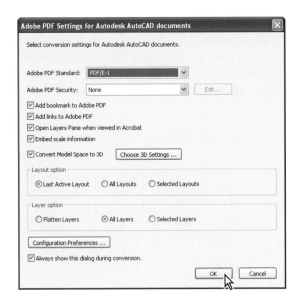

4 Click Choose Layers. This dialog box allows you to choose which layers to display in the PDF file.

For this part of the lesson, you'll convert all layers.

5 Click Add All Layers, and click Convert.

6 Leave all the other settings at their default values in the Adobe PDF Settings For Autodesk AutoCAD Documents dialog box, and click OK.

Your DWG file is converted to PDF with all the layers fully functional. It is that easy to convert your drawing files to fully layered PDF files.

7 When you have finished with the file, choose File > Save As, and save your PDF file in the Lesson13 folder using the name **Remodel_Convert.pdf**. Close the file.

Printing custom sizes

Printing an oversized document: Although you can create a PDF file as large as 15,000,000 inches (38,100,000 cm) in either direction, most desktop printers cannot print such large pages. To print an oversized document on your desktop printer, you can print each page in pieces, called tiles, and then trim and assemble those pieces.

You can also increase the scale of a standard-sized document and print it on multiple pages.

1   Choose File > Print.

2   From the Page Scaling menu, choose Tile All Pages if all pages of the document are oversized. If some of the pages are standard-sized, choose Tile Large Pages.

3   (Optional) Set any of these options, referring to the Preview image to check the output results:

  • **Tile Scale** adjusts the scaling. The scaling affects how the sections of the PDF page map to the physical sheet.

  • **Overlap** specifies the minimum amount of duplicated information you want printed on each tile for ease in assembly. The Overlap option uses the unit of measure specified for the document. The value should be greater than the minimum nonprinting margins for the printer. You can specify up to half the size of the shortest side of the document page to overlap. For example, tiles for a page that measures 11-by-17 inches (279.4mm-by-431.8mm) can overlap up to 5.5 inches (139.7mm).

  • **Labels** includes the PDF name, date of printing, and tile coordinates on every sheet. For example, Page 1 (1,1) means row 1, column 1 of the first page. Tile coordinates are used for reassembling the tiles.

  • **Cut Marks** prints marks on each corner of a tiled page for ease of assembly. Use this option in conjunction with the Overlap option. When you specify an overlapping edge and then superimpose those edges, you can use the cut marks to line up the tiles.

Scaling a document for printing: To print an oversized PDF on paper that has smaller dimensions, you can scale the document's width and height to fit.

1   Choose File > Print.

2   From the Page Scaling menu, choose Fit To Printable Area or Shrink To Printable Area.

—From the Adobe Acrobat 9 Help

Permanently removing text from PDF documents

Often you need to remove sensitive personal information from a document before passing it on to a client or colleague. Acrobat 9 offers the redaction feature, which allows you to permanently remove sensitive data from your documents. You can remove data in both horizontal and vertical formats. For more information, see Lesson 12, "Using the Legal Features."

Using the PDF Maps feature

Acrobat 9 offers the PDF Maps feature that allows you to create, view, and interact with PDF maps that contain geospatial coordinates. You can import geospatially enabled TIFF, JPEG 2000, SHP, and PDF map files and convert them to Adobe PDF maps. You can mark locations and find locations on PDF maps by entering coordinates, and you can determine distances using real-world units—kilometers, miles, etc. You can copy a location from a PDF map to a Web mapping service such as Google Maps, Yahoo Maps, or Mapquest.

With 3D maps, you can use the Fly tool (✈) on the 3D toolbar to zoom in close to the surface of the earth. You have finer control as the Fly Tool slows down as it gets close to earth.

All Acrobat 9 users can use the geospatial measurement and location tools and default views. Users of Acrobat 9 Pro and Pro Extended can also create PDF maps, import map content, and export geospatial markups. Only users of Pro Extended can use the geospatial registration tool and 3D navigation feature.

1   In Acrobat, choose File > Open, navigate to the Lesson13 folder, select the SanJose_Geo.pdf file, and click Open.

2   Choose View > Toolbars > Analysis.

You'll use the Geospatial Location tool (▦) to locate the Adobe San Jose office.

3 Select the Geospatial Location tool. Right click (Windows) or Control-click (Mac OS) in the document pane, and select Find A Location from the context menu.

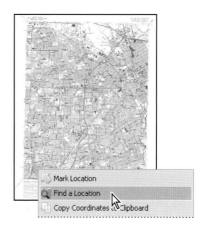

4 In the floating window at the bottom of the page, enter the latitude and longitude values for the Adobe San Jose office. (We entered 37.3310 for the latitude and -121.8901 for the longitude.) Press Enter or Return.

The location of the office is marked with a small square.

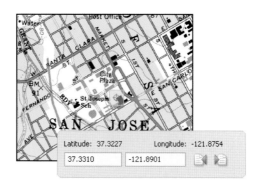

5 To mark the location of the office with an annotation, move your pointer over the small blue square, right-click (Windows) or Control-click (Mac OS), and choose Mark Location from the context menu. (Double-click on the annotation to open it and check on the coordinates.)

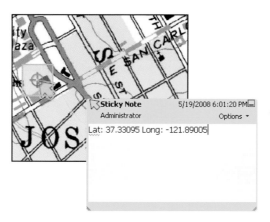

6 Choose File > Save As, and save your annotated map in the Lesson13 folder using the name **SanJose_Geo1.pdf**. Close the file.

You can also determine the coordinates of a location on the map and export the coordinates to a mapping service.

Geospatial registration (Acrobat Pro Extended)

Geospatially enabled PDF files from third-party providers can be imported into Acrobat Pro Extended, or latitude and longitude coordinates can be added to an existing PDF map to make it geospatially enabled.

If you are working with a geospatially enabled PDF, you can find locations, measure distances, add location markers, and export location data to a web mapping service.

In this section of the lesson, you'll geospatially enable a PDF map.

1   In Acrobat, navigate to the Lesson13 folder, and open the MtRainier.pdf file. Then choose File > Save As, and save the file in the Lesson13 folder using the name **MtRainier_Enabled.pdf**.

This is a simple image of a map. The bottom left corner of the map describes the projection that the map is based on. You can use the Marquee Zoom tool if you want to zoom in and read this information.

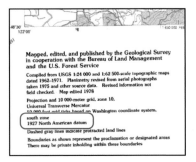

2   Select the Geospatial Registration tool (⊕) on the Analysis toolbar. Enter a name for your map. We entered **MtRainier**. Click Next, and select Use Page Bounds As Neatline. Click Next again.

While the neatline helps define the map area, it is the coordinate input that defines the area that is registered. You'll need four coordinates (the four corners of the map) to geospatially register the page.

3   If necessary, drag the Geospatial Registration box into the middle of the map, away from the corners. Click on the upper-left corner of the map, and for point 1, enter **47** for the latitude and **-122** for the longitude.

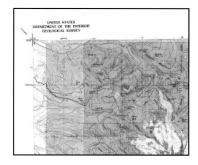 

- Click the upper-right corner, and enter Lat **47,** Long **-121** for point 2.

- Click the lower-left corner, and enter Lat **46.30**, Long **-122** for point 3.

- Click the lower-right corner, and enter Lat **46.30**, Long **-121** for point 4.

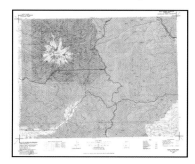 

4   Click Next.

5   Click the arrow to open the Projected menu, and scroll down to select NAD_1927_StatePlane_Washington_ South_FIPS_4602.

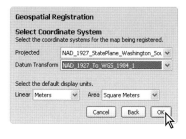

6   Click the arrow to open the Datum Transform menu, and scroll down to select NAD_1927_to_WGS_1984_1. Click OK, and click OK again to close the message box.

7 Select the Geospatial Location tool (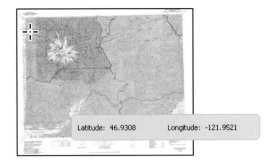), and click in the area of the summit of Mt . Rainier. Note that the coordinates are now visible. Your map is geospatially enabled.

Latitude: 46.9308   Longitude: -121.9521

8 When you are finished, choose View > Toolbars> Reset Toolbars, and then choose File > Close to close the work file.

Review questions

1   In general, where do layers in an Adobe PDF file originate? How are they added to the file?

2   Can you permanently expunge or remove text and illustrations from a PDF document?

3   How can you create a geospatially enabled PDF map?

Review answers

1   Generally, layers come from the authoring program, such as AutoCAD, Microsoft Visio, Adobe Illustrator, or Adobe InDesign. They are created in these programs and exported as a component of the PDF when the PDF file is generated.

2   Yes, you can use the Redaction tool to "ink over" selected text and illustrations, maintaining the original look of the document but obliterating sensitive material.

3   With Acrobat 9 Pro Extended, you can geospatially enable any PDF map using the Geospatial Registration tool.

14 USING ACROBAT IN PROFESSIONAL PRINTING

Lesson Overview

In this lesson you'll do the following:

- Create Adobe PDF files suitable for high-resolution printing.

- Preflight an Adobe PDF file to check for quality and consistency.

- View how transparent objects affect a page.

- Configure color management.

- Use Acrobat to generate color separations.

 This lesson will take approximately 60 minutes to complete. Copy the Lesson14 folder onto your hard drive if you haven't already done so.

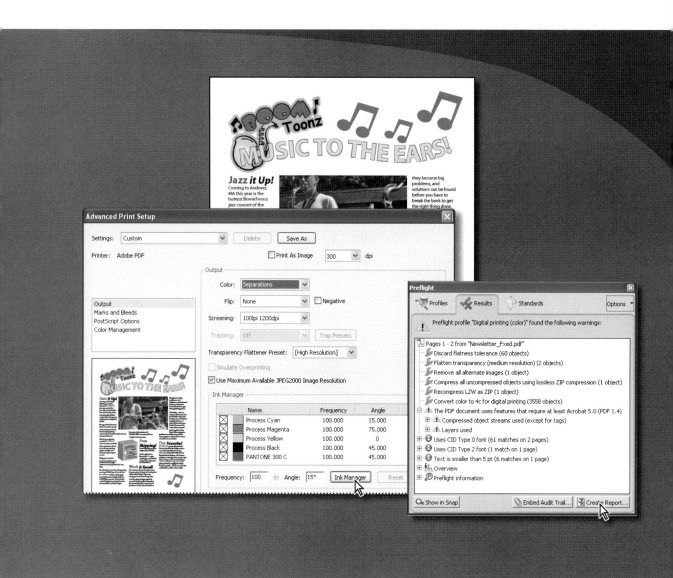

Getting started

● **Note:** The features and tools discussed in this lesson are primarily available only for users of Acrobat Pro and Acrobat Pro Extended. However, you can create Adobe PDF files suitable for high-resolution printing using Acrobat Standard.

In this lesson, you'll select the appropriate PDF settings file to convert a document to Adobe PDF for high-resolution printing. You will then check a converted file using the Acrobat preflight tools and view its color separations. You will also work with a file that contains transparency, and generate a color-separated proof.

Guidelines for creating print-ready PDF files

By the time you submit a PDF file to a printer, the die has been cast. A printer can coax a quality print-out from some less-than-optimal PDF files, but for the most part, the printer is restricted by decisions made during the creative process. Following these guidelines, you can deliver the strongest, highest quality PDF file to a printer:

- **Remember that the end product is only as good as its components.** For high-quality printing, a PDF file must contain the appropriate images, fonts, and other components.

- **Convert only when absolutely necessary.** Every time you convert text, objects, or color, you compromise the integrity of the file. Therefore, the printed product will most closely resemble your original intent if you minimize conversions. Keep text in its original form, as fonts, rather than outlining or rasterizing it. Keep gradients live. Maintain live transparency as long as possible. And don't convert colors from device-independent or high-gamut color spaces, such as RGB, to device-specific or low-gamut color spaces, such as CMYK, unless advised to do so.

- **Use transparency efficiently.** Transparency comes into play any time you apply a blending mode or change the opacity of an object. For the best results, keep transparency live as long as possible; place objects you don't want the flattener to affect (such as text and line objects) above all nearby sources of transparency, preferably on a separate layer; and use the highest quality flattener settings if and when you flatten transparency.

- **Proof and preflight before creating the PDF file.** Early in the workflow, you have more context for problems, and more options for fixing them. Carefully proof the content and formatting before creating a PDF file. Additionally, if the authoring application provides a preflight feature, use it to identify missing fonts, unlinked images, or other issues that could result in problems down the road. The earlier you can identify and fix a problem, the easier and less expensive it is to fix. Certainly, technical problems found while you're still working in the authoring program are easier to fix than problems found in Acrobat or on a printing press.

- **Embed fonts.** To minimize the chance of complications, embed fonts in the PDF file. Read the end user license agreement (EULA) before purchasing a font to ensure it permits embedding.

- **Use the appropriate PDF settings file.** When you create the PDF file, make sure you're using the appropriate settings. The PDF settings file determines how image data is saved, whether fonts are embedded, and whether colors are converted. By default, Acrobat PDFMaker in Microsoft Office creates PDF files using the Standard settings file, which does not meet the requirements for most high-end printing. No matter where you're creating a PDF file for professional printing, ensure that you're using the Press Quality PDF settings file or the settings file recommended by your printer.

- **Create a PDF/X file if appropriate.** PDF/X is a subset of the Adobe PDF specification, and it requires that PDF files meet specific criteria, resulting in more reliable PDF files. Using PDF/X-compliant files eliminates the most common errors in file preparation: fonts that aren't embedded, incorrect color spaces, missing images, and overprinting and trapping issues. PDF/X-1a, PDF/X-3, and PDF/X-4 are the most popular formats; each is designed for a different purpose. Ask your printer whether you should save your file in a PDF/X format.

Creating PDF files for print and prepress

There are many ways to create a PDF file from your original document. No matter which method you choose, however, you need to use the appropriate PDF preset for your intended output. For high-resolution, professional printing, specify the Press Quality PDF preset or a custom PDF preset provided by your printer.

You can create a PDF file from any application using the Adobe PDF printer, which is automatically installed with Acrobat 9. Because we do not know which applications you use, we have not included a file for this exercise. You can use any existing document or create a new document.

1 Open any document in its original application.

2 Choose File > Print.

3 Select Adobe PDF from the list of available printers.

4 In Windows, click Properties, Preferences, or Setup, depending on the application. In Mac OS, choose PDF Options from the pop-up menu beneath the Presets menu to select the PDF conversion settings. (If there is no Presets menu in an application in Mac OS, you may need to select default settings in Distiller. See Acrobat 9 Help for more information.)

5 Choose Press Quality or a custom PDF settings file.

6 On Windows, select Prompt For Adobe PDF Filename from the Adobe PDF Output Folder menu, and then click OK. If you do not select this option, the Adobe PDF printer saves the file in the My Documents folder. (On Mac OS, you will be prompted for a filename and location automatically.)

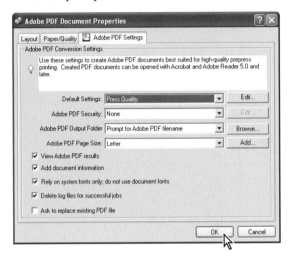

7 Click Print.

8 Specify a filename and folder for the PDF file when prompted, and click Save.

9 Close the PDF file and the original document.

For a description of each of the default PDF presets, see the "Adobe PDF presets" sidebar in this lesson and Adobe Acrobat 9 Help.

Adobe PDF presets

A PDF preset is a group of settings that affect the process of creating a PDF file. These settings are designed to balance file size with quality, depending on how the PDF file will be used. Most predefined presets are shared across Adobe Creative Suite applications, including InDesign, Illustrator, Photoshop, and Acrobat. You can also create and share custom presets for your unique output requirements.

Some PDF presets are not available until you move them from the Extras folder to the Settings folder. For more detailed descriptions of each preset, see Adobe Acrobat 9 Help.

- **High Quality Print** creates PDFs for quality printing on desktop printers and proofing devices.

- **Oversized Pages** creates PDFs suitable for viewing and printing engineering drawings larger than 200 x 200 inches.

- **PDF/A-1b: 2005 (CMYK and RGB)** is used for the long-term preservation (archival) of electronic documents.

- **PDF/X-1a (2001 and 2003)** standards minimize the number of variables in a PDF document to improve reliability. PDF/X-1a files are commonly used for digital ads that will be reproduced on a press.

- **PDF/X-3 (2003)** files are similar to PDF/X-1a files, but they support color-managed workflows and allow some RGB images.

- **PDF/X-4 (2007)** has the same color-management ICC color specifications as PDF/X-3, but it includes support for live transparency.

- **Press Quality** creates PDF files for high-quality print production (for example, for digital printing or for separations to an imagesetter or platesetter).

- **Rich Content PDF** creates accessible PDF files that include tags, hyperlinks, bookmarks, interactive elements, and layers.

- **Smallest File Size** creates PDF files for displaying on the web or an intranet, or for distribution through an email system.

- **Standard** creates PDF files to be printed to desktop printers or digital copiers, published on a CD, or sent to a client as a publishing proof.

Creating PDFs with Distiller

You can also convert PostScript files to PDF using Distiller, which is automatically installed with Acrobat. How you print a document to PostScript depends on the authoring application. Some applications include specific options for printing a PostScript file; in others, you must set up a printer using a port set up to print to file. To create the PDF file, open Distiller, choose the settings you want to use, and then open the PostScript file in Distiller. Distiller converts the document using the settings you've selected.

To start Distiller within Acrobat, choose Advanced > Print Production > Acrobat Distiller.

Preflighting files (Acrobat Pro and Pro Extended)

Before you hand a PDF file off to a print service provider, preflight it to verify that the document meets the criteria for print publishing. Preflighting analyzes a document against the criteria listed in the preflight profile you specify; in addition to identifying potential issues, many preflight profiles contain fixups that can correct problems for you.

Ask your print service provider which preflight profile to use to accurately preflight your document. Many print service providers provide custom preflight profiles to their customers.

Now you'll preflight a newsletter file to determine whether it's ready for digital printing.

1   In Acrobat, choose File > Open and navigate to the Lesson14 folder. Select the Newsletter.pdf file, and click Open.

2   Choose Advanced > Preflight.

The Preflight dialog box lists the available preflight profiles, grouped into categories that describe the tasks they perform.

3 Click the triangle next to Digital Printing And Online Publishing to expand the category.

4 Select the Digital Printing (Color) profile.

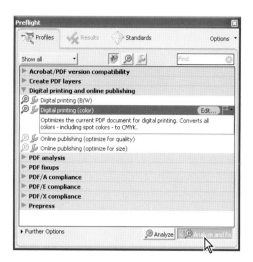

The full magnifying glass icon next to the profile indicates that it performs analysis; the full wrench icon indicates that it also performs fixups. When you select the profile, Acrobat displays its description. If a profile does not include analysis, or checks, the magnifying glass appears as an outline. If a profile does not include fixups, the wrench appears as an outline.

5 Click Analyze And Fix.

6 In the Save As dialog box, name the fixed file **Newsletter_fixed.pdf,** and click Save.

Because the profile applies fixups, it makes changes to the file. Saving the file to a different name ensures that you can return to the original if you need to.

7 Review the results of the preflight.

Acrobat displays the results of the preflight in the Results pane. In this file, Acrobat performed several fixups, applying compression, color conversion, and transparency flattening, as well as other changes.

The Results pane also notes that the PDF document uses features that require PDF 1.4 or later, includes CID Type 0 and CID Type 2 fonts, and contains text smaller than 5 points. If you were professionally printing this document, you might want to contact your print service provider to ensure that these factors won't cause problems when your document is printed.

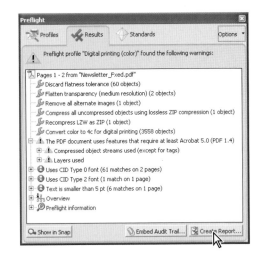

8 Click Create Report.

▶ **Tip:** You can hide or show individual layers that were created in the authoring application, and determine which ones will print. To learn about showing, hiding, and printing layers, see Lesson 13, "Using the Engineering and Technical Features."

9 Click Save to save the report in the Lesson14 folder with the name **Newsletter_ fixed_report.pdf**.

Acrobat creates the preflight summary report as a PDF and opens it in Acrobat.

10 Close the Preflight dialog box and review the preflight summary report.

You can send the preflight summary report to your print service provider if you have any questions about preparing the file.

11 Close the preflight summary report and the Newsletter_fixed.pdf file.

PDF standards

PDF standards are internationally defined standards designed to simplify the exchange of graphic content (PDF/X), archived documents (PDF/A), or engineering workflows (PDF/E). The most widely used standards for a print publishing workflow are PDF/X-1a, PDF/X-3, and PDF/X-4.

You can validate PDF content against PDF/X, PDF/A, or PDF/E criteria in Acrobat 9 Pro or Pro Extended and save a copy of the document as PDF/X, PDF/A, or PDF/E, provided it complies with the specified requirements. You can also save a PDF file as a PDF/X or PDF/A file when you create the file using the Adobe PDF printer or the Export or Save command in an Adobe application.

When you open a PDF/X or PDF/A file in Acrobat 9 or Reader 9, the Standards pane automatically opens to show you information about the file's conformance. If you are using Acrobat 9 Pro or Pro Extended, you can also click Verify in the Standards pane to verify that the PDF file is a valid PDF/X or PDF/A file, using the preflight feature.

To save a copy of an existing PDF file as a PDF/X , PDF/A, or PDF/E file in Acrobat 9 Pro or Pro Extended:

1   Choose Advanced > Preflight.

2   In the Preflight dialog box, click Standards.

3   Select Save As PDF/X, Save As PDF/A, or Save As PDF/E, and then click Continue.

4   Specify the version of the standard, and click Continue.

5   Select a conversion profile and one of the available viewing or printing conditions.

6   If you want to apply corrections during the conversion, select Apply Corrections.

7   To convert the PDF file based on the selected profile and settings, click Save As.

8   Do one of the following, depending on the results of the conversion:

   •   If the conversion succeeds, save the PDF file. A green check mark appears in the Preflight dialog box.

   •   If the conversion fails, view the results in the Results list. A red X appears in the Preflight dialog box.

Custom preflight profiles

You can customize the preflight profiles included with Acrobat, import profiles provided by your print service provider, or create your own custom profiles. To create a new profile, open the Preflight dialog box and choose Options > Create New Preflight Profile. To modify an existing profile, click Edit next to its name, and then, if it's locked, choose Unlocked, and give the custom version a new name. Next, choose a group for the profile. Then, click a category of criteria, and add or remove specific checks or fixups. Save the profile when you're done.

To import a preflight profile, open the Preflight dialog box, and choose Options > Import Preflight Profile. Navigate to the custom profile, which has a .klp extension, and click Open.

To export a profile, select the profile you want to share and then choose Options > Export Preflight Profile. Define the display name of the profile and then specify the location where you want to save it.

Working with transparency (Acrobat Pro and Pro Extended)

Adobe applications let you modify objects in ways that can affect the underlying artwork, creating the appearance of transparency. You may create transparency by using an opacity slider in InDesign, Illustrator, or Photoshop, or by changing the blending mode for a layer or selected object. Transparency also comes into play whenever you create a drop shadow or apply feathering. Adobe applications can keep transparency "live," or editable, as you move documents from one application to another, but transparency must typically be flattened before printing. It's important to know which areas of your document are affected by transparency, and how those areas will print.

Previewing transparency

Note: If your print service provider is using a RIP that includes the Adobe PDF Print Engine, you may not need to flatten transparency.

When you print to most printers, transparency is flattened. The flattening process separates overlapping areas of artwork into discrete sections that are either converted into separate vector shapes or rasterized pixels to retain the look of the transparency.

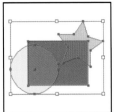 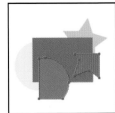

Objects before flattening   Objects after flattening
(Overlapping art is divided when flattened.)

Before flattening occurs, you can determine how much of the transparent area remains vector, and how much becomes rasterized. Some effects, such as drop shadows, must be rasterized in order to print correctly.

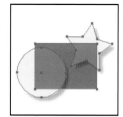 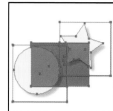

What is rasterization?

Rasterization is the process of changing vector objects, including fonts, into bitmap images to display or print them. The number of pixels per inch (ppi) is referred to as the *resolution*. The higher the resolution in a raster image, the better the quality. When flattening occurs, some objects may need to be rasterized, depending upon flattening settings.

Vector Object   Rasterized at 72 ppi   Rasterized at 300 ppi

If you received a PDF file created by someone else, you may not know if or where transparency has been applied. The Acrobat transparency preview shows you where transparency is used in a document. This feature can also help you determine the best flattener settings to use when printing the document.

You'll preview transparency in the newsletter.pdf file.

1 Open the Newsletter.pdf file from the Lesson14 folder.

2 Navigate to page 2 of the newsletter. If the entire page is not visible, press Ctrl+0 (Windows) or Command+0 (Mac OS) to fit the entire page in the window.

3 Choose Advanced > Print Production > Flattener Preview.

The Flattener Preview shows a preview of page 2 of the newsletter on the right side of the dialog box.

Specifying flattener preview settings

1   In the Flattener Preview dialog box, choose All Affected Objects from the Highlight menu. The photo and three musical notes are highlighted in red, indicating that they have transparent properties or interact with objects that have transparent properties.

2   Choose High Resolution from the Preset dialog box in the Transparency Flattener Preset Options area. The preset determines how much of the artwork remains vector and how much is rasterized. For professional printing, use the High Resolution preset unless your print service provider advises you differently.

3   Click the left end of the Raster/Vector Balance slider or type 0 in the box. Then click Refresh, and choose All Affected Objects from the Highlight menu. Everything on the page is highlighted in red, indicating that everything would be rasterized at this setting.

4   Make other selections to see how the settings affect the document. When you are finished, click the close button in the upper-right (Windows) or upper-left (Mac OS) corner of the window to close the Flattener Preview window without applying your settings.

▶ **Tip:** You can find more information on transparency output issues on the Adobe website at www.adobe.com.

If you wanted to use the selected transparency flattener settings when printing, you would click Apply in the Flattener Preview dialog box.

About flattening options

- **Line Art And Text Resolution:** Because line art and text involve a sharper contrast around the edges, they need to be rasterized at a higher resolution to maintain a high-quality appearance. A resolution of 300 ppi is sufficient when proofing, but this should be increased to a higher resolution for final high-quality output. A resolution of 1200 ppi is typically sufficient for high-quality output.

- **Gradient And Mesh Resolution:** Gradients and meshes, which are sometimes called *blends*, will be rasterized, and should have a resolution appropriate for your specific printer. For proofing to a general purpose laser printer or inkjet printer, the default setting of 150 ppi is appropriate. For printing to most high-quality output devices, such as a film or plate output device, a resolution of 300 ppi is usually sufficient.

- **Convert All Text To Outlines** ensures that the width of all text in the artwork stays consistent. However, converting small fonts to outlines can make them appear noticeably thicker and less readable (especially when printing on lower-end printing systems).

- **Convert All Strokes To Outlines** ensures that the width of all strokes in the artwork stays consistent. Selecting this option, however, causes thin strokes to appear slightly thicker (especially when printing on lower-end printing systems).

- **Clip Complex Regions** ensures that the boundaries between vector artwork and rasterized artwork fall along object paths. This option reduces stitching artifacts that result when part of an object is rasterized while another part of the object remains in vector form (as determined by the Raster/Vector slider). Keep in mind that selecting this option may result in extremely complex clipping paths, which take significant time to compute, and can cause errors when printing.

- **Preserve Overprint** blends the color of transparent artwork with the background color to create an overprint effect. Overprinted colors are two or more inks printed on top of each other. For example, when a cyan ink prints over a yellow ink, the resulting overprint is a green color. Without overprinting, the underlying yellow would not be printed, resulting in a cyan color.

Setting up color management

Using color management can help you achieve consistent color throughout your workflow. Color profiles describe the characteristics of each device. Color management uses those profiles to map the colors possible for one device, such as a computer monitor, with the colors possible on another device, such as a printer.

1   Choose Edit > Preferences (Windows) or Acrobat > Preferences (Mac OS) and select Color Management in the list on the left.

● **Note:** You can synchronize color management settings for all the Adobe Creative Suite applications in Bridge. See Bridge Help for more information.

2   From the Settings menu, choose North America Prepress 2. With this setting, Acrobat will display colors as they generally appear when printed using North American printing standards.

The setting you select determines which color working spaces are used by the application, what happens when you open and import files with embedded profiles, and how the color management system converts colors. To view a description of a setting, select the setting and then position the pointer over the setting name. The description appears at the bottom of the dialog box.

ACE (Adobe Color Engine) is the same color management engine used by other Adobe graphics software, so you can be confident that color management settings applied in Acrobat will mirror those applied in your other Adobe applications.

3   Click OK to close the Preferences dialog box.

Previewing your print job

You've already previewed how transparency will print. Now you'll preview color separations, and look at individual objects to verify their resolution. You'll also perform a soft proof; that is, you'll proof the document on the screen without having to print it out.

Previewing color separations

To reproduce color and continuous-tone images, printers usually separate artwork into four plates (called process colors)—one plate for each of the cyan, magenta, yellow, and black portions of the image. You can also include custom pre-mixed inks, called spot colors, which require their own plates. When inked with the appropriate color and printed in register with one another, these colors combine to reproduce the original artwork. The plates are called color separations.

You will preview color separations from this document using the Output Preview dialog box.

1 Choose View > Zoom > Fit Page.

2 Navigate to page 2 of the newsletter, if it's not already visible.

3 Choose Advanced > Print Production > Output Preview.

4 Select Separations from the Preview menu.

The Separations area of the dialog box lists all the inks that are included in this document for printing. There are four process inks (cyan, magenta, yellow, and black) and one spot color (PANTONE 300 C).

5 Drag the Output Preview dialog box to the side so that you can see the document, and in the Output Preview dialog box, deselect every ink except PANTONE 300 C. The items that remain on the page use the selected ink.

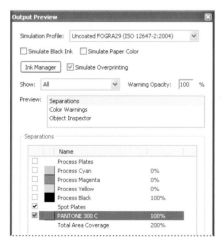

Tip: If you wanted to remap a spot color to a process color, in order to limit the number of plates, and thus the expense, of a print job, you could use the Ink Manager, also available in the Output Preview dialog box.

6 Deselect PANTONE 300 C, and select Process Magenta. Only those items that would print on the magenta plate appear.

7 Select all the inks again.

Soft-proofing your document

You can use the Output Preview dialog box to *soft-proof* a document, so that you can see onscreen how your document will look when printed. Use the simulation settings to approximate the color.

1 Choose U.S. Web Coated (SWOP) v2 from the Simulation Profile menu.

2 Go to page 1 of the newsletter.

3 Choose Apple RGB from the Simulation Profile menu.

4 Choose Adobe RGB from the Simulation Profile menu.

As you change the simulation profile, color shifts on the monitor. When you soft-proof a document, select the simulation profile that matches your output device. If you use accurately calibrated ICC profiles and have calibrated your monitor, the onscreen preview should match the final output. If you haven't calibrated your monitor or your profiles, the preview may not provide an exact match. For information about calibrating your monitor and profiles, see Acrobat 9 Help.

5 Choose U.S. Web Coated (SWOP) v2 from the Simulation Profile menu again.

Inspecting objects in a PDF file

You can take a closer look at individual graphics and text in a PDF file using the Object Inspector. The Object Inspector displays the image resolution, color mode, transparency, and other information about the selected object.

You'll check the resolution of the image on page 2.

1 Select Object Inspector in the Preview menu.

2 Scroll to page 2, and click the image of the waterside village.

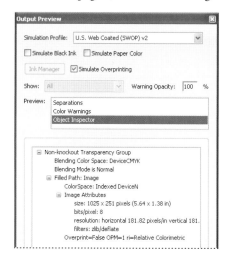 

► **Tip:** Overprinting is automatically displayed accurately in PDF/X files in all versions of Acrobat 9 and Adobe Reader 9. You can change the settings to display overprinting accurately for all files in the Acrobat Preferences dialog box.

The Object Inspector lists attributes of the image you clicked, including the image resolution: 181.82 pixels by 181.82 pixels.

3 Close the Output Preview dialog box.

Advanced printing controls

In this section, you'll use the advanced printing features of Acrobat 9 Pro and Pro Extended to produce color separations, add printing marks, and control how transparent and complex items are imaged.

1 Choose File > Print.

2 In the Print dialog box, choose a PostScript printer. If you do not have a PostScript printer available, choose Adobe PDF from the Name menu.

Some advanced printing options, including color separations, are available only for PostScript printers. The Adobe PDF printer uses a PostScript printer driver, so it will give you access to the options covered in this lesson.

3 In the Print Range area, select All.

4 In the Page Handling area, select Fit To Printable Area from the Page Scaling menu.

The Fit To Printable Area option reduces or enlarges each page to fit the paper size.

5 Click Advanced.

There are four options on the left side of the dialog box: Output, Marks And Bleeds, PostScript Options, and Color Management.

6   Select Output, and then choose Separations from the Color menu.

7   Click the Ink Manager button in the Ink Manager area.

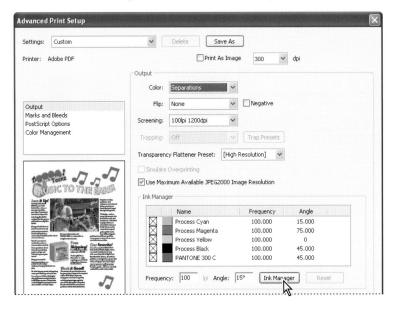

8   In the Ink Manager dialog box, select the icon to the left of the PANTONE 300 C name. The icon changes into a CMYK color swatch, indicating that this color will be printed as a process color, using the cyan, magenta, yellow, and black plates.

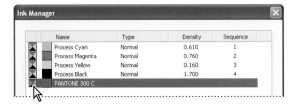

Acrobat will mix cyan and black to simulate the dedicated ink that is used to produce the PANTONE 300 C spot color. In many cases, it is more cost-effective to use a mixture of CMYK inks than to add an entirely new spot color ink.

To globally convert all spot colors to their CMYK equivalents, select Convert All Spots To Process.

9   Click OK to close the Ink Manager dialog box.

10 In the Advanced Print Setup dialog box, select Marks And Bleeds from the list on the left. Select All Marks to enable trim marks, bleed marks, registration marks, color bars, and page information to print on each plate, outside the edges of the document.

11 Select Color Management from the list on the left.

12 Choose Acrobat Color Management from the Color Handling menu.

13 Choose Working CMYK: U.S. Web Coated (SWOP) v2 from the Color Profile menu.

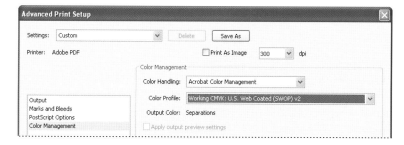

The color profile you select should match the device you will be printing to.

14 Click Save As at the top of the Advanced Print Setup dialog box, and save your settings using the name **Newsletter**. Then, click OK.

Saved settings are added to the settings menu, so you can re-use them for future print jobs without having to re-enter the settings you use for certain jobs or specific output devices.

15 Click OK to exit the Advanced Print Setup dialog box. Then either click OK to print this document, or click Cancel if you prefer not to print at this time.

16 Close the document and quit Acrobat.

Review questions

1 What is the Adobe PDF printer, and how do you use it?

2 What problems can Preflight detect within a PDF?

3 What is a spot color and how can you remap it to a process color?

Review answers

1 Adobe PDF printer is a printer installed by Acrobat 9 Standard, Acrobat 9 Pro, or Acrobat 9 Pro Extended. You can use it to print to a PDF file from any application. Simply choose it as the printer in the application's Print dialog box.

To change settings for the Adobe PDF printer in Windows, click Setup, Properties, or Preferences, depending on the application. To change settings in Mac OS, choose PDF Options from the pop-up menu beneath the Presets menu.

2 Use the Preflight command to check for all areas of concern within a PDF. For example, if you are sending a PDF file to a professional printer, preflight the document to verify that fonts are embedded, graphics have the appropriate resolution, and colors are correct.

3 A spot color is a special premixed ink that is used instead of, or in addition to, CMYK process inks, and that requires its own printing plate on a printing press. If absolute color accuracy is not critical, and it is not practical to print a spot color plate as well as CMYK plates, you can remap the spot color to a process color using the Ink Manager. In the Advanced Print dialog box, select Separations, and then click Ink Manager. In the Ink Manager, click the icon to the left of the spot color to remap it to a process color for the print job.

15 WORKING WITH 3D IN PDF FILES

Lesson Overview

In this lesson, you'll do the following:

- Explore the Acrobat 3D toolbar.

- Manipulate a 3D model.

- Explore the Model Tree.

- Convert a 3D design file to 3D PDF and explore the different conversion settings for creating 3D PDF files.

- View product manufacturing information associated with a 3D model.

- Export dimensioning and tolerancing information.

 This lesson will take approximately 60-90 minutes to complete. Copy the Lesson15 folder onto your hard drive if you haven't already done so.

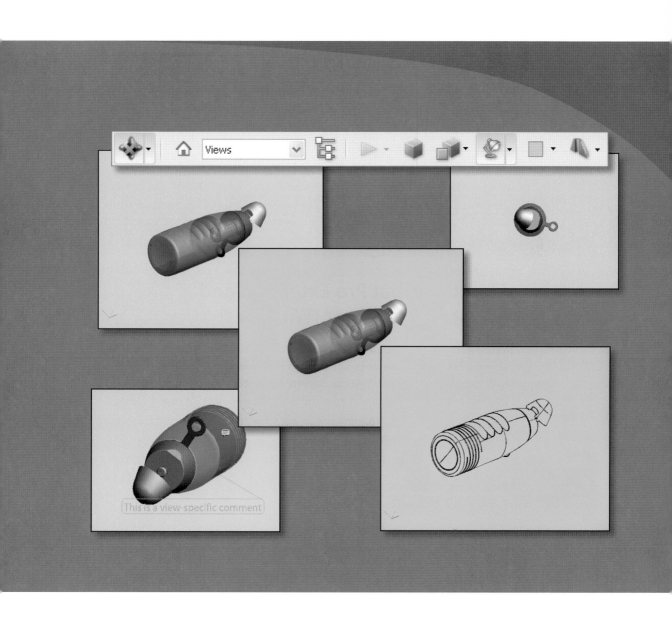

This is a view-specific comment

Adobe Acrobat 9 offers an improved 3D design collaboration process combined with powerful CAD data interoperability. Acrobat Pro Extended (Windows) allows users to rapidly convert virtually any CAD file into highly compressed, more secure Adobe PDF files that can be used by customers, suppliers, and co-workers to review and mark up 3D designs using the free Adobe Reader software. And the exact geometry in these Adobe PDF files can be leveraged by manufacturers for downstream CAD, CAM, or CAE-based processes without the need for expensive CAD translators.

3D models can also be used to create content-rich documentation. Technical writers, illustrators, and graphic designers can create 2D vector art and rasterized illustrations from 3D CAD files. They can incorporate 3D models into PDF files, creating rich, interactive documents.

Because the PDF files retain the appearance of your original documents, you don't need to worry about losing document quality. Your PDF files can be viewed, manipulated, and interrogated on Windows, Mac OS, or UNIX using the free Adobe Reader software, so anyone (with your permission) can work with your PDF files without having the source applications.

About Acrobat Pro Extended and Adobe 3D Reviewer (Windows)

Adobe Acrobat Pro Extended (Windows) allows you to create 3D PDF files, add 3D models to PDF documents, and interact with existing 3D content using the 3D toolbar and a Model Tree. You can convert 3D content directly from supported 3D CAD files or you can capture content from within your 3D CAD applications.

When you install Acrobat Pro Extended, Adobe 3D Reviewer is installed automatically. You can use 3D Reviewer to edit most 3D models in native file formats and in PDF. 3D Reviewer is particularly useful if you want to change or remove entities from a 3D model but don't have the source application installed. Right-click an embedded 3D model in a PDF file, and choose Edit In 3D Reviewer to open that model for editing.

To create a PDF file from a file open in 3D Reviewer, simply choose File > Export and export the file to PDF.

Users of Adobe Reader can interact with 3D models, create and save camera views, capture product views, and use the Model Tree. If the creator of a 3D-enhanced PDF has extended usage right, users of Adobe Reader can also use comment and mark-up tools and use the 3D measurement tools.

Working with 3D content in PDF files

You'll open a 3D PDF file and see how easily you can work with the rich 3D content without the need for complex CAD, CAM, or CAE applications.

1 Start Acrobat.

2 Choose File > Open. Navigate to the Lesson15 folder, select the Aquo_Bottle.pdf file, and click Open.

The file opens in the Acrobat document window.

Working with the 3D toolbar

The default Acrobat work area is streamlined to ensure easy access to the tools you'll use most often as you work with PDF files. In this part of the lesson, you'll use the tools on the 3D toolbar to turn parts around as if you were holding them in your hands, and to create views that you can use across files.

You interact with models using the 3D toolbar and the Model Tree.

1 Click on the bottle in the work area to activate the 3D model. (The Hand tool (✋) changes to a pointing finger when it is over a 3D model.) The 3D toolbar appears automatically across the top of the model. When you shift the focus away from the 3D content, the toolbar disappears.

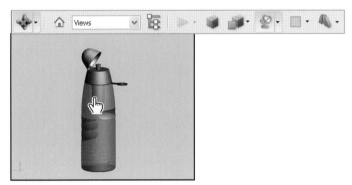

You cannot move the 3D toolbar but you can hide it.

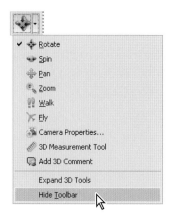

2 To hide the 3D toolbar, click the arrow next to the Rotate tool (⬦) to expand the menu, and choose Hide Toolbar.

3 To show the toolbar, right-click (Windows) or Control-click (Mac OS) on the 3D model and choose Tools > Show Toolbar.

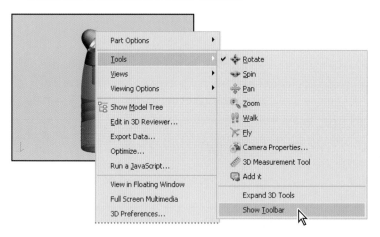

The 3D toolbar has several types of tools. You use the tools hidden under the Rotate tool on the left of the toolbar to manipulate the 3D model. You use the Default View button, the Views menu, and the Model Tree button to manage views of the model. And you use the buttons on the right of the toolbar to control animations embedded in the 3D file, toggle between perspective and orthographic projections, change the rendering mode, lighting, and background color, and show and hide cross-sections.

You can show the names of the tools or buttons by resting the pointer over the icons on the 3D toolbar.

4   Hover the pointer over the leftmost tool on the 3D toolbar. The tool tip shows the name of the tool—the Rotate tool.

Note: The 3D Tool, which is used to insert 3D models or animations into PDF documents, is located on the Multimedia toolbar in Acrobat.

5   Click the arrow next to the Rotate tool to show the hidden tools.

6   Choose Expand 3D Tools to add these hidden tools to the toolbar. (You can hide the additional tools at anytime by right-clicking on the 3D content in the document pane, and choosing Tools > Collapse 3D tools.) For now, leave the additional tools on the 3D toolbar.

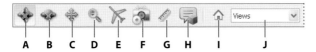

A. Rotate tool B. Spin tool C. Pan tool D. Zoom tool E. Fly tool
F. Camera Properties G. 3D Measurement tool H. Add 3D Commer
tool I. Default View J. Views Menu

You manipulate a 3D model by selecting the appropriate tool and dragging with your pointer in the document pane. When you manipulate a model, it may help to think of viewing the stationary 3D model from a camera's perspective.

A tool stays selected until you choose another tool or until you click the Hand tool on the Acrobat toolbar.

Manipulating a 3D model

Now you'll manipulate the 3D model.

1   If necessary, move your pointer over the 3D model to show the 3D toolbar again.

2   On the Acrobat 3D toolbar, click the Rotate tool (✥) to select it, and then drag your pointer in the work area to rotate the model. Experiment by dragging your pointer down, up, and across and watching the degree and direction of rotation of the model.

3   To spin the model, select the Spin tool (✥). Drag up and down, and from side to side. Notice that the vertical up and down motion is limited. Spinning turns a 3D model parallel to two fixed axes, the x-axis and the z-axis. Rotation with the Rotate tool is not constrained in this way.

Tip: You can use the Hand tool to rotate an object if Enable Selection For The Hand Tool is selected in the 3D & Multimedia Preferences.

4   To pan the model, select the Pan tool (✥). Drag up and down, and across the document pane. The model moves vertically and horizontally.

You can also pan with the Rotate tool by holding down the Ctrl key as you drag. With a double-button mouse, holding down both buttons allows you to pan.

5   To zoom in and out, select the Zoom tool (🔍). Drag up in the document pane to make the image larger; drag down to make the image smaller.

6   Select the Fly tool (✈) to navigate through the model while maintaining the surface orientation. To rotate the camera view, move your pointer into the document pane, click the left mouse button, and drag to turn the camera view.

The Camera Properties button (📷) opens the Camera Properties dialog box, where you set the camera angle, alignment, and other properties that define the lens through which the 3D model is viewed.

You use the 3D Measurement tool (📏) to measure part sizes and distances in 3D models. The enhanced 3D Measurement tool in Acrobat 9 supports four types of measurements: perpendicular distance between two straight edges, linear distance between two points, the radius of circular edges, and the angle between two edges (or three points). When the 3D Measurement tool is selected, as you move the pointer over the 3D model, specific points and edges are highlighted. Measurements are associated with specific views and are added to the view hierarchy in the Model Tree. Measurement markups are preserved after the document is closed. You can also convert measurements to comments.

The 3D Comment tool (💬) allows you to add a sticky note that is view-specific.

7   Click the Default View button (🏠) to return to the default view of the model.

Accessing the Walk tool

The Walk tool, used primarily when working with architectural 3D models, pivots the model horizontally around the scene when you drag horizontally in the document pane and moves forward or backward in the scene when you drag vertically. The elevation is constant.

1   To access the Walk tool (🚶), right-click on the 3D model, and choose Tools > Walk.

2   Drag in the model area to see how the Walk tool works.

If you lose sight of the model at any time, click the Default View button to return to the opening view.

Using the Views menu

The Views menu on the 3D toolbar lists any views defined for the current 3D model. At a minimum, most designers will create the standard views—Left, Top, Front, Right, Bottom, and Back.

Note: Users of Adobe Reader and Acrobat Standard can use views; only users of Acrobat Pro and Pro Extended can create views.

1   To switch to a predefined view of a model, expand the Views menu and select a view.

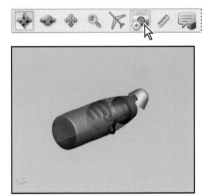

2   When you are finished, click the Default View button ( ) to return to the opening view of the 3D model.

Now you'll create and save a camera view that you can apply to other 3D models.

3   First, select the Rotate tool ( ) and drag over the 3D model to create any new view. Then click the Camera Properties button ( ) on the 3D toolbar to open the Camera Properties dialog box.

Camera properties define the precise angle and positioning for a view of an object. These properties make up a camera view that can be used across files. For example, if you need the same view of a number of models, you can create a camera view that you can use across all your model files. For Alignment, you can select Target to align the camera properties to the target position, or you can select Camera And Target to align the camera properties to both the camera direction and the target position.

4   Leave Target as the selection.

5   Click Select Model and then click the 3D model in the document to record the current camera position in the dialog box. You may need to drag the dialog box away from the model.

6   Click Save As, and name your camera view. We named the view **Test**.

7   Click OK to save the view.

8   In the Camera Properties dialog box, click Save Camera View, and click OK to clear the View Properties dialog box. Click the close button to close the Camera Properties dialog box.

● **Note:** Any view that you save retains the object's conditions for that view (background color and illustration mode, for example). Reverting to the default view returns all the object's conditions to their original status.

9   Display the Views menu and notice that Test is displayed as a view. You can test the view by selecting any other view and then selecting the Test view.

Your newly created view is also available across files.

10 Choose File > Open, and open the Bottle_Mold.pdf file. Click the 3D model to open the 3D toolbar. Click the Camera Properties button. In the Camera Properties dialog box, expand the Camera Preset menu, and select Test. Click Save Camera View. Click OK to clear the message box, and click the close button to close the Camera Properties dialog box. Expand the Views menu and select Test. Note that the view is the view you defined for the water bottle. Close the Bottle_Mold.pdf file when you are finished. You don't need to save changes.

Acrobat Pro and Pro Extended users can create a new view of a 3D model at any time by clicking the Create View button in the Views pane of the Model Tree. When you are finished working with your model, you can delete any views that are not useful. You can even create views when you create your 3D PDF file. In the Acrobat 3D Conversion dialog box, select the Add Default Views option, and select views from the adjacent pop-up menu. Also, if you add a comment, measurement, or annotation to your 3D model, a new view associated with that comment, measurement, or annotation is created automatically.

Using the viewing options

The buttons on the right of the 3D toolbar allow you to control any animations embedded in the 3D file, toggle between perspective and orthographic projections, change the rendering mode, lighting, and background color, and show and hide cross-sections.

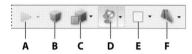

A. Play Animation **B.** Projection Mode **C.** Model Render Mode **D.** Enable Extra Lighting **E.** Background Color **F.** Toggle Cross Section

● **Note:** The Play Animation button is available only if the model has an associated animation.

You can change the background color of your model.

1 In the Aquo_Bottle.pdf document window, click the arrow next to the Background Color button (▢) to open the Background Color swatch. Select a color swatch, or choose Other Color to define a custom color for the space surrounding the 3D object. We chose orange. Note that this changes only the background color on your monitor.

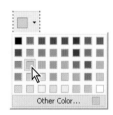

2 Click the arrow next to the Model Render Mode button (🔲) to show the menu.

The Model Render Mode menu lets you specify how the 3D shape appears.

3 Choose Illustration to see a line art version of the 3D model.

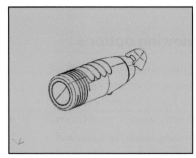

4 When you have finished experimenting with the rendering mode, choose Solid from the Model Render Mode menu. You can also restore the original background if you wish. Click the arrow next to the Background Color button (■) to open the Background Color swatch, and select gray.

Next, you'll change the lighting effects using the Enable Extra Lighting menu.

5 Expand the Enable Extra Lighting menu (🕯). Experiment to get the visual effects you want. When you are finished, choose White Lights from the pop-up menu.

The Toggle Cross Section menu allows you to show and hide cross-sections of the object as well as create your own cross-sections.

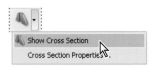

6 Click the arrow to expand the Toggle Cross Section menu (🔪) and choose Show Cross Section. A horizontal cross-section of the model is created automatically (Z-axis).

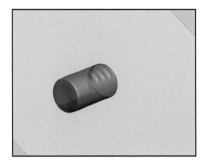

7 Click the arrow to expand the Toggle Cross Section menu again and choose Cross Section Properties.

You change the cross-section view in this dialog box.

8 Drag the dialog box to the side so that you can see the model. (Drag the dialog box by its title bar.)

9 In the Cross Section Properties dialog box, select the Enable Cross Section option. Choose Y-Axis. Select the color box next to the Show Intersections option and choose the highlight color. We chose blue. Select a color for the cutting plane in the same way. We chose red.

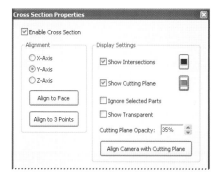

▶ **Tip:** To define a custom cutting plane, select the Align to 3 Points option in the Cross Section Properties dialog box, and click on three points on your 3D model. If necessary, use the Position and Orientation sliders to refine the cutting plane.

10 Click Save Section View to save your cross-section view. Click OK to close the View Properties dialog box. After you have saved the values, you can access this view from the Views menu on the 3D toolbar. Click the close button to close the dialog box.

Now you'll rename the cross-section view that you just created—SectionView*n*. You'll rename the view using the Manage Views command in the Views menu.

11 Click the arrow to expand the Views menu, and choose Manage Views. You may need to move the pointer over the 3D model in the document pane to show the 3D toolbar.

12 In the Manage Views dialog box, select the name of the view you just created (SectionView*n*). Select the name in the text box next to the Rename button, type **CrossSection**, and click Rename.

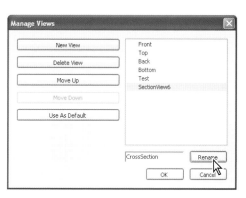

13 Click OK to close the dialog box.

You've created and named a view. (You can also create and name views using the Options menu in the Views pane.)

Now you'll test your new view.

14 Click the model to activate it. Use any of the tools on the toolbar to change the view. We rotated the model to bring the cross-section plane to the front.

15 Expand the Views menu, and choose CrossSection to return to the view you just created.

▶ **Tip:** If you want a view to be available for use with other files, use the Camera Properties button to save the view.

16 Click the Toggle Cross Section button to turn off the cross-section feature.

17 Click the Default View (⌂) button to return to the default view of the model.

18 Choose File > Save As, and save the file using the name **New_Bottle.pdf**.

Showing and hiding parts with the Model Tree

Now you'll see how the Model Tree enables you to work with parts or views of the model.

The Model Tree opens in the navigation pane, to the left of the document pane in the work area. You use the Model Tree to show, hide, or isolate parts in the 3D model, to create views that you can return to, and to display any metadata that was included for the 3D model in the authoring program. (Metadata could include object properties such as mass, material, and center of gravity, for example.)

1 To open the Model Tree, do one of the following:

- Click the Model Tree button (▦) in the navigation pane to the left of the document pane.

- Click the Toggle Model Tree button (▦) on the 3D toolbar.

- Right-click (Windows) or Control-click (Mac OS) the 3D model and choose Show Model Tree from the context menu.

The Model Tree has three panes.

- The Structure pane at the top of the
  Model Tree shows the tree structure
  of the 3D object. You expand the
  model's structure by clicking the plus
  sign or arrow next to any component.
  Selecting any part in the Structure
  pane highlights the part in the 3D
  model. Selecting any part in the model
  automatically expands the structure
  and highlights the part's label in the
  Structure pane. A blue check mark
  indicates that the part is visible in the
  3D model.

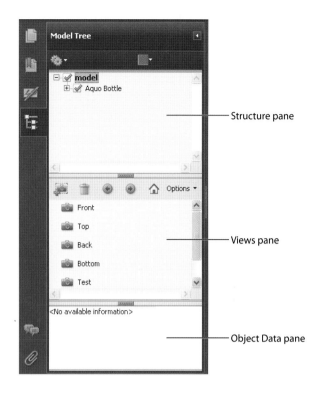

Structure pane

Views pane

Object Data pane

If product manufacturing information
(PMI) has been added to the model, it will
appear as a group of items on the same
hierarchical level as its related object or
assembly.

- The Views pane in the middle lists the
  defined views of the model. You can
  define new views and edit existing
  views. For example, after you isolate
  and rotate a part, you can save that
  particular view. Any views created
  with the Camera Properties tool are
  also listed in this pane.

- The Object Data pane at the bottom
  displays properties or any available
  metadata for the object or part selected
  in the model. You cannot edit this
  information for 3D objects in Acrobat.

Now you'll use the Model Tree to hide the outer cover of the water bottle to show
the filter.

2   In the document window, click the 3D model to automatically open the 3D
    toolbar.

3 In the upper pane of the Model Tree (the Structure pane), click the plus sign or triangle next to Aquo_Bottle to expand the list of parts.

4 If necessary, widen the navigation pane by dragging its right border to the right. Enlarge the Structure pane by dragging the lower border down.

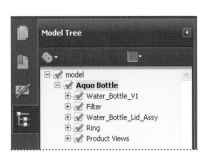 

Notice that all the parts in the Structure pane are selected. Selected parts are visible in the 3D model in the work area.

5 Deselect Ring to remove the check mark. This hides the ring around the neck of the water bottle. You may need to scroll down in the Structure pane.

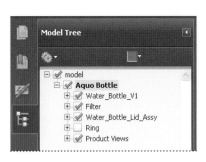 

6 Select Ring to restore the check mark and display the ring.

Selecting parts

You can easily identify a part in the 3D model by selecting the part in the Structure pane.

1　In the Structure pane, expand the structure, and select the label Water _Bottle_ Lid_Assy. The water bottle cap assembly is highlighted in the 3D model.

You can change the highlight color using the color swatch at the top of the structure pane.

2　At the top of the Model Tree, click the arrow next to the color swatch. Choose a color from the color swatches or create a custom color. We chose blue.

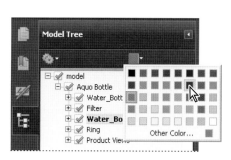

You can also identify a part in the model by selecting the part in the 3D model in the document pane.

3　In the 3D model in the document pane, select the body of the water bottle.

4　In the Structure pane, notice that the Water_Bottle_V1 node label is highlighted. This is the part you selected in the 3D model.

Zooming in on a part

Now you'll zoom in on a part you want to work with.

- In the Structure pane, if necessary, expand the Water_Bottle_Lid_Assy component. Then select the Water_Bottle_Nozzle label. Right-click (Windows) or Control-click (Mac OS) to open the context menu, and choose Zoom To Part.

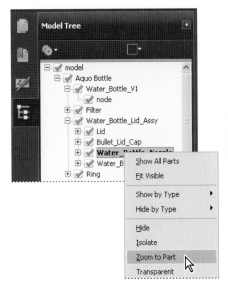
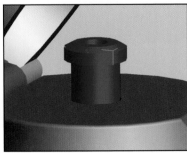

▶ **Tip:** When you use Zoom To Part, the focus changes from the model to the part, which allows you to rotate around the center of the part versus the center of the model.

You can also use the Zoom tool on the 3D toolbar to zoom in on a part.

Isolating a part

Now you'll isolate the nozzle so that you can see it more clearly and manipulate it independently of the rest of the model.

The nozzle should still be selected in the work area and in the Structure pane.

- Click the arrow next to the Options button at the top of the Structure pane to expand the menu, and choose Isolate.

All the other components are hidden, leaving only the nozzle displayed. You can use any of the tools on the 3D toolbar to manipulate this one part. (Simply move the pointer into the work area to display the 3D toolbar.)

Showing and hiding parts

Now you'll show and hide parts to see details of the filter.

1 In the 3D toolbar, expand the Views menu, and choose Front. In the Structure pane of the Model Tree, select the Water_Bottle_V1 label. Right-click (Windows) or Control-click (Mac OS) to open the context menu, and click Hide.

Now you are viewing only the filter and the cap assembly.

2 Use any of the tools on the 3D toolbar to manipulate the model.

3 When you are finished, click the Default View button (⌂) on the 3D toolbar.

Reviewing and commenting on 3D models

For the most part, reviewing and commenting on 3D PDF files is very much the same as reviewing and commenting on any PDF file. With 3D PDF files, however, your collaborators can explore all aspects of the 3D model, from hidden internal structures to exploded animations. They can rotate, cross-section, and measure parts while adding their comments in notes, drawings, and other markups.

If you add comments or markups to 3D files using the Acrobat comment and markup tools, comments and markups apply to all views. However, if you add comments using the Add 3D Comment button (📝) on the 3D toolbar, Acrobat creates a new view associated with the comment or markup. When you change the view, the comment is hidden in the work area.

1 On the Acrobat Tasks toolbar (not the 3D toolbar), click the Comment button (☺) and select Add Sticky Note. In the sticky note box, type in a message. We typed **This comment applies to all views**.

You can close the note and you can drag the note icon anywhere in the document pane.

2 Expand the Views menu on the 3D toolbar and notice that there is no view associated with the sticky note. Select several views in turn, and note that the sticky note is always visible.

3 Select the Rotate tool on the 3D toolbar, and drag the model to a new view. The view is not important, but it shouldn't be a view currently listed in the Views menu.

4 On the 3D toolbar, select the Add 3D Comment tool (🖐). Your pointer changes to a crosshair. Move the pointer over the model and double-click anywhere on the 3D model. In the Enter Comment String box, enter your message. We typed **This is a view-specific comment**. Click OK to close the box.

Notice that a new view is created for the comment. You can add multiple comments to a view, or you can add comments to different views of a model.

5 Click the Default View button (⌂) on the 3D toolbar to return to the opening view.

Now you'll see how the comments appear in the Views pane of the Model Tree.

6 If necessary, drag the upper margin of the Views pane to enlarge the pane. Scroll down to see 3DCommentView*n*. Click the camera icon (📷) to go to the view you annotated. Click the comment icon in the Views pane to highlight the comment in the document pane. The comment is also displayed in the Object Data pane.

7 To review all the comments added using the Comment button in the Tasks toolbar and the Add 3D Comments tool, click the Comments button at the bottom of the navigation pane to open the Comments pane.

8 Close any open files when you are finished. You do not need to save your work.

For information on using the Comments panel, deleting comments, and editing comments, see Lesson 9, "Using Acrobat in a Review Cycle."

The remainder of this lesson is for users of Acrobat Pro Extended.

Converting 3D design files to PDF (Acrobat Pro Extended)

From drawing board to manufacturing plant, Adobe PDF can ease the flow of computer aided design, manufacturing, and engineering (CAD, CAM, and CAE) information. You can quickly convert a design file to an Adobe PDF file that is a fraction of the original file size, while retaining exact geometric dimensioning and tolerancing and other product specifications. You can even add product manufacturing information (PMI). Manufacturers and suppliers can manipulate and interrogate your design without installing the original CAD application or a CAD translator. All they need is the free Adobe Reader. They can view product manufacturing information and export geometry to a standard file format that can be reused in CAM applications to cut, build, and assemble parts.

Acrobat supports major design and modeling applications.

How you create 3D PDF files depends very much on your workflow.

If you have the design application

You can use the Print Screen command in your design application (SolidWorks®, CATIA®, and Pro/ENGINEER®, for example) in conjunction with the 3D Capture utility to create a 3D PDF file.

> **Note:** With Capture, the original structure is not preserved. The hierarchy is flattened into one layer; parent-child relationships are not retained.

If you don't have the design application or don't have the design application running

You can use the Create > PDF From File command in Acrobat, the Create task button, or you can simply drag a supported 3D application file into the Acrobat window or onto the Acrobat desktop icon. In most cases, you don't have to have the original source application on your system.

If your 3D model is in a format that Acrobat doesn't support

You can probably open the 3D design file in 3D Reviewer and save it in a supported format, such as U3D or RH.

Converting your PDF file from within the authoring application, using the Create command, or dragging the file into the Acrobat window gives you the most options for representing the 3D model and preserving the original file structure. Relationships between parts, subparts, and assemblies look the same as in the original 3D file.

If a CAD file includes 2-dimensional (2D) drawings with layers

You must use PDFMaker to convert the files to PDF if you wish to retain the layers. If your 2D files do not contain layers or if you don't wish to retain the layers, you can convert 2D drawings to PDF using Acrobat Distiller. From within your software application, use the Print command and choose the Adobe PDF printer. You do not have to launch Distiller manually.

Dragging a file onto the Acrobat icon

In this part of the lesson, you'll convert a file that you want to send to colleagues and suppliers for preliminary review.

▶ **Tip:** You can check the file types that you can convert to PDF by choosing File > Create PDF > From File and expanding the Files Of Type menu in the Open dialog box.

1   On your desktop, navigate to the Lesson15 folder and drag the Water_Bottle.CATPart file onto the Acrobat icon on your desktop. (You can also choose File > Open to convert the file, or you can drag the file into the Acrobat document pane to create a new PDF file.)

2   In the Acrobat 3D Conversion dialog box, expand the 3D Conversion Settings menu. Select any of these presets to see an explanation of the settings in the Description text box.

You can also create, name, and save custom conversion settings in this dialog box. If you change any of the settings on the General, Document, Import, or Optimize tabs, the name of the 3D Conversion Setting automatically changes to Custom. Click the plus button (+) to name and save any custom preset that you create.

3 In the Acrobat 3D
   Conversion dialog box, select
   Visualization/Small File from
   the 3D Conversion Settings
   menu because you want
   the 3D PDF file to be small
   enough to email to colleagues.
   Because this is a preliminary
   review, fine detail isn't
   important.

4 Click the Optimize tab.

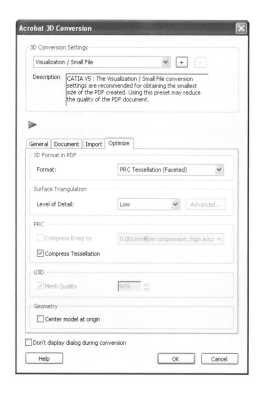

Before you continue with the conversion, notice that the format is PRC Tessellation. PRC is a B-rep (or boundary representation) precise format that lets you create different representations of a 3D model. You can save a visual representation that consists of polygons, or you can save the precise geometry that the model is based on. You can apply compression during conversion to decrease file size, or afterward to save time opening the file. PRC files are interoperable with computer aided manufacturing (CAM) and computer aided engineering (CAE) applications.

5 Click the Import tab. Notice that the 3D PMI & Views option is selected. This embeds product manufacturing information from the CATPart file.

6 Click OK.

7 Click OK to close the message box.

The progress of the conversion is shown onscreen, and the PDF file opens automatically in Acrobat when the conversion is complete.

8 Choose File > Save As, and save the file in the Lesson15 folder using the name **My_Water_Bottle.pdf.**

9 Choose File > Close to close your file. It's that easy to create 3D PDF files.

In the Document tab of the Acrobat 3D Conversion dialog box, you have the option to import your 3D content into an existing PDF template. Creating a PDF template with a placeholder for 3D content allows you to give consistent layout and structure to your files. You can create the template in any Microsoft Office application in which PDFMaker is available to convert the file to PDF.

Changing the conversion settings

You just used the Visualization/Small File preset, selected in the Acrobat 3D Conversion dialog box, to convert your file. You can also set the conversion settings in the Preferences menu.

1 In Acrobat, choose Edit > Preferences, and in the left pane of the Preferences dialog box, select Convert To PDF.

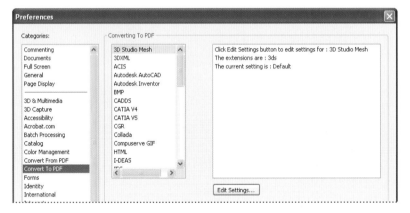

The dialog box lists all the file types that can be converted to PDF.

2 In the Converting To PDF list, choose your design application program, then choose Edit Settings.

3 Take a moment to select various presets and page through the tabs to review the values for each of the presets. A description of each preset is given in the text box below the preset name. When you are finished, click Cancel to close the Preferences dialog box without making any changes.

Using 3D PDF files in your manufacturing workflow (Acrobat Pro Extended)

When you use Acrobat in your workflow, you can create a 3D PDF file that is much smaller than your CAD drawing file but still contains necessary dimensioning and tolerancing data. You can include product manufacturing information in your 3D PDF file. And you can include model geometry that can be exported in common CAM and CAE formats.

Incorporating PMI and model geometry

To include product manufacturing information in your Adobe 3D PDF file, the 3D PMI & Views option must be checked on the Import panel of the Acrobat 3D Conversion dialog box when you create the Adobe 3D PDF file.

To include your model's geometry when converting a CAD file to Adobe 3D PDF, choose a PRC B-rep format option in the Import tab of the Acrobat 3D Conversion dialog box.

Viewing product information

Product manufacturing information usually consists of notes that are added to one or more of the standard or custom views in the Model Tree. Anyone with access to your 3D model can view the product manufacturing information in the Model Tree and in the 3D model.

1   Choose File > Open. Navigate to the Lesson15 folder, select the Water_Bottle.pdf file, and click Open. This is equivalent to the file you created earlier in the lesson.

As you'll recall, the 3D PMI & Views option was selected on the Import panel of the Acrobat 3D Conversion dialog box in order to embed the product manufacturing information from the CATPart file.

2   With the Hand tool (🖐) selected, click the 3D model. Then click the Model Tree button (🔳) in the 3D toolbar.

3 Scroll down the Views pane and observe that you have three product views—Projected View.1, Projected View.2, and Projected View.3.

▶ **Tip:** You can view the physical properties of any part in your 3D model in the Model Tree. First, expand the Option menu at the top of the Structure pane, and choose Show Physical Properties. Then select a part in the 3D model in the document pane. The physical properties of the part are listed in the Object Data pane at the bottom of the Model Tree.

4 Move the pointer over the model to open the 3D toolbar and expand the Views menu. In turn, select Projected View.1, Projected View.2, and Projected View.3. Product manufacturing information is associated with Projected View.1. Select that view.

You can move between product information views using the Next View and Previous View buttons in the Views pane. You can also change views in the work area. You can right-click on the 3D content, choose Views from the context menu, and select a view. You cannot toggle between views using the Structure pane.

5 In the Structure pane, expand the Water_Bottle_V1 label and the 3D PMI label and click on the Text.1 label to highlight it in the work area. To hide the label in the work area, deselect the label. When the check mark is visible, the notation is visible.

The entries in the Structure pane reflect the information contained in the original CAD file.

▶ **Tip:** You can make the Structure pane longer by dragging the lower margin down.

6 To return to the default view at any time, click the Default View button (⌂) at the top of the Views pane or in the 3D toolbar.

7 When you are finished, close the file. You need not save your work.

Exporting geometry from a 3D model

If the geometry of the 3D model was retained during the conversion of the CAD file to Adobe PDF, you can export the geometry in IGES, STEP, ParaSolid, VRML, or STL file formats. (Product manufacturing information is not exported.)

To save your model's geometry when converting the CAD file to Adobe PDF, be sure to choose a PRC B-rep format option (boundary representation) in the Import tab of the Acrobat 3D Conversion dialog box.

1 Choose File > Open, navigate to the Lesson15 folder, and open the Bottle_Mold.pdf file.

2 Click to activate the 3D model in the work area, right-click on the model, and then choose Export Data from the context menu.

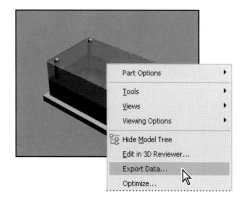

3 Choose a file type from the Save As Type menu, and click Settings to specify options for that file type. We chose STEP for the file type and used the default settings.

4 Click Save to save the file in the Lesson15 folder using the same file name and the .stp extension.

5 You can then import this file into your CAM application.

6 Close any open files.

Note: Acrobat may modify the exported data to improve the results without changing the geometry. For example, if the source CAD application is loose-tolerant and the export format is tight-tolerant, Acrobat may add a tolerance to the exported file.

Using 3D models in technical publishing (Acrobat Pro Extended)

Depending on your workflow, you have several ways to bring a 3D model or animation into a PDF version of your technical publication:

- You can use the 3D tool on the Multimedia toolbar in Acrobat to insert a 3D model or animation into a PDF document or presentation.

- You can convert your 3D model or animation to a one-page 3D PDF file and insert the page in the appropriate place in your existing document or presentation.

- In Microsoft Office applications, you can use the Embed 3D button on the Acrobat ribbon (2007) or the Insert Acrobat 3D Model button on the toolbar (earlier versions of Office) to add a 3D model file to your document.

Users of your 3D-enhanced PDF electronic document can manipulate the 3D models and run any animations using the 3D toolbar that is available in Adobe Reader and all of the other Acrobat applications.

In this part of the lesson, you'll add a one-page PDF version of a 3D model to an existing one-page technical specification.

You can convert any supported 3D file to Adobe PDF by dragging it into the Acrobat work area or onto the Acrobat icon on your desktop.

1   Use the Restore Down button (■) or drag the corner of the Acrobat window to reduce its size.

2   On your desktop, navigate to the Lesson15 folder, select the Aquo_Bottle.u3d file and drag it into the Acrobat work area.

3   In the Acrobat 3D Conversion dialog box, select Publishing from the 3D Conversion Settings menu. Leave all the other settings at their default values, and click OK.

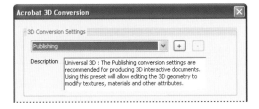

4   Click OK to clear any message boxes.

The PDF file opens in its own window.

5   Maximize the Acrobat work area.

6   Click the model to open the Acrobat 3D toolbar.

7   Use the Background Color button to set a new background color. We chose pale yellow.

8 Use the tools on the 3D toolbar to manipulate the model and create a new view.

9 After you have created a new view, choose Manage Views from the Views menu on the 3D toolbar.

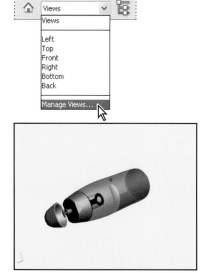

10 In the Manage Views dialog box, click New View, and then click OK in the View Properties dialog box.

11 Select the new view, New7, from the view list. Type the new name **Ad** in the text box, and click Rename.

12 Click Use As Default, and then click OK.

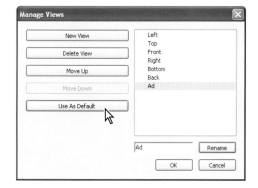

13 Choose File > Save As, and save your file in the Lesson15 folder as **3D_model.pdf**.

Now you'll open the technical specification document.

14 Choose File > Open. Navigate to the Lesson15 folder, select the Cover_Letter.pdf file, and click Open.

15 Choose Document > Insert Pages > From File.

16 In the Select File To Insert dialog box, navigate to the Lesson15 folder, and select the 3D_Model.pdf file. Click Select.

17 In the Insert Pages dialog box, select After for Location, and click OK.

18 On the Acrobat toolbar, click the Next Page button ().

Your cover letter now has two pages, the second of which is the 3D model.

19 Click the model to activate it. The view switches to the new default view that you set.

20 Choose File > Close, and save your new document. Quit Acrobat.

For information on adding 3D content to Microsoft Office files, see Lesson 4, "Creating Adobe PDF from Microsoft Office Files."

Recipients of your new two-page technical specification can read the specification and then manipulate the 3D model using the tools on the 3D toolbar, which are available in Adobe Reader.

Creating graphics from 3D content

Adobe 3D Reviewer allows technical publications professionals to quickly and easily create 2D graphics from 3D models, simplify 3D models, and prepare 3D animations for use in presentations and documents. These presentations and documents are easily updated and provide much more information and context than a flat, printed illustration.

To open Adobe 3D Reviewer, choose Start > Programs or All Programs > Adobe 3D Reviewer. Reviewer has its own online Help.

Review questions

1   Can you manipulate a part in a model without manipulating the entire model?

2   Where do you change the settings used to convert your design file to Adobe PDF?

3   When would you use PRC format rather than U3D format?

4   How do you get product manufacturing information into a 3D PDF file?

5   How do you include model geometry in a 3D PDF file?

Review answers

1   Yes. First you would select the part you want to manipulate. (Select the part in the 3D model or in the Structure tree.) Then isolate the selected part by choosing Isolate from the Options menu in the Structure pane.

2   You change the conversion settings in the Adobe 3D Conversion dialog box. You can also change the conversion settings in the Convert To PDF preferences dialog box.

3   If you need to include product manufacturing information in your file and if you want to retain geometry for reuse in CAD, CAM, or CAE applications, you must use the PRC format.

4   You import the product manufacturing information when you convert your 3D model to Adobe PDF. On the Import tab of the Acrobat 3D Conversion dialog box, make sure that the 3D PMI & Views option is selected.

5   To include model geometry, you must select a PRC B-rep format in the Import tab of the Acrobat 3D Conversion dialog box when you create your 3D PDF file.

INDEX

Production Notes

The *Adobe Acrobat 9 Classroom in a Book* was created electronically using Adobe InDesign CS3. Art was produced using Adobe InDesign, Adobe Illustrator, and Adobe Photoshop. The Myriad Pro and Warnock Pro OpenType families of typefaces were used throughout this book.

References to company names in the lessons are for demonstration purposes only and are not intended to refer to any actual organization or person.

Images

Photographic images and illustrations are intended for use with the tutorials.

Typefaces used

Adobe Myriad Pro and Adobe Minion Pro are used throughout the lessons. For more information about OpenType and Adobe fonts, visit www.adobe.com/type/opentype/.

Team credits

The following individuals contributed to the development of this edition of the *Adobe Acrobat 9 Classroom in a Book*:

Project Manager and Production Editor: Lisa Fridsma
Technical Editors: Jo Davies and Brie Gyncild
Proofreader: Betsy Shafer
Technical Reviewers: David Van Ness and Dawn Dombrow
Indexer: Brie Gyncild
Cover design: Eddie Yuen
Interior design: Mimi Heft

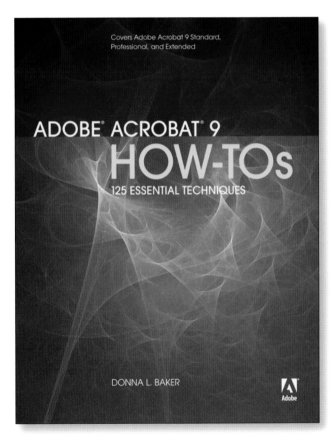